The Grantseeker's Handbook of Essential Internet Sites

2000–2001 Edition

Aspen Grants & Nonprofit Development Group

Mollie Mudd
Senior Editor

Introduction by
David Lamb
Director of Prospect Research and Training
University of Washington
Seattle, Washington

AN ASPEN PUBLICATION®
Aspen Publishers, Inc.
Gaithersburg, Maryland
2000

Jane Garwood, Publisher
Jo Gulledge, Executive Director
William Reinhard, Acquisitions, Grants
Mollie Mudd, Senior Editor
Jodi Wick, Database Editor
Rosette Graham, Senior Production Manager
Jennifer Barnes Eliot, Marketing Manager

Orders: 800-638-8437
Customer Service: 800-234-1660
ISBN 978-0-8342-1800-0

Printed in the United States of America

1 2 3 4 5

Table of Contents

Preface v

Introduction vii

Corporations 1

Foundations and Associations 61

Government 143

Research 163

Resources 175

Index to Sites by Alphabetical Order 195

Index to Corporate and Foundation Sites by Major Category of Giving 211

Preface

The Internet is an essential tool for today's grantseeker. From researching a foundation's priorities and tracking down financial figures on a corporate giving program, to catching up on the latest developments in fundraising and grantmaking trends, the Internet offers something for everyone — all from the convenience of your personal computer.

Note that we didn't say that the process can be done from the "comfort" of your PC. Surfing the Web often is anything but comfortable. That is where this book comes in.

Grantseekers have found themselves in a love/hate relationship with the Internet. Developed as a way to save time, the Internet can easily become a burden. Sifting through the proliferation of marketing, advertising and consumer-oriented sites is a bit like looking for loose change on the beach without benefit of a metal detector. Even if one finds a few coins, the result doesn't add up to much.

The Grantseekers Handbook of Essential Internet Sites, 2000–2001 Edition, is designed to guide fundraisers to the motherlode. This unique resource reviews more than 750 Internet sites — over 250 more sites than last edition. Each entry includes the resource's Internet address and a description of the site. For ease of use, the sites have been classified into five categories: corporations, foundations and associations, government, research and resources.

Benefits to the User

This fourth edition of *The Grantseeker's Handbook of Essential Internet Sites*, published in both book and online formats, offers three special features designed to help readers put the Internet to work.

An introduction from David Lamb, Director of Prospect Research and Tracking at the University of Washington is featured. Lamb, who is among the handful of development researchers who can truly be called an "expert" in this field (although many claim to be), offers his thoughts on Internet usage for grantseekers.

Each site listed has been analyzed by our team of experienced researchers. Descriptions provide users with a brief look at the site and note any special features that may be helpful or of interest to grantseekers.

Two indexes allow grantseekers to focus their research efforts. Sites are indexed alphabetically by name and corporate and foundation sites are indexed by major category of giving.

We trust that you will find *The Grantseeker's Handbook of Essential Internet Sites, 2000–2001 Edition*, to be a useful addition to your research library.

Mollie Mudd
Senior Editor

Introduction

Internet Temptations for Prospect Researchers

by David Lamb

"Discover hidden secrets about your neighbors." The e-mail subject line whispers suggestively like a devil on your shoulder tempting you to peek through the windows of the house next door. If you've been using e-mail for very long, you've probably been spammed by a similar offer.

The message is from "spyonyou@...." That's enough of a clue that this is high-grade snake oil, but perversely fascinated, you read on.

> "The SOFTWARE they want BANNED in 27 countries! Why? Because these secrets were never intended to reach you [sic] eyes...
>
> *"Get the facts on anyone using the Internet."*

Really? Could this be the professional researcher's guilty dream come true? What do they mean by "the facts?" Read on!

> "Find out SECRETS about your relatives, friends, enemies and everyone else! — even your spouse!
>
> "Get anyone's name and address with just a license plate number! (find that girl you met in traffic!)
>
> "Get anyone's driving record!
>
> "Get anyone's phone number with just a name – even unlisted numbers!
>
> "Discover dirty secrets your in-laws do not want you to know!
>
> "Use the sources that private investigators use (all on the Internet) secretly!

"Learn how to get information on an ex-spouse that will help you win in court! (dig up old skeletons)

"Criminal background check! Find out about your daughter's boyfriend (or her husband)!

"Learn all about your mysterious neighbors! Find out what they have to hide!

"Be astonished by what you will learn about people you work with!"

At this point you're either drooling at the prospect of getting your hands on all this juicy stuff, or you're retching at the suggested violation of the privacy of your friends, relatives, acquaintances and, since you're not the only person who received this message, yourself. Most prospect researchers I know would be in the retching camp.

A savvy reader will recognize that the "software" promised in this message is about as good as those X-ray glasses and voice-throwing devices that we used to buy from ads in the back of comic books. (Come on, I wasn't the only one who bought one of those, was I?) True, there are Web sites where you can find *some* of this information in limited amounts about *some* people, but these broad claims are patently false. The biggest lie of all is that you can access all of this information for the low, low price of $19.95 if you act NOW! At best your money will buy you a list of Web sites, if you get anything at all. These will include some Web-based phone directories and links to a few public information sites. The book you're holding in your hands is a far better value. Additionally, there are several "meta-sites" (lists of categorized links to useful Web sites – you can find a good sampling of them in the Resources section) created by prospect researchers for prospect researchers with no snake-oil content whatsoever.

Even though we know better than to bite on this line, this kind of advertisement poses a very real threat to the prospect research profession in at least two ways. First, it perpetuates the myth that you can find *anything* on the Internet. This false but widely held belief creates unrealistic expectations in our clients about what we can and can't find. I have to admit that I had a momentary twinge of professional jealousy when I first started seeing ads like this. If they can find everything there is to know about a person for $19.95, why does my office spend thousands of dollars every year to find only limited data? The truth is, they can't make good on their claim. For the most part, the private information this message promises to reveal requires either the resources of professional law enforcement or an investment of considerably more than $20 to discover it.

The second threat may ultimately be the greater one. Messages like this one feed the general perception and anxiety felt by many that our privacy has been seriously eroded in the late 20th, early 21st century. While you may be interested in learning if your daughter's boyfriend has a criminal record, none of us want anyone prying into *our* private affairs. If I believe that by buying a certain product I can learn secrets about my neighbors, my own sense of privacy is instantly diminished.

Why is this a threat to prospect research? Research on major donors is significantly aided by the free flowing exchange of information that is a cornerstone of the strong economies of the developed world. When unscrupulous people take advantage of the information that is available in ways that injure others, the natural reaction is to reduce the information that is available, to take special measures to hide from prying eyes. Where once most people never gave a thought to privacy (because the right to privacy was assumed), it is now very much in the public consciousness. Evidence of this is the increase in the number of unlisted phone numbers over the last couple of decades. Contrary to the promise of Mr. Spyonyou, you will have a very hard time ever obtaining an unlisted number, except from the person who holds the number.

Paradoxical as it may seem, it is up to professional researchers to safeguard the privacy of the very people who are the subjects of our searches. There is an element of truth to the general sense that the walls that kept others out of our private business are coming down. It's not that the amount of publicly available information has significantly increased in recent years. Instead, the mechanisms for accessing the information that is already legally available have become remarkably easier to use. Often the point of access is a dial-up connection to an online database or the Internet.

This fact has been a great boon to professional researchers, but it can also aid others whose intent might not be as benign. Therefore it is incumbent on those of us who make our living sipping from the fast flowing stream of electronic data to make sure that the privacy of the individuals we research is respected and preserved. Our motto should echo the Hippocratic oath, "First, do no harm." Our goal must never be to exploit information to our organization's good and another person's or organization's harm. But it is not enough to stop there. The prospect's interests and desires should ultimately underlie any development activities, including prospect research.

A number of years ago, the Association of Professional Researchers in Advancement (APRA) adopted a statement of ethics that directly addressed these issues. It says, in part:

> APRA members shall support and further the individual's fundamental right to

> privacy and protect the confidential information of their institutions. APRA members are committed to the ethical collection and use of information. Members shall follow all applicable federal, state and local laws, as well as institutional policies governing the collection, use, maintenance and dissemination of information in the pursuit of the missions of their institutions. APRA members shall respect all people and organizations...Prospect researchers must balance the needs of their institutions to collect, analyze, record, maintain, use and disseminate information with an individual's right to privacy...

The statement goes on to outline fundamental principles of ethical collection of information and suggested best practices. You can read the entire APRA statement of ethics at http://www.aprahome.org/apra_statement_of_ethics.htm.

There will always be someone like Mr. Spyonyou, tempting the susceptible to buy his paper and plastic X-ray glasses and peer into things that are none of their business. Let there be no doubt about this: he does not speak, and never has spoken for the professional prospect researchers.

Guidelines for Internet Research

When conducting Internet research, you should not only keep in mind the strengths and weakness of the Internet but also follow these general guidelines.

Focus, focus, focus. The information you find on the Web is fascinating, but not all is relevant. When you stop finding relevant data, stop searching for more and start analyzing what you have.

Limit your search time. If you haven't found anything useful in 20 minutes, you're probably better off using a different resource. It is important to remain familiar with what the Internet offers, so set aside a period of time for general Web surfing. At all other times, however, the Internet must be used in a disciplined way.

Have a plan of attack. Know which resources are relevant to your search, both on and off the Internet. This is where those free surfing sessions can inform your later activities. You also need to know your dial-up vendors and off-line resources like CDs and print materials. Start with the source that is least expensive, but also likely to provide good quality data. Don't waste your time on sources that are constantly disappointing. And know when to give up the search. Ultimately, experience is the best way to determine that, but when your sources start repeating each other, it's probably time to stop gathering data and start processing them.

Check for relevance and validity. Data go stale quickly. Just because you found something on a Web site doesn't mean it is the "latest and greatest." Try to determine the material's date and origin. If you can't find a corporate or a personal author, don't trust the information. If a search engine takes you to a document deep within a site, back up to the home page to find information about the source that will help you qualify the validity of the document. You can usually back up to the home page by eliminating from the Web address everything but the site name. For example, if the document you've found has the address www.sitename.com/directory/document.html, the home page can usually be found by going to www.sitename.com.

Handle information carefully, especially if you paid for it. If you download something from a fee-based Internet site, it is probably in the form of a Web page and the charge goes to your credit card at the time you download the page. If, while you have that page on your screen and you go to another site, the Web page you paid for is probably lost and you'll have to repeat your search. Better to print out a hard copy or save the page before you do anything else. Similarly, Web sites that contain important information come and go. Site addresses change. If you find a page with information to which you wish to refer later, it's better to print off a copy than to risk the possibility of not finding it later.

Capitalize on the experience and knowledge of others. You don't need to personally investigate all the sites that might have useful information related to your research. Others have been there before you. This book will direct you to Internet sites that previous users have found to be most valuable. Additionally, some Internet researchers have created Web pages designed to help others find information. You can find references to those meta-indexes, as they're sometimes called, in the sections of this book titled "Research" and "Resources."

Use the Right Tool

The Internet is a marvelous tool for gathering information from around the globe. It has not yet, however, replaced the other tools like dial-up databases and CD-ROM directories. And let's not forget the venerable and still important public library! The book you have in your hands will guide you to some of the most useful Web sites for grantseekers and prospect researchers. Like the prospectors of old, we must use the right tool for the right situation to uncover those nuggets of gold for our organizations.

* * *

David Lamb is the Director of Prospect Research and Tracking at the University of Washington. Lamb is also the developer of the Prospect Research Page (http://staff.washington.edu/dlamb) on the Web, a useful list of Internet sites for prospect researchers. Lamb's bachelors and masters degrees are in Sociology (Sterling College, Kansas, and Wichita State University). He also received a Masters of Divinity from San Francisco Theological Seminary. In his current incarnation, he has taught about prospect research and the Internet at events sponsored by the Association of Professional Researchers in Advancement, Council for Aid and Support of Education and Northwest Development Officers Association.

Corporations

◆ 3M in the Community

http://www.3m.com/profile/community/index.html

The 3M Company's major areas of giving include: education, health and human services, the arts and the community. The company's support of education is targeted at higher education in science, technology and business. Grantseekers will find descriptions of programs funded in the past and a list of its priorities. Grantseekers, however, will not find application procedures or giving guidelines. The Web site also provides links to the company's home page for information on its products, services, financials and press releases.

Giving Category (ies): arts, education, environment, health, international, social services

◆ 7-Eleven Stores

http://www.7-eleven.com/store/community.html

People Who Read Achieve is a nationwide initiative of 7-Eleven to help people learn to read, read better and read more. The Web site offers general financial and application information for the program. Important dates and deadlines are stated, as is contact information.

Giving Category (ies): education

◆ Adobe Philanthropic Council

http://www.adobe.com/aboutadobe/philanthropy/main.html

This site, sponsored by Adobe Systems Inc., provides information on the company's philanthropic and community relations programs, including funding priorities and guidelines for requests for cash or product donations, equipment, supplies and volunteerism. Adobe makes their latest versions of software available to nonprofit organizations throughout the United States and Canada that do the following: service disadvantaged youth, the homeless, people with disabilities, minorities, the elderly and victims of abuse; provide disaster relief, medical and hospice care and meal service; provide education and literacy programs; support human rights; support the arts; protect the environment; and support animal rights. Users can also download a Volunteer Support Request Form. Users can download both a donation request form and an annual report, included — appropriately enough — in Adobe Acrobat format.

Giving Category (ies): arts, education, environment, health, social services

◆ Aetna Foundation

http://www.aetna.com/foundation/

The Aetna Foundation reflects the company's mission of helping people with what matters most, their health and financial well-being and a long standing commitment to the communities in which employees live and work. The Aetna Foundation Web site offers grantseekers brief profiles of some of the major programs it has supported. Major health issues are women's cardiovascular health and the Quality Care Research Fund. "The major area of education is the financial literacy program for high school students. Application guidelines and restrictions are provided. The foundation also sponsors a number of employee programs, including a matching grants program for higher education. Users also may link to the company's home page to get a list of services provided, view financial and stock information and order a copy of the corporate annual report.

Giving Category (ies): arts, education, health

◆ Alliant Energy Foundation

http://www.alliantenergy.com/ourinvolvement/charity.php3

Formerly known as Wisconsin Power & Light, Alliant Energy is a new company and a new foundation comprised of three energy services providers: IES Industries, Interstate Power and WPL Holdings. This new foundation's mission is to improve the social and economic environment with an emphasis on human needs, education, culture and the arts, civics and nature. Users can e-mail foundation contacts with comments, questions or concerns. The company's 1998 grant totals and corporate giving report can be downloaded in Adobe Acrobat. A printable application form is also available in Adobe Acrobat. Grantseekers are provided with information on how to apply and are given the foundation's guidelines. Users can link to the corporate home page for information on products, services and financials.

Giving Category (ies): arts, civic, education, environment, social services

◆ American Express Company

http://home3.americanexpress.com/corp/philanthropy/

American Express Web site provides descriptions of the company's funding priorities and major programs as well as a list of its most recent grants (without the amount of the award). A major initiatives section details funding in the company's three major program areas: community service, cultural heritage and economic independence. Funding includes employee volunteer activities, support to local United Ways and grants to the American Red Cross and other relief agencies. Detailed application procedures are provided.

Giving Category (ies): arts, civic, social services

◆ Ameritech Corporation

http://www.ameritech.com/community/index.html

Ameritech's Web site offers the grantseeker a copy of the company's contributions report, information and detailed application guidelines regarding the company's digital grant competition with the Library of Congress and its ongoing teacher awards competition. Innovations in Communications Technology is a new program that Ameritech sponsors with the National Council on Aging. Its goal is to improve the quality of life for older people and people with disabilities by fostering the development, adaptation and broad use of innovations in communications technology. The National Crime Prevention Council, with Ameritech, established the Ameritech Awards of Excellence in Crime Prevention in 1997 to honor ordinary individuals who have done extraordinary things to prevent crime and build safer, more caring communities. Grantseekers also can search the Web page for corporate financial information. The home page has a link to the company's annual report.

Giving Category (ies): civic, education, social services

◆ Amway

http://www.amway.com/ourStory/o-comm.asp

Amway provides financial and human support to different community programs in the areas of human services, education, environment, arts and culture and sports. A list of previously funded organizations and projects is listed under each category. Unfortunately, application procedures are not provided. Users can link to Amway's home page for a description of its products and services.

Giving Category (ies): arts, education, environment, international, social services

◆ Apple Computer

http://www.apple.com/education

Apple's home page offers a brief overview of the company and its interests. Primarily concerned with revitalizing learning and teaching through the effective use of its technology, Apple targets its limited giving on education programs with a focus on grades K-12 and also offers a link that deals with higher education. A link to the corporate home page offers visitors information on products and services.

Giving Category (ies): education

◆ ARCO Foundation

http://www.arco.com/Corporate/reports/foundation/AR1998/pages/index.html

ARCO's Web site offers a look at the foundation's most recent annual report. It lists the company's giving priorities, namely, education, community, arts and humanities, environment and public information. Grantseekers will find funding guidelines for each of the giving areas and regions of interest, as well as application procedures. Users can link to the sponsoring company's home page for detailed information on its products and services, financials and career opportunities. This Web site offers a look at the foundation's annual reports from 1995/1996 through 1998/1999. Also gives a breakdown of grants by category for 1998.

Giving Category (ies): arts, civic, education, environment, health, international, social services

◆ Arizona Cardinals Charities

http://www.azcardinals.com/community/

The Arizona Cardinals Charities focuses on children and youth, social services, women, cancer research and the United Way. Brief summaries are given on each of the charity's recent fundraising events.

Giving Category (ies): social services, youth

◆ Ashland Foundation

http://www.ashland.com

The Ashland Foundation's portion of the corporate Web page details the company's giving program, which is primarily focused on education. The company and its foundation contribute more than half of donations to education programs annually. A Teachers Achievement Award program is offered along with a list of 1999 recipients. Grantseekers can link to the Putting the Power of Education to Work page to learn more about Ashland's programs. The Parent Power newsletter is available online, as are sample lesson plans for educators. Ashland Inc. annually honors a diverse group of projects and individuals with its Chairman's Challenge Award for demonstrating excellence in environmental, health and safety practices. The corporate home page describes Ashland's products and services, lists financial data and includes an online version of its annual report.

Giving Category (ies): arts, civic, education, environment, social services

◆ AT&T Foundation

http://www.att.com/foundation/

The AT&T Foundation Web page provides information on its philanthropic programs, giving guidelines, application procedures and funding restrictions. Currently, 25 percent of the AT&T Foundation's grant budget is allocated to support regional and local programs. Support covers three primary areas: education, civic and community service and arts and culture. Additionally, corporate grantseekers will find a list of the foundation's staff and trustees and links to other organizations who have received AT&T funding. The site includes a "grant search" to identify the specific organizations that received funding from the AT&T Foundation from 1996 to 1999. The site also provides links to the sponsoring company's home page, which contains information on the company's product and services, a list of other Internet resources and links to online phone directories.

Giving Category (ies): arts, education, health, international, social services

◆ Autodesk Foundation

http://www.autodesk.com/foundation/index.htm

The Autodesk Foundation was founded in 1990 "to identify and develop strategies and model programs for improving public schools and expanding educational opportunities beyond the walls of the classroom." This corporate foundation's Web site provides a description of its funding programs, list of staff members, online application form for the high school internship program and online newsletter. The site does not contain funding guidelines or sample grants. Due to setbacks in the marketplace, Autodesk, Inc., will no longer be able to sponsor the foundation, which has been in operation since 1991. The 1999-2000 school year will be the final year of the Autodesk Foundation. During that time the foundation will honor its present commitments and work to transfer its programs and initiatives to other partner organizations.

Giving Category (ies): education

◆ Avon Products Foundation

http://www.avon.com/about/women/foundation/foundation.html

The Avon Products Foundation is dedicated to supporting endeavors that understand and respond to the unique needs of women and their families and enable women to reach their full potential. The four major categories that receive funding are health, education, community and social services, arts and culture. Grant application guidelines, contact information and a listing of grant recipients are provided.

Giving Category (ies): arts, civic, education, health, social services

◆ Baltimore Gas and Electric Company Corporate Contributions

http://www.bge.com/aboutbge/contrib/contrib.html

The Baltimore Gas and Electric Company Corporate Contributions Web site offers grantseekers a list of program objectives; giving history, including a graphic display of its most recently available distributions by program area; application guidelines; and information on the grant request process.

Giving Category (ies): arts and humanities, civic, environment, health, social services

◆ Bank of America Foundation

http://www.bankofamerica.com/foundation

The Bank of America Foundation supports education, community development, health, human services and arts and culture. The application process is reviewed for grantseekers. The company's annual report can also be found on this Web site. Links are available for information on Catalyst Grants, the Volunteer Grants Program, Educational Partnerships, Joe Martin Scholarships and Matching Gifts Program. Users can also view current foundation press releases.

Giving Category (ies): arts, civic, education, health, social services

◆ BankBoston and the Community

http://www.bankboston.com/today/community/

The company's philanthropic approach includes partnerships with local organizations and government agencies through financial support, volunteer involvement and technical assistance. There is a list of upcoming and ongoing events sponsored by BankBoston. Grantseekers will find minimal information on this corporate giver's support of the arts and social services on this site. Broad descriptions of previously supported organizations and projects are listed. Users will not find application procedures or giving guidelines, but you can link to the company's home page for a brief history of the bank, information on its services and a list of employment opportunities. There also are links to sponsorships.

Giving Category (ies): arts, social services

◆ Bankers Trust Foundation

http://www.bankerstrust.com/corpcomm/communi/report/index.html

The Bankers Trust Web site provides detailed information on the company's grantmaking program, including its report on contributions, application policies, guidelines and giving priorities. Giving in the areas of arts and culture, health, hospitals and the environment is focused on the New York City area. The site also allows grantseekers to browse press releases, a company profile and current issues, investor relations, a 1999 interim report and a short biography of the board of managing directors.

Giving Category (ies): arts, civic, education, environment, health, international, social services

◆ Baxter International Corporate Citizenship

http://www.baxter.com/investors/citizenship/index.html

Grantseekers will find a brief overview of this corporate giver's funding programs on this Internet site. Information on the Baxter Allegiance Foundation, formerly the Baxter Foundation, also is provided. The Baxter Allegiance Foundation's grantmaking initiatives extend across international borders, helping to improve access to healthcare on three continents. The foundation provides philanthropic gifts in the United States, Europe, Latin America and Mexico. The foundation will further expand its geographic reach to include Japan and Asia. Reflecting Baxter's commitment to community service, Baxter employees across the globe are active in a variety of volunteer activities. Unfortunately, the site does not provide guidelines or application procedures. The company's home page provides details on Baxter International's corporate vision, products, services and financials.

Giving Category (ies): education, environment, health, international, social services

◆ Bell Atlantic Foundation

http://www.bellatlanticfoundation.com

Bell Atlantic has a foundation site with a variety of information of interest to grantseekers. It includes grant guidelines, application procedures and links to programs it funds. The site has a "Meet the Foundation Team" section, that allows the user to directly e-mail any of the members of the foundation team, including the foundation's director. There is also a section that summarizes the organizations that this foundation supports. Links are included to take the user directly to each organization's Web site. There is an online grant application. News releases and special events are included on this site as well.

Giving Category (ies): arts, education, health, social services

◆ BellSouth Foundation

http://www.bellsouthcorp.com/bsf/

BellSouth's site contains an online version of its giving guidelines, including application forms and recent grants. The site also contains information on the foundation's operating activities and NetDay involvement along with links to other philanthropy-related sites. Grantseekers can link to the sponsoring company's home page for information on its products and services. No new unsolicited grant proposals are being considered after September 1, 1999. New grant guidelines for the BellSouth Foundation will be issued for 2001-2005. "Foundation Matters," a semi-annual newsletter highlighting the work of the BellSouth Foundation is also found on this Web site. A search can be done online to find out who has received grants from the BellSouth Foundation. Users can e-mail the foundation by completing and submitting the form found on the site.

Giving Category (ies): education

◆ Ben & Jerry's Foundation

http://www.benjerry.com/foundation/index.html

The Ben & Jerry's Foundation Web site includes information on the foundation's history, its mission, areas of philanthropic interest, restrictions and application deadlines. Recent grant recipient lists also are provided, as are ideas for other funding sources. This site offers application information as well as tips for writing a grant proposal.

Giving Category (ies): social services

◆ Blue Cross and Blue Shield of Michigan Community Sponsored Events

http://www.bcbsm.com/foundation.shtml

Their mission is to support research and service projects that seek to improve healthcare for the people of Michigan by focusing on the following: enhancing the quality and appropriate use of healthcare; improving access to appropriate health services; and controlling healthcare costs. Visitors to the Blue Cross and Blue Shield of Michigan site will find a detailed foundation site, with information on research grant programs and a copy of its 1998 annual report. Users can link to the company's home page for details on services and health-related information, browse through an abridged version of a recent annual report or download the complete report using the Adobe Acrobat viewer.

Giving Category (ies): health, social services

◆ BOC Group

http://www.boc.com/foundation/index.html

The BOC Group awards grants for projects proposing practical solutions to environmental problems in the UK. Visitors to this site can view the listing of the foundation's board of directors, as well as the foundation's current newsletter. Contact information is provided. Past and current foundation projects are listed and include links to Web pages for each one. Application procedures and funding criteria are reviewed.

Giving Category (ies): environment

◆ Boeing

http://www.boeing.com/companyoffices/aboutus/community/

The Boeing Web site includes the corporation's three most recent citizenship reports, which detail gifts, contributed services and volunteer efforts of the corporation, as well as the corporation's philanthropic priorities. Boeing's efforts include corporate contributions, the Boeing Charitable Trust and the Boeing-McDonnell Foundation. The latter is the result of recent the McDonnell-Douglas merger with Boeing.

Giving Category (ies): arts, education, social services

◆ BPAmoco Corporation

http://www.amoco.com/

BPAmoco's Web site provides only limited information regarding the company's philanthropic activities. Information is included on the BP Grants for Schools-Western Australia and limited grants for the arts. Grantseekers can find information on the company's giving priorities and operating locations, search press releases for recent grants or browse its annual report for corporate data. Grantseekers, however, will not find contact information, guidelines or application information.

Giving Category (ies): arts, education, international

◆ Bristol-Myers Squibb Foundation

http://www.bms.com/aboutbms/index.html

The Bristol-Myers Squibb Web site contains information on its contribution guidelines, philanthropic initiatives and programs, application procedures and funding restrictions. Grantseekers will find information regarding the company foundation, including a deadline schedule, list of recent grant recipients and a PDF format version of the annual report. The site also provides links to the corporate home page, where grantseekers can find data on its products, services and financials.

Giving Category (ies): civic, education, health

◆ British Telecom in the Community

http://www.bt.com/World/community

The company spends money on projects that benefit the community, most of which are being directly managed through their Community Partnership Programme (CPP). British Telecom (BT) coordinates major national charitable events. These include the BT Swimathon and BT Children's Swimathon and telethons for Children in Need and Comic Relief. The CPP aims to address the key concerns of education and the communications skills that enable people to overcome problems and gain jobs. Included on this Web site are the latest news stories from BT's CPP and their new magazine, Tomorrow's Generation, a guide to the partnership opportunities for young people with BT. Giving is primarily available regionally and nationally with the exception of the Disasters Emergency Committee.

Giving Category (ies): education, international, social services

◆ Brooklyn Union

http://www.bug.com/commune/invest.htm

Brooklyn Union offers support in the areas of children and youth, human services, education, culture and community activities. Funding has supported the Queens Botanical Gardens, the Brooklyn Academy of Music and the Brooklyn Historical Society.

Giving Category (ies): arts, civic, education, social services, youth

◆ Brown Brothers Harriman & Company Community Involvement

http://www.bbh.com/career/community.htm

The Brown Brothers Harriman & Company Community Involvement home page briefly describes the company's volunteer initiatives. Company volunteers primarily support social service organizations in the greater Boston area. Users also can link to Brown Harriman's home page to learn more about the company, its products, services and career opportunities.

Giving Category (ies): social services

◆ Burger King

http://www.burgerking.com/home.htm

The corporate Web site outlines BK Cares, the company's official community service policy which is primarily a volunteer coordination effort. BK Cares' ongoing projects include KAPOW (Kids and the Power of Work); providing volunteers to feed the homeless at Community Partnership for Homeless; Community In Schools (CIS) Burger King Academy's partner for which Burger King Corporation provides space at their headquarters; Back to School Backpack Drives; a holiday angel gift tree for the Children's Home Society; and mentoring. Burger King also recently established the Burger King/McLamore Youth Opportunities Foundation, which will launch programs to provide education scholarships to youth. It is not a grantmaking body.

Giving Category (ies): education, social services

◆ Cable & Wireless Corporate Community Involvement

http://www.cwplc.com/about/comm/coindex.htm

The Web site contains a section of key figures for 1998/1999, including a breakdown of giving by category and by country. There is also a section of planned projects for the year 2000. News releases, a policy statement and requirements for community sponsorships are made available. Users can also find a step-to-step guide for applying for corporate funding for community projects. The site gives guidelines to help in writing a proposal. Users can contact community affairs with comments and opinions.

Giving Category (ies): arts, civic, education, environment, health, international, social services, youth

◆ Cabot Corporation Social Responsibility

http://www.cabot-corp.com/

The Cabot Corporation Social Responsibility home page provides only limited information on the Cabot Corporation Foundation and Cabot's employee volunteer program. The Cabot Corporation Foundation provided nearly $1 million to Cabot communities throughout the world for projects that are related to science, technology, education, community improvement, culture and the environment. Cabot's Community Relations Teams, comprised of Cabot employee volunteers, are active in the communities in which the company operates. These teams review requests for funding from local educational and charitable institutions and help identify projects in their communities that would benefit from the support of the Cabot Corporation Foundation. The site does not provide contributions guidelines or application procedures.

Giving Category (ies): arts, education, environment, science, social services

◆ Canon U.S.A. Society and Environment

http://www.usa.canon.com/cleanearth/index.html

Canon's Clean Campaign focuses on four major areas of giving: recycling and conservation in the workplace, conserving environmental resources, scientific research and education and outdoors appreciation. The Canon Cartridge Recycling Program has collected millions of cartridges. Canon's Expedition into the Parks program funds high priority conservation projects that contribute to the overall well-being of the parks, their inhabitants and the information needed to set habitat management priorities. Through the Clean Earth Campaign, Canon supports the Wings of the Americas program. Cannon also supports the Nature Conservancy. The company sponsors the Canon National Parks Science Scholars program, as well as Envirothon. Cannon also underwrites PBS's Nature series. News releases can be found on this Web site. Grantseekers, however, will not find funding guidelines and restrictions on the site. A link to the corporate page home provides users with a brief profile of the company, its products and services.

Giving Category (ies): environment

◆ Carolina Power & Light in the Community

http://www.cplc.com/community/

The Carolina Power & Light in the Community Web site provides a brief description of this direct giver's funding programs. The company focuses on three primary areas - education, economic development and the environment. An application form is included on the site. In addition, a number of environmental programs are outlined, including the TreeSmart program and Project Share, which supplies needy families with necessary heating fuel. Visitors can link to other pages for more information on the company, financial news, industry issues and employment opportunities.

Giving Category (ies): arts, education, environment, social services

◆ Ceridian Corporation Community Involvement

http://www.ceridian.com/who_community.asp

The primary emphasis of Ceridian's corporate giving is on innovative policy initiatives and programs that help people balance the growing demands of work and home life. Ceridian's secondary focus is on giving in the areas of health, education and the arts. Ceridian offers a Community Action Field Program that provides up to $500 for programs of nonprofit organizations in which employees are active. Community organizations that have benefited from this program range from Meals on Wheels to the Girl Scouts and Boy Scouts and the Animal Humane Society. Application guidelines and restrictions are included.

Giving Category (ies): arts, education, health, social services

◆ Chevron Corporation

http://www.chevron.com/community/

Chevron's program initiatives include international community development, education and environment projects. The company has an extensive Wildlife Protection Program and focuses on math and science in their educational programs. Chevron does not currently use an application process nor do they have any formal grant guidelines. The Web site offers an annual report of contributions.

Giving Category (ies): education, environment, international

◆ Cisco Systems Community Involvement

http://cio.cisco.com/warp/public/750/involve.html

Cisco Systems is committed to funding organizations that fulfill basic needs within the community, including education, food, healthcare, shelter, vocational training and assistance with earning a living. The Cisco Systems Community Involvement Web page contains detailed information on the company's direct grants program. Corporate grantseekers also will find links to specific programs funded by Cisco Systems and a link to the company's home page for facts on its products, services and financials. Users can contact the community development department with any concerns or questions they may have.

Giving Category (ies): education, health, international, social services

◆ Citigroup Foundation

http://www.citigroup.com/citigroup/foundation/index.htm

Formerly known as the Citibank Foundation, the Citigroup Foundation's mission is to improve the quality of life now and in the future for children, families and the communities in which the company's employees live and where they do business. The foundation supports a wide range of educational programs that start with an interest in early childhood learning, pre-K education and child care. The foundation partners with a variety of community development corporations to increase the availability of affordable housing, encourage small-business development and establish neighborhood facilities/amenities such as child care centers and recreational space. The Citigroup Foundation supports a new Volunteer Incentive Program through which employees can earn grants of $500 for organizations that benefit from their service. Grantseekers will find giving guidelines and can download the 1998 report in Adobe Acrobat format.

Giving Category (ies): civic, education, international, youth

◆ Clorox Community Affairs

http://www.clorox.com/company/foundation/

Users will find 1999 annual report highlights and a link to Clorox's 1999 grant list. Grant application guidelines, how to apply for a grant and where to apply are all included in this Web site. The three main areas for giving are education and youth development, culture and civic programs and employee involvement (volunteerism). Grantseekers are able to contact the foundation directly through e-mail and a mailing address is also given.

Giving Category (ies): arts, civic, education, health, social services, youth

◆ Coca-Cola Scholars Foundation

http://www.thecoca-colacompany.com/scholars/index.html

The Coca-Cola Scholars Foundation home page provides details on Coca-Cola scholarships, merit-based awards granted to 150 high school seniors each year. Fifty are $20,000 scholarships and the remaining 100 are $4,000 scholarships. Basic guidelines, restrictions and deadlines can be found on this site. Application forms are available only at local high school guidance counseling offices. Grantseekers also can see a breakdown of scholarships by state and by education institution within a particular state. Users can search 1999 finalists and 2000 semifinalists by state.

Giving Category (ies): education

◆ Comdisco, Inc.

http://www.comdisco.com/about/foundation/

The primary focus of the Comdisco Foundation is organizations and programs that promote the welfare of children and young adults. Grant guidelines, eligibility restrictions and contact information are provided on the site.

Giving Category (ies): social services, youth

◆ Compaq Computer Corporate Contributions

http://www.compaq.com/corporate/contrib/index.html

Compaq provides technology, product and cash contributions and encourages employee involvement. Visitors to Compaq Computer Corporate Contributions Internet site will find a description of this direct giver's giving priorities and contribution guidelines. Its funding program focuses on organizations that focus on health, social services, the environment and the arts. Users also can link to the company's home page for information on its products and services, as well as corporate job opportunities.

Giving Category (ies): arts, education, environment, health, international, social services

◆ Computer Associates

http://www.cai.com/charity/

The Computer Associates Foundation supports community service, including the support of victims of natural disasters, children with medical problems, holiday shopping for needy children and helping the National Center for Missing and Exploited Children.

Giving Category (ies): civic, social services, youth

◆ Conoco

http://www.conoco.com/index_dynamic.html

Conoco has a long history of philanthropy and civic involvement in its operating locations throughout the world. Conoco supports projects in the areas of education, health and human services, the arts, civic and community affairs and the environment. Grantseekers can do searches from the company's home page that will take them to links in the areas of philanthropy, giving, volunteerism and the community. Otherwise, there is very limited information about what the company funds. Grantseekers can link to additional information about the company, such as financial statistics, global business, news releases and employment opportunities.

Giving Category (ies): arts, civic, education, environment, health, international, social services

◆ Conseco Community Action Report

http://www.conseco.com/about/community.htm

Conseco believes in reinvesting in the communities where their employees live and work. Through various programs and grants, Conseco supports nonprofit organizations that provide direct services or deliver effective solutions to improve the quality of life. The company contributes to the United Way, the Special Olympics, the March of Dimes and raises funds for U.S. Olympians. Grantseekers will find a sampling of organizations and programs that receive support from this corporate giver's Internet site. A link to the corporate home page provides some background on the company along with information on its products, services, financials and employment opportunities.

Giving Category (ies): arts, civic, education, health, international, social services

◆ Dai Nippon Printing Company-Dynamic Corporate Citizenship

http://www.dnp.co.jp/eng/dnp/annual95/05citizens.html

This Japanese corporate giver offers limited funding information on its Internet site. The home page offers a description of company-sponsored programs and projects, along with links to several of the nonprofit organizations. Users can link to both the English and Japanese versions of Dai Nippon's corporate home page and from there can view the annual report, including corporate citizenship information, in PDF format.

Giving Category (ies): arts, environment, social services

◆ Delta Air Lines

http://www.delta-air.com/gateway/about/comaware/index.html

This site outlines the mission and focus areas of the company sponsored Delta Air Lines Foundation, as well as it's direct giving program and employee giving policies. The focus area is the support of families with young children. Delta Air Lines supports non-profit organizations that provide young people with positive reinforcement and support at an early age to help build self-esteem and establish a solid value system. Delta also supports organizations and programs that help bridge the gap between our world's varied cultures, primarily in the visual and performing arts. The Delta Foundation manages an employee matching gift fund that matches employee contributions to educational institutions. Links are included to organizations which have received funding in the past.

Giving Category (ies): arts, civic, education, social services

◆ Dial Corporation

http://www.dialcorp.com/corporate-giving.html

The Dial Corporation focuses its charitable giving on the following areas: children and youth; education; human services; and arts and culture. However, the centerpiece of Dial's Corporate Giving Program is the United Way. Grantseekers will find a list of grant guidelines, including contact information, funding restrictions and application procedures.

Giving Category (ies): arts, education, social services, youth

◆ Dole Food Company

http://www.dole.com/company/business/community.ghtml

The Dole Food Company's charitable contribution program provides cash donations to hospitals, churches, schools, environmental programs and social and cultural programs. In addition, Dole provides a tremendous amount of in-kind giving each year. Summaries of several of the company's funding programs can be found on this Web site, including their food donation program.

Giving Category (ies): arts, civic, environment, health, religion, social services

◆ R.R. Donnelly & Sons Company

http://www.rrdonnelley.com/public/community/

This company gives high priority to activities that support the written word. R.R. Donnelly & Sons also gives priority to activities that serve children and youth at-risk, as well as programs that enhance the overall quality of life in the communities where they work and live. This Web site provides contact and financial information, including an annual report. For each of the company's three initiatives, grantseekers will find a list of past grant recipients, an overview of each funding program and grant guidelines.

Giving Category (ies): civic, education, youth

◆ Charles Stark Draper Laboratories Community Outreach

http://www.draper.com/

Grantseekers will find a brief overview of the Charles Stark Draper Community Outreach program on its home page. The site offers a basic description of this corporate giver's funding initiatives and in-kind giving program. Draper provides quarterly grants to deserving nonprofit organizations and institutions in the Cambridge community. Particular emphasis is placed on educational programs in engineering, mathematics and science, followed by human services. Administered by a review committee of Draper volunteer employees, proposals are reviewed and over $100,000 in funds are disbursed annually. Users will find a PDF file of 1998-1999 grant allocations. Users may contact the company via e-mail to obtain a copy of the most recent community involvement report and grant application guidelines. A link to the company's Web site provides information on the research and engineering efforts, as well as career opportunities.

Giving Category (ies): civic, education, social services

◆ Dreyer's Grand Ice Cream Corporate Philanthropy

http://www.dreyers.com/thecompany/index.html

Dreyer's Grand Ice Cream Corporate Philanthropy Web site provides grantseekers with information on its mission, purpose and list of sample grants. The Dreyer's Grand Ice Cream Charitable Foundation was established in 1987 to provide more focused community support, particularly for youth and K-12 public education. The mission of the Dreyer's Foundation is to promote family, school and community environments which enable young people to develop individual initiative and talent in order for them to become contributing members of their communities and caretakers of the communities' values and ideals for the next generation. Users will find giving guidelines and application procedures for the following contribution programs: Grand Expectations Program, Rocky Road Community Bus Program, Employee Community Involvement Fund, small grants and product donations and Dream the Dream competition. Information on the company along with financials can be accessed via a link to the corporate home page.

Giving Category (ies): education, social services

◆ DuPont-Social Responsibility

http://www.dupont.com/corp/gbl-company/social.html

The Web site gives a history of "a strong sense of social responsibility" that started back in 1802. DuPont's giving program contributes more than $30 million a year. On this Web site, a brief description of its giving priorities is provided. Corporate funding focuses on environmental programs, education and community and civic activities. DuPont also is committed to supporting minority businesses. Users can link to the company's home page for a description of products, services and financials and view the corporate annual report online.

Giving Category (ies): civic, education, environment, international, social services

◆ Eastern Enterprises Foundation

http://www.efu.com/foundation.html

The Eastern Enterprises Foundation represents the interests of Eastern Enterprises and its operating subsidiaries: Boston Gas Company, Colonial Gas Company, Essex Gas Company, ServicEdge Partners Inc. and Midland Enterprises Inc. Eligibility guidelines and restrictions are listed along with a contact person, who can be e-mailed directly. The Eastern Enterprises Foundation currently focuses its major grantmaking on programs that build long-term capacity to improve the quality of life for young people. Information about application reviews, requirements and deadlines is provided to users. A list of areas in Massachusetts and Ohio that are serviced by the foundation is supplied.

Giving Category (ies): education

◆ Eastman Chemical Company and the Community

http://www.eastman.com/corp/emncommunity.html

The Eastman Chemical Company site provides a description of its giving program and includes a graphic display of its major funding areas. Grantseekers also will find basic giving guidelines and restrictions. Information on the company's products, services, financials and employment opportunities is available by linking to the corporate home page.

Giving Category (ies): arts, civic, education, health, social services

◆ Eaton Corporation

http://www.eaton.com/corp/contribute/index.html

Eaton Corporation includes the 1998 Report of Contributions in Adobe Acrobat format. The report gives grantseekers information on the company's giving priorities, recent giving totals, overviews of its giving programs, examples of recent grants in the priority areas, grant criteria, matching gifts policies and application procedures. The site also includes a directory of the company's corporate contributions committee.

Giving Category (ies): civic, education, health

◆ Eddie Bauer, Inc.

http://www.eddiebauer.com/about/frame_comrelmain.asp

The Eddie Bauer Foundation focuses on the environment, education, empowering women and community volunteering. The Web site offers summaries on each of the four funding initiatives and provides an overview on the programs the foundation currently supports. Contact information, as well as application procedures are offered to grantseekers.

Giving Category (ies): civic, education, environment

◆ Electronic Data Systems (EDS) Community Affairs

http://www.eds.com/about_eds/about_eds_ community.shtml

The EDS Community Affairs home page offers grantseekers information on its employee volunteer and loaned executive programs, including its technology grants program. Additional information is provided on EDS' Global Volunteer Program. Users also can link to the corporate Web page and learn more about the company by browsing through its annual report online.

Giving Category (ies): education, social services

◆ EMI Group

http://www.emigroup.com/profile/charity.htm

In 1997, the EMI Group established a new charity called the "Music Sound Foundation," for the promotion of musical education. All EMI Group sponsorship efforts are targeted towards the foundation to safeguard and ensure the future of music. Visitors to this site will find foundation history, grant guidelines and application procedures. A mailing address for the foundation is provided, as this is where grantseekers must obtain an application form.

Giving Category (ies): arts

◆ Enron

http://www4.enron.com/corp/pr/cr/

The company supports three main areas for funding: education, environment and healthy families. Company programs in each area of giving are reviewed. Enron is also committed to supporting their employee-driven volunteer initiatives. The company is involved in matching gifts and discretionary grants, as well. Enron may be contacted through their mailing address or via e-mail.

Giving Category (ies): education, environment, social services

◆ Estée Lauder Companies

http://www.elcompanies.com/company/philanthropic.html

The company's corporate philanthropy program supports the activities and growth of organizations dedicated to health and human services, education, the environment and the arts. Estée Lauder's corporate fund drives help local public schools and needy charities. This fund also works to preserve the environment through broad-based recycling programs. The company strongly endorses employee volunteerism. The company's most important philanthropic initiative is the Pink Ribbon Breast Cancer Awareness Campaign, to help support the Breast Cancer Research Foundation and to raise public awareness of the disease.

Giving Category (ies): arts, education, environment, health, social services

◆ ExxonMobil Corporation

http://www.exxon.com/community/index.html

Formerly known as the Exxon Corporation, the company and foundation is now known as ExxonMobil. On November 30, 1999, Exxon Corporation and Mobil Corporation formally merged to form ExxonMobil Corporation. The ExxonMobil Corporation's Internet site provides detailed information on its six major funding program areas: environment; public policy; health; community services; women and minorities; arts, museums and historical associations and the Exxon Education Foundation. The site provides information about applying for a grant, where to send proposals, as well as general advice to grantseekers. Additionally, the foundation continues to support its Tiger Conservation Project to aid in saving the world's tigers from extinction. A listing of major ExxonMobil communities is also provided.

Giving Category (ies): arts, civic, education, environment, health, social services

◆ Fannie Mae Foundation

http://www.fanniemaefoundation.org/grant/index.htm

The Fannie Mae Foundation has nationwide grantmaking programs with a focus on supporting affordable homeownership, rental housing opportunities and community development. Grantmaking and geographical priorities, eligibility, as well as application procedures and requirements are all provided to grantseekers. The Fannie Mae Foundation Web site contains information on the foundation's mission, its Regional and Community Initiatives Grants, Signature Grant Programs, Capital City (Washington, DC) Initiative Grants and Research Grants Program.

Giving Category (ies): civic, social services

◆ Fina

http://www.fina.com/en/ch9/index.asp

Fina's Web site offers users information on the company's links with the educational world, including teacher education programs at all levels and dedicated chairs in different universities. The company also offers educational brochures and resources specifically for university students and those at school. These include information about the environment and pollution, education for Europeans and information on petroleum and plastics.

Giving Category (ies): education

◆ Fleet Bank

http://www.fleet.com/ceccpg.html

The goal of this company's charitable giving program is to help build and sustain strong, successful communities that serve their members well. By funding community-based agencies and other nonprofit organizations, Fleet supports programs and creates opportunities, especially for children, families and individuals in low/moderate-income areas and provides resources to support community and economic development, education, healthcare, human services and the arts and humanities. Priorities, guidelines and evaluation criteria are presented in an easy-to-read fashion and a grant application form is available to download.

Giving Category (ies): arts, education, health, social services

◆ FMC Foundation

http://www.fmc.com/community/community.html

The FMC Foundation Web page contains information on the corporate giver's philanthropic philosophy; a percentage breakdown of its giving, including detailed descriptions of each funding category; foundation guidelines; and submission requirements. Grantseekers also will find links to the sponsoring company's home page where they can find information about FMC's products and services. Users will find a link that enables them to view the company's 1998 annual report on FMC's home page.

Giving Category (ies): education, health, social services

◆ Ford Motor Company

http://www.ford.com/corporate-info/culture/cares/index.htm

Ford's elaborate "Ford Cares" site includes corporate philosophy and a variety of anecdotal evidence portraying its good work. The entire contributions report is available online, featuring priorities, guidelines and application assistance. It also offers an opportunity to obtain the report in paper form.

Giving Category (ies): arts, education, environment, health, social services

◆ France Telecom

http://www.francetelecom.fr/vanglais/apropos/actions.htm

France Telecom supports education and local development, healthcare and special services for the disabled, protecting the environment and supporting new businesses. Each funding initiative is defined. There is also a link to the France Telecom Foundation whose actions focus on promoting human expression in the fields of singing, gymnastics and offers support for autistic people and their families.

Giving Category (ies): civic, education, environment, health, social services

◆ Fred Meyer Stores

http://www.fredmeyer.com/fms/contributnoo1.shtml

Fred Meyer Stores' Web site includes information about the corporation's new foundation, as well as its corporate sponsorship activities. Grant guidelines are included, in addition to a description of the evaluation process.

Giving Category (ies): education, social services

◆ Freddie Mac

http://www.freddiemacfoundation.org/

The Freddie Mac Foundation is dedicated to brightening the future of children, youth and families at-risk. Contact information, news and events and an extensive list of grant guidelines for each priority area are provided on this Web site. The Web site also spotlights several of the foundation's programs, such as "Wednesday's Child."

Giving Category (ies): youth

◆ Fuji Bank Group-Corporate Citizen

http://www.fujibank.co.jp/eng/fb/topics/philan.html

Fuji Bank Group-Corporate Citizen Web page contains limited information on the company's giving program. Primary support goes to education; the promotion of social welfare, to which the Fuji Memorial Foundation is dedicated; and a traffic safety campaign. Additional information on Fuji Bank is available via a link to the corporate Web site.

Giving Category (ies): civic, education, social services

◆ Fujitsu-Social Commitment

http://www.fujitsu.co.jp/hypertext/organization/index-new-e.html

Grantseekers can find information on the Fujitsu Asia Pacific Scholarship Program on this Internet site. In this program, Fujitsu offers scholarships to Asians who want to obtain a Japanese MBA. The scholarships are offered through the Japan-focused Executive MBA (JEMBA) joint program between JAIMS, a nonprofit education institute that Fujitsu established in 1972 and the University of Hawaii. Asian students study the American and Japanese cultures and their different approaches to management at the institute. The corporate home page offers users information on Fujitsu's products and services, publications and employment opportunities.

Giving Category (ies): education

◆ Gap, Inc. Community Relations

http://gapinc.com/community/community_relations/community_relations.htm

Grantseekers can find basic information on the Gap's giving program on its community relations page. The revamped program concentrates on youth and business, as well as HIV/AIDS prevention and education. The company also does gift certificate and merchandise donations. The site provides information on submitting funding inquiry letters. Users can link to the company's home page to learn more about its products, store locations and financials.

Giving Category (ies): arts, education, environment, health, social services

◆ Genentech, Inc., Corporate Responsibility

http://www.gene.com/Company/Responsibility/

Genentech's Web page contains information on the company's assistance program and its two corporate-sponsored foundations: Genentech Foundation for Biomedical Sciences and Genentech Foundation for Human Growth and Development. The Genentech Assistance Program has provided more $200 million worth of pharmaceuticals free-of-charge through various programs for un- or underinsured patients in the United States. It also provides information on the Genentech Endowment for Cystic Fibrosis and the Access Excellence and Collaborative Research Materials Programs and links to the company's home page. The site includes limited information on application procedures and giving guidelines.

Giving Category (ies): education, health, science

◆ General Electric Co.

http://www.ge.com/fund/

General Electric's Web site provides information on the GE Fund, its programs and grant application procedures. Grantseekers will find information on the fund's directors and advisors, a list of recent grants and dollar amounts and an online version of its 1998 annual report. Grantseekers also can link to the sponsoring company's home page for information on its product, services and operating locations.

Giving Category (ies): arts, education, international, social services

◆ General Mills

http://www.genmills.com/explore/community/

This Web site offers foundation news, recent grants, a staff directory and grantmaking guidelines. General Mills' funding priorities include: arts and culture; education; family life; and health and nutrition. Contact and application information are given.

Giving Category (ies): arts, education, health

◆ General Motors Corporation-Philanthropy

http://www.generalmotors.com/company/community_involvement/philanthropy/home.html

The GM foundation, founded in 1976, is dedicated to improving the environmental, economic, social, educational and cultural well-being of the communities in which General Mills operates. Grantseekers will find a list of 1998 contributions made. This list is broken down by giving category and does include dollar amounts donated. Grantseekers will not find giving guidelines or applications for the foundation.

Giving Category (ies): arts, civic, education, environment, health, social services

◆ Gillette Company

http://www.gillette.com/frames.asp?top=citizenship/citizenship.html&f=27&mmf=1

The Gillette Company contributes to the communities in which they operate, which includes international funding programs. The Web site notes that the company supports education, children and youth, healthcare, social services and the environment. The company's programs include the Women's Cancer Programs and the Corporate Wetlands Restoration Partnership. An annual report is available for viewing.

Giving Category (ies): education, environment, health, social services, youth

◆ Glaxo Wellcome in the Community

http://www.glaxowellcome.co.uk/about/fr_about.html

Glaxo Wellcome in the Community Web page contains descriptions of the company's philanthropic programs along with projects it funds in the communities in which it operates. The Web page excludes application procedures or giving guidelines. Users can link to the company's home page for information on products and services.

Giving Category (ies): arts, education, environment, health, international

◆ GTE Foundation

http://www.gte.com/AboutGTE/community/foundat.html

The GTE Foundation Web site contains very limited information regarding the foundation's giving program and the company's employee volunteer program. The site does not list recent grants. The GTE Foundation gives nearly $27 million annually to education, scientific and charitable organizations. Brochures can be downloaded. Foundation contact information such as address, phone and fax numbers are also available. Users can link to the company's home page for details on products and services.

Giving Category (ies): civic, education, science

◆ Guardian National Insurance Company

http://www.guardian.co.za/corporate/social.html

The Guardian National Insurance Company supports funding in the areas of the environment, wildlife preservation, education, community betterment, healthcare and youth and children. Programs include: the Red Cross Children's Hospital Trust; the Holbane Community Complex; and the Alexandra Health Clinic. As part of its ongoing commitment to conservation and community development, Guardian National Insurance Company has sponsored the insurance premiums for the Endangered Wildlife Trust (EWT) for a year.

Giving Category (ies): civic, education, environment, health, youth

◆ H. E. Butt Grocery

http://www.hebgrocery.com/export/H-E-B/publications/aboutheb/community.html

H. E. Butt Grocery (H-E-B) is involved in making the communities it serves a better place by investing in civic and charitable causes. The H-E-B Community Investment Program accepts requests year-round, but does request that organizations contact them during September with applications for funding that apply to the following calendar year. There are no formal guidelines. The company's major areas of interest include, but are not limited to education, hunger awareness, economic opportunity development, recreation and the arts.

Giving Category (ies): arts, civic, education, social services

◆ Hallmark Cards

http://www.hallmark.com

The Hallmark Cards Company strives to share their resources and talents in communities where their employees live. The company focuses their giving on communities and social services. Programs include an annual food drive, support of Kansas City's new Science City museum and a Santa's Helpers volunteer project.

Giving Category (ies): civic, social services

◆ HEI Charitable Foundation

http://www.hei.com/heicf/heicf.html

The HEI Charitable Foundation Web site contains information on the foundation's mission and program descriptions, recent community reports, application procedures and giving restrictions. Grantseekers also can link to Hawaiian Electric Industries home page for information on its services.

Giving Category (ies): arts, education, environment, health, international, social services

◆ Hershey Foods Corporation

http://www.hersheys.com/about/contributions/index.html

Corporate giving for the Hershey Foods Corporation focuses on education, health and human services, civic and community initiatives, arts and culture and the environment. Particular emphasis is placed on the needs of communities in which the corporation employs a substantial number of people. Grantmaking restrictions are included on this Web site.

Giving Category (ies): arts, civic, education, environment, health, social services

◆ Hewlett Packard Corporate Philanthropy

http://webcenter.hp.com/grants/

This Web site contains the Hewlett Packard (HP) Philanthropy Annual Report for 1998. A list of recent grants for 1999, as well as previous grants for the years 1996 through 1998 can also be found. The listing is broken up into two categories: university grants and non-university grants. There is a "Commonly Donated Product List" available in a PDF format. The HP Corporate Philanthropy Web site has links to the different types of causes they give to, such as: universities, K-12, health/human services, civic and environmental, arts and culture and global philanthropy. There also is a frequently asked questions section where grantseekers can go to a link and get a copy of all the foundation's guidelines information. Grantseekers can find out about donations made to a specific country or continent by clicking on the appropriate link. The site links to both the Hewlett and Packard family foundations.

Giving Category (ies): arts, civic, education, environment, health, international, science

◆ Hitachi Foundation

http://www.hitachi.co.jp/Int/E/HKG-115.html

Only minimal information is provided on the Hitachi Foundation page. Users will find only a brief description of Hitachi's giving priorities in the United States and abroad. The foundation, established in 1985, has made more than 500 grants and related investments in American communities. Details on the company's products and services are provided through a link to the corporate Web site.

Giving Category (ies): arts, education, social services

◆ Home Depot

http://www.homedepot.com

The Web site contains a 1998 Home Depot Social Responsibility Report. The company contributes to affordable housing, youth-at-risk, the environment and disaster relief. Each area of giving has a link where grantseekers can find out more information, such as the specific organizations that received funding. The Web site does include grant application information and tells how to apply.

Giving Category (ies): environment, health, social services

◆ Huntington Bancshares Incorporated

http://www.huntington.com/corp/about/phil/index.shtml

Through grants and charitable donations, Huntington Bancshares supports a variety of community focused initiatives that benefit children, education, economic development, health, social service housing and the arts. Huntington Bancshares revamped philanthropy Web page offers limited information on this direct giver's funding program. A contact person is listed from which a corporate contribution application form may be requested. Huntington encourages employees to engage in philanthropic efforts and volunteer activities.

Giving Category (ies): arts, civic, education, health, social services

◆ IGA

http://www.igainc.com/

IGA focuses its giving on communities and education. Examples of funding programs are listed and include helping local schools purchase computers, sponsoring recreational softball teams and community tree planting programs.

Giving Category (ies): civic, education

◆ Intel and the Community

http://www.intel.com/intel/community

The Intel and the Community Web page contains information on the company's philanthropic philosophy and giving programs, including national grants, community grants and various education partnerships. There is a very thorough list of contacts from around the world for further information about specific areas of funding. Users also can link to the company's online version of its 1998 annual report.

Giving Category (ies): civic, education

◆ International Business Machines (IBM) Philanthropy

http://www.ibm.com/IBM/ibmgives/

The IBM Philanthropy Web page contains information on the company's funding priorities, including K-12 education, workforce development and the environment; recent grants; matching gift and employee charitable contributions; and application procedures and giving guidelines. The site, essentially an online version of its corporate responsibility report, also contains a list of the current operating locations and links to other philanthropy-related sites. The IBM grant process is reviewed. Grantseekers also can visit the company's home page for information on its products, services and financials.

Giving Category (ies): arts, civic, education, environment, social services

◆ International Paper

http://www.internationalpaper.com/our_world/outreach_frame.html

The company and its employees contribute volunteer hours and financial support to educational, recreational and cultural programs in the communities in which they conduct business. In 1998, International Paper and the International Paper Company Foundation donated more than $8 million to education and charities (including the United Way) in communities where they do business. The company's foundation funded educational programs, environmental organizations, programs that enable children to stay in and succeed in school and arts programs that supplement school curriculums. Environmental funding included grants to the annual National 4-H Forestry Invitational. These programs are discussed in detail on the Web site. Details about eligibility or other application information are not included.

Giving Category (ies): arts, education, environment

◆ Intimate Brands

http://www.intimatebrands.com/who/philanthrp.asp

Intimate Brands targets programs that are responsive to the needs of women, children, education and communities. Each target area for funding is clearly defined. A listing of grant recipients is grouped in alphabetical order, some with corresponding links to the organization's Web site. Contact information is given for those who are seeking information about funding.

Giving Category (ies): education, social services, youth

◆ Ipalco

http://www.ipalco.com/

Ipalco funds educational projects, specifically in the fields of math and science, as well as environmental projects. One such program is the Golden Eagle Environmental Awards. Recent and past recipients are listed, along with a description of each individual project. Another program that Ipalco supports is the Golden Apple Awards for Central Indiana educators who excel in utilizing math, science or technology in the classroom. Information about this program, nomination forms and procedures, as well as an application form can all be viewed in PDF format.

Giving Category (ies): education, environment

◆ Itochu-Contributing to Society

http://www.itochu.com/main/coy_9e.html

The Itochu Corporation focuses on environmental concerns in Japan, but it also donates to programs and projects in fields such as education, scientific research, art and culture, sports, international exchange, regional societies and welfare, primarily in its home country. The foundation primarily supports child- and youth-related causes. The foundation's fellowship program provides study expenses to Japanese students in foreign universities or graduate schools concentrating on social welfare, pedagogy, library science or physical education. The foundation provides assistance to individual volunteers and private organizations promoting children's use of libraries. A brief company history and information on its products and services can be found by linking to the corporate home page.

Giving Category (ies): arts, education, environment, international, science, social services

◆ Jacksonville Jaguars Foundation

http://www.jaguars.com/jag_web/nav2.cfm?page=/jag_web/fanzone/roar/menu.htm

The Jacksonville Jaguars Foundation supports economically and socially disadvantaged youth and families. Grantseekers will find grant guidelines and restrictions, as well as contact information.

Giving Category (ies): social services, youth

◆ JCPenney Community Involvement

http://www.jcpenney.net/company/commrel/index.htm

JCPenney Community Involvement site provides grantseekers with an online version of its 1998 community relations annual report detailing the corporate giver's major funding areas. Recent annual contributions totaled more than $28 million. Most of this support was made by JCPenney stores and other facilities in their home communities. The remaining funds were contributed by the JCPenney home office to national organizations or those which serve the company's home state of Texas. Major home office contributions are listed. Grantseekers will find a list of major grant recipients, application guidelines, restrictions and a description of the company's national volunteer awards. A link to the corporate home page offers visitors information on the company's history and philosophy, products, services and career opportunities.

Giving Category (ies): arts, civic, education, health, social services

◆ JM Family Enterprises

http://www.jmfamily.com/community.htm

JM Family Enterprises supports various charities, civic and economic groups, diversity relations programs, arts and cultural organizations and community events. JM Family Enterprises focuses their philanthropy in the areas of at-risk youth, education, the arts and multi-cultural diversity. A contact person is listed along with an accompanying e-mail address and telephone number. A listing of the company's "African-American Achievers" winners is also available for viewing.

Giving Category (ies): arts, civic, education, social services, youth

◆ Johnson & Johnson

http://www.johnsonandjohnson.com/who_is_jnj/sr_index.html

Johnson & Johnson's well-regarded social responsibility program is outlined on the corporate Web site. Although the corporation's giving program no longer accepts unsolicited grant proposals, its various health and family programs may be of interest to grantseekers in those categories. Recent social responsibility reports are available for downloading.

Giving Category (ies): health, social services

◆ Kansas City Power & Light Company Community Outlets

http://www.kcpl.com/communit/index.htm

The company invests more than $1 million in the Kansas City community each year through community relations activities. The company's Dollar-Aide program helps people in need pay their utility bills year-round. Kansas City Power & Light works to create and support educational initiatives for students in and around the greater metropolitan area through their various educational partnership programs. This site provides links to information on the company, its products and services, employment opportunities and other corporate facts.

Giving Category (ies): civic, education, social services

◆ Kimberly-Clark

http://www.kimberly-clark.com/who/citizenship/

Kimberly Clark funding supports social services, medical research, disaster relief, the environment, communities, education and arts and culture. The Web site provides news and financial information about the company. Some of the programs funded are the Nature Conservancy, the Girls and Boys Club and Junior Achievement. The company has supported minority scholarship funds, symphony orchestras and zoos.

Giving Category (ies): arts, civic, education, environment, health, science, social services

◆ Kingfisher in the Community

http://www.kingfisher.co.uk/social.htm

Grantseekers will find a description of this British giver's funding areas on this Internet site. Primary support goes to child and youth development. Kingfisher supports the Entente Cordiale Scholarship scheme which enables the most outstanding students of both England and France to study or carry out research for a year on the other side of the Channel. Another of the company's sponsorship programs is the "Kingfisher Challenge 2000." There is a link that grantseekers can look at which is entirely devoted to information on this new program. Users can link to the corporate home page for information on products, services and financials. This Web site can now also be viewed in French.

Giving Category (ies): education

◆ KN Energy

http://www.kne.com/pages/community/funding.htm

The KN Energy Foundation makes charitable contributions to programs emphasizing youth, leadership, arts and culture, education and economic development. This Web site offers an extensive funding history, including past and present grants made, along with dollar amounts donated. Grant recipients include Opera Colorado, Creighton Library Foundation, National Historic Trails Foundation and the Young Americans Education Foundation.

Giving Category (ies): arts, civic, education, youth

◆ Kodak Corporation

http://www.kodak.com/us/en/corp/community.shtml

Kodak Corporation Web site contains basic corporate giving information as well as links to selected organizations that receive Kodak funding. Grantseekers also can link to information on organizations and events that Kodak sponsors, including the National Women's Hall of Fame. The Web site also contains links to the company's home page for an online version of its annual report or information on its products and services.

Giving Category (ies): arts, civic, education, health, social services

◆ LEGOLAND California

http://www.legolandca.com/education.idc

LEGOLAND California provides grants in the field of education. Programs include the LEGOLAND California Educational Grant and the Heart of Learning Awards. The Web site describes each program, provides contact information and grant guidelines. An application may be printed from this Web site in PDF format.

Giving Category (ies): education

◆ Levi Strauss & Company

http://www.levistrauss.com/index_about.html

Levi Strauss & Company (LS&CO) donates more than $20 million annually in combined charitable gifts to organizations in over forty countries. Levi's Global Giving Program is carried out in the United States through the Levi Strauss Foundation (LSF). LS&CO and the LSF channel resources to communities where the company has a business presence. They sponsor AIDS education and prevention programs, support anti-racism and social justice initiatives, promote economic empowerment for the poor and disenfranchised and fund projects that engage youth in decision-making and social action. Included in this Web site are several giving case studies. Grantseekers will find global giving guidelines, directions on how to apply and mailing addresses for inquiries.

Giving Category (ies): civic, education, health, international, social services

◆ The Limited Inc. Foundation

http://www.limited.com/philanthropy/

The Limited Inc. Foundation supports education, arts and culture, social services, healthcare and research and community betterment programs. Grantseekers will find a listing of the company's past funding recipients.

Giving Category (ies): arts, civic, education, health, science, social services

◆ Lotus Development Corporation Philanthropy Program

http://www.lotus.com/home.nsf/welcome/corporate

The Lotus Philanthropy Program was formally merged into the IBM corporate contributions program in late 1998. The Lotus Web site details the organization's historic link to philanthropy, celebrates its accomplishments and links to the IBM Web site. Among the decisions that have been made concerning strategic shifts in program focus, the following are in effect: the Massachusetts-based Grantmaking Program has introduced new guidelines, offering support primarily to technology-based projects focused on K-12 education reform, workforce development, global workforce diversity or technology enhancements for the nonprofit sector. The geographic focus has broadened to cover Massachusetts as a whole and the priority is on grants providing IBM and Lotus technology as opposed to pure cash contributions; The US-based Product Donations Program continues, focusing on organizations working in K-12 education reform, workforce development and global workforce diversity, with donations also available for technology enhancements for the nonprofit sector.

Giving Category (ies): civic, education

◆ Lowe's Companies

http://www.lowes.com/lowes/findex.asp

Grantseekers will find a list of company-sponsored projects and organizations. Giving programs include Clean and Green and Lowe's Charitable and Educational Foundation. Recently the board established K-12 education as the primary focus for this foundation. There is a link to specific education and charitable projects. On a separate link, information is given about the Lowe's/Ferry Morse School Program. Grantseekers also can link to the corporate home page for information on the company and its products, "how to" and home safety tips and a list of career opportunities.

Giving Category (ies): education, environment, social services

◆ Lubrizol Foundation

http://www.lubrizol.com/aboutlubrizol/lz_foundation/index.htm

The Lubrizol Corporation awards financial support to educational institutions and charitable organizations in communities primarily within the United States where Lubrizol operates major facilities (i.e. Greater Houston and Cleveland). The application process is reviewed and contact information is given. A recent annual report may be viewed in Adobe Acrobat.

Giving Category (ies): education

◆ Marks & Spencer

http://www.marks-and-spencer.co.uk/corporate/

The Marks & Spencer Web site provides an online version of its 1998/1999 annual report. The company has seven main areas of support which include: People Care (the elderly), those with disabilities, mental health, family and parenting issues, addiction, homelessness and children. Under the company's "Community and Cultural and Opportunities," there exists four main areas of support: education, training and employment; crime reduction and victims of crime; community services; and environment. Support is also given to cultural programs, including the arts. Application guidelines and tips for applying can also be found on this site.

Giving Category (ies): arts, education, environment, health, social services

◆ Mary Kay

http://www.marykay.com/MKACF/MKACF.html

The Mary Kay Ash Charitable Foundation provides funding for cancer research throughout the United States at leading institutions and universities. Contact information is available, as are links to cancer related Web sites. Past grant recipients are listed.

Giving Category (ies): health, science

◆ Mattel, Inc.

http://www.mattel.com/corporate/company/mattel_foundation/

The Mattel Children's Foundation promotes the spirit of philanthropy and community involvement among its employees and makes charitable investments aimed at furthering the company's goal to better the lives of children in need. The Web site offers a history of the company, news and employment opportunities.

Giving Category (ies): youth

◆ McDonald's-Our Community

http://www.mcdonalds.com/community/index.html

The McDonald's Community Internet site offers details on the company's four major giving areas: Ronald McDonald House Charities; McDonald's Earth Effort; education; and health (immunization). Grantseekers will find basic application guidelines for Ronald McDonald House Charities grants. There are several links with specific information and programs under each of the company's four main giving categories. Users can link to the corporate home page for a variety of information on the company.

Giving Category (ies): education, environment, health, social services

◆ MCI WorldCom

http://www.wcom.com/marcopolo/index.shtml

Details of the MCI WorldCom Marco Polo education initiative are on this site. The MarcoPolo program provides no-cost, standards-based Internet content for the K-12 teacher and classroom, developed by the nation's content experts. Grant opportunities for education programs and teacher training kits are offered by the program and are detailed on the Web site.

Giving Category (ies): education

◆ Medtronic Foundation

http://www.medtronic.com/foundation/

The Medtronic Foundation Web page contains information on the foundation's mission, most recent giving figures, including a percentage breakdown of giving by category and highlights of its STAR (Science and Technology Are Rewarding) program. Grantseekers also can link to guidelines and application procedures for each of the foundation's giving programs. Also included are the communities where grants are available. A 1998-1999 grants list and grantmaking summary are also found on this Web site.

Giving Category (ies): art, civic, education, health, science, social services

◆ Men's Wearhouse

http://www.menswearhouse.com/html/community_commitments.html

The Men's Wearhouse offers funding in the following areas: social services, healthcare, children and youth, religion, arts and culture, community events, education and animal welfare. Although the Men's Wearhouse focuses on spending its charitable donation dollars in the same markets where their stores are in operation, the company does make contributions to national organizations. These include the American Red Cross, Girl Scouts of America and the Jane Goodall Institute. A listing of recent local and national grants is provided.

Giving Category (ies): arts, education, health, religion, social services, youth

◆ Merck & Co.

http://www.merck.com/philanthropy/

The mission of the Merck Company Foundation is to advance the company's philanthropic goals to support biomedical science training and education and to improve healthcare worldwide. Where appropriate, funding is also given to support social service, art and cultural, civic, environmental and other programs. The foundation also supports employee giving to qualified nonprofit organizations through the Matching Gift Program and Employee Giving Campaign. Grantseekers will find an electronic version of their 1998 annual report, information on products and services, a statement of corporate responsibility and a description of the UNCF/Merck Science Initiative. Grantseekers, however, will not find any specific giving guidelines or application procedures. Contact information is provided. The Merck & Co. home page links users to basic information about this corporate giver.

Giving Category (ies): arts, civic, education, environment, health, international, social services

◆ Metropolitan Life Insurance Company

http://www.metlife.com/

The Metropolitan Life Foundation was established in 1976 by MetLife for the purpose of supporting various educational, health and welfare, civic and cultural organizations. MetLife's Web site offers an array of information on its direct giving program and its company-sponsored foundation. Overviews are provided for the Social Investment program, the Targeted Suppliers program and the foundation. Grantseekers will find application procedures for program funding and foundation giving. The foundation Web page breaks down its most recent contributions by major giving category and offers links to philanthropic resource sites and several nonprofit sites.

Giving Category (ies): arts, civic, education, health

◆ Microsoft Community Affairs

http://www.microsoft.com/giving/

Microsoft's national corporate philanthropy is focused on creating greater access to information technology in disadvantaged communities. The Microsoft Community Affairs home page contains basic information on Microsoft funding programs, namely, employee giving, including a matching gifts program and volunteer efforts; community giving; and its education programs. The corporation's community support and software donations also are featured, as are Microsoft's three national initiatives: Libraries Online, Working Connections/America's Community Colleges and Open Studio/The Arts Online. Highlights of the 1998 annual giving report can be found on the Web site. Grantseekers can find recent and archived giving related press releases. Users can link to the corporate home page for information on Microsoft products and services.

Giving Category (ies): arts, civic, education, environment, health, social services

◆ Millipore Foundation

http://www.millipore.com/corporate/mf.nsf/docs/42YSSX

Grantseekers will find information on the foundation's mission, giving programs and application guidelines on Millipore's Internet site. A financial summary lists its most recent giving totals. An "ask the director" page allows users to e-mail questions to the foundation about its programs. A link to the company's home page allows users to learn more about Millipore's products and services.

Giving Category (ies): civic, education, science, social services

◆ Mintz Levin Community Service

http://www.mintz.com/

This legal firm's Web site informs visitors of its pro bono policy, highlighting the firm's help with the Vilna Center for Jewish Heritage and major community initiatives. Among them are programs designed to fight domestic violence. The firm also has recently initiated an Internet Access Project, introducing Boston-area students and educators to the resources and capabilities of the Internet.

Giving Category (ies): civic, education, social services

◆ Mitsubishi Electric America Foundation

http://www.meaf.org/

Grantseekers will find on this corporate foundation's Internet site the foundation's history, mission statement, list of officers and directors, information on important projects funded by the foundation, press releases and an overview of current and past grant recipients. An online guidelines brochure offers detailed application procedures and giving restrictions. The Web page also provides a link to the sponsoring company's Web page where grantseekers can learn more about the company's product and services.

Giving Category (ies): education, health

◆ Monsanto Fund

http://www.monsanto.com/monsanto/mediacenter/default.htm

The Monsanto Fund Web site does not provide its giving guidelines or details on how to apply for funds, but grantseekers can find a general overview of the company's giving program and examples of recent grant winners from the company's media center, which lists recent press releases and background on the fund.

Giving Category (ies): arts, education, social services

◆ J. P. Morgan and Company Community Relations

http://www.jpmorgan.com/CorpInfo/CRA/CommunityDevel.html

J. P. Morgan makes charitable contributions to a wide range of organizations in the arts, education, the environment, health and human services, international affairs and urban affairs. In 1998 contributions totaled more than $17 million. The Web site contains links with more specific information on each of the major giving areas. The company's charitable giving is concentrated in New York City, where their headquarters are located, but their philanthropy does extend globally. The entire 1998 annual report is available in PDF format or highlighted details of the report can be viewed without Adobe Acrobat. Additional information is provided on the company via a link to the corporate Web site.

Giving Category (ies): arts, civic, education, environment, health, international, social services

◆ Motorola

http://www.mot.com/General/Sponsors/

The Motorola Web site provides links to company-sponsored organizations and projects in the areas of arts and culture, education and research and sports and athletics. One such project highlighted on this Web site is the Ocean Planet hosted by the Smithsonian's Museum of Natural History and sponsored by Motorola. The company's home page provides details on its products and services.

Giving Category (ies): arts, civic, education

◆ National Semiconductor Community Care

http://www.national.com/community/

National Semiconductor Community Care Web site offers grantseekers information on its funding initiatives and volunteer activity, namely improving education and addressing critical community needs; describes its employee volunteerism program and employee giving campaigns; and lists guidelines and restrictions on funding. A link to the corporate home page provides details on the company.

Giving Category (ies): education, social services

◆ NatWest Group Community Relations-Group Community Review

http://www.natwestgroup.com/comm/index.html

This British corporate giver's site contains information on its funding programs in the United Kingdom and worldwide. Community initiatives include working with, among others, secondary school children, vulnerable youngsters, those caring for disabled and elderly people and community enterprises. Financial literacy, community development and volunteerism are high priorities. Grantseekers can link to the corporate home page for more information on NatWest Group. Users can look at a 1998/1999 Social Impact Review.

Giving Category (ies): civic, education, social services

◆ NEC Foundation of America

http://www.nec.com/search/index.html

Detailed community relations and foundation information can be found under the corporate citizenship heading on the site. The NEC Foundation supports programs with national reach and impact in science and technology education, principally at the secondary level, and/or assistive technology for people with disabilities. This corporate foundation's Web site provides grantseekers with all the necessary information to apply for funding, including guidelines, application procedures, giving restrictions, deadline information and giving priorities, as well as a listing of recent grants. There is a listing of board and committee members as well. Grantseekers can also link to other philanthropic sites on the Internet. The Web site has a "Quick Test for Eligibility" link, as well as a "Top Ten Turn Down Reasons" link.

Giving Category (ies): education, science, social services

◆ Nellie Mae Foundation

http://www.nelliemaefoundation.org

This site is currently under construction, but should be launched soon. For guidelines and funding information, please contact wboussicaut@nmfdn.org or call 781-348-4200.

Giving Category (ies): education

◆ Nordstrom

http://www2.nordstrom.com/shop/default.asp?section=aboutus&content=%2Faboutus%2Fdiversity%2Fmission%5Fstatement%2Ehtml

Under its diversity affairs program, Nordstrom provides support to community organizations through contributions, outreach programs, special events and volunteerism. The company's financial contributions target education, human services, the arts and community development. Nordstrom encourages employees to volunteer in regional activities such as food and blood drives, walk-a-thons for AIDS and other causes, such as penpals or mentors to local students and adopting families in need over the holidays.

Giving Category (ies): arts, education, social services

◆ Nortel Networks

http://www.nortelnetworks.com/Corporate/Community/citizenship/html/index.html

Nortel Networks, formerly known as Bay Networks, does not believe in the traditional approach to corporate citizenship. They have instead focused their corporate citizenship efforts in three main areas: business fundamentals, science and technology education and community support. The company offers awards to Nortel Network Scholars. The Web site gives a very brief overview of this program, but does list a contact person for more information. NetKnowledge provides teachers with networking curriculum and training, all at no cost to their schools. The community support link describes some of the recent volunteer activities of Nortel Network's employees. Users can also find news releases discussing recent support given by the company to various causes.

Giving Category (ies): education, international, social services

◆ Northeast Utilities Community Services

http://www.nu.com/partners/commun.htm#contributions/

Visitors to this Internet site will find information on Northeast Utilities' direct corporate giving program and its employee volunteer activities. Funding primarily supports education, social and health programs and environmental causes. Company support is given in the states of Connecticut, Massachusetts and New Hampshire. Northeast Utilities offers numerous nature trails, information and science centers and recreational facilities for the general public and school groups. The company's partnerships in education focus on helping high-risk students; enhancing science, math, engineering and computer skills; and strengthening public education and adult literacy programs. In addition, Northeast Utilities Community Services donates funds to the United Way, shelters and soup kitchens. Giving priorities are outlined and contact information is also provided in the forms of e-mail, a toll free phone number and regular mailing address. Users can link to the corporate home page for additional information on the company.

Giving Category (ies): civic, education, environment, health, social services

◆ Northern States Power Company Community Involvement

http://www.nspco.com/co/co.htm

The Northern States Power Company (NSP) Community Involvement site offers information on the company's corporate affairs and charitable contributions. NSP's corporate contributions focus on the citizens in its operating communities. Employees and retirees are actively involved in community events, a speakers bureau, education initiatives, power plant tours and other services coordinated by the community affairs department.

Giving Category (ies): education, social services

◆ Northwest Airlines

http://www.nwa.com/corpinfo/aircares/

Northwest Airlines has two major funding programs, the AirCares Program and the KidCares Program. Contact information is supplied, as is an e-mail address to request an application for the KidCares Program. Both initiatives are defined, as are guidelines and eligibility requirements. Grantseekers can view a listing of all of Northwest Airlines AirCares partners.

Giving Category (ies): social services

◆ Novartis Foundation for Sustainable Development

http://www.foundation.novartis.com/

The company is engaged in programs in developing countries that directly contribute to an improvement in the quality of life of the poorest people. The Novartis Foundation for Sustainable Development Web site provides information on the corporate foundation's history, philosophy and giving priorities. Development assistance programs focus on the areas of agriculture, health, social development and emergency aid. Grantseekers can browse recent foundation articles and publications and visit the sponsoring company's home page. Included on the site are the results of a survey that assesses the foundation's work.

Giving Category (ies): health, international, social services

◆ Novell

http://www.novell.com/careers/college/cr/index.html

Novell corporate philanthropy consists of software donations and employee volunteer efforts in the areas of education, critical community needs and cultural development. Grantseekers will find contact information and corporate giving guidelines. Also available is a listing of past recipients. The company's scholarship program is reviewed and software donation recipients are listed.

Giving Category (ies): arts, education

◆ Occidental Petroleum Corporation

http://www.oxy.com/html/soc_resp.htm

The Occidental Petroleum Corporation focuses its giving on giving back to the environment. Current environmental projects include working to establish an artificial reef at the company's Idd el Shargi EOR project offshore Qatar; waste management and pollution prevention activities; and becoming a member of the Wildlife Habitat Council, whose goal is to increase the number and enhance the quality of wildlife habitat on corporate, private and public lands.

Giving Category (ies): environment

◆ Olin Corporation

http://www.olin.com/about/communities.asp

Recently, the Olin Corporation Charitable Trust's program of giving has become more focused on three priority categories: education with a science and technology emphasis; programs that include Olin employees as volunteers and that impact communities in which employees work and live; and conservation, environmental education and environmental research. One program highlighted in the Web site is the Science Education for Public Understanding Project (SEPUP). The Web site also has a list of winners of Olin Corporation's 1999 Environmental Recognition Awards.

Giving Category (ies): education, environment

◆ Oshman's SuperSports USA

http://www.oshmans.com/womensports/oshmanwomen.html

The company seeks to acknowledge the importance of sports in the lives of girls and women. The Web site offers a calendar of events, past grant recipients and an application form.

Giving Category (ies): youth

◆ Owens Corning World Community Support

http://www.owens-corning.com/owens/acquainted/support/

Owens Corning World Community Support Internet site provides details on its giving philosophy and programs. Owens strives "to enhance and enrich local communities through a variety of civic and environmental projects, through monetary contributions, donation of materials, expertise and volunteer time." Users will find descriptions of select company-sponsored projects and organizations. Visitors can link to the corporate home page for details on products and services, investor information and home improvement tips.

Giving Category (ies): arts, civic, education, environment, health, international, social services

◆ Pacific Gas & Electric Contributions Program

http://www.pge.com/about_us/communities/giving.html

The Pacific Gas & Electric (PG&E) Contributions Program Web page contains general information on the corporate giver along with brief descriptions of its major funding areas of economic development, environment and education. Each year, PG&E gives up to $2.25 million to Relief for Energy Assistance through Community Help (REACH). Donations are also made to the United Way and to the American Red Cross. Additionally, the foundation provides funding for emergency preparedness and response.

Giving Category (ies): civic, education, environment, social services

◆ Patagonia Environmental Grants Program

http://www.patagonia.com/main.ehtml?section=enviroaction&return=1

Patagonia's environmental work is divided into two categories: what they do internally to reduce the impact of manufacturing their products and what they do to support and promote environmental activism. Patagonia, which contributes one percent of its sales to environmental issues, provides limited information on its Patagonia Environmental Grants Program, including funding cycles and contact information. Each organization that received a Patagonia grant in fiscal year 1999 is listed by category, with a brief description of what the grant was used for and projects the group is working on. There is a link to a number of essays compiled over the years by the company, that provide insight into who they are and what causes they care about. The Web page contains no application procedures or giving guidelines; however, grantseekers can link to the company's home page for information on its products.

Giving Category (ies): environment

◆ PECO Energy Community Development

http://www.peco.com/communit/

PECO Energy supports community activities and organizations. PECO Energy is a sponsor of PECO Primate Reserve at the Philadelphia Zoo. The company is a sponsor of many exhibits and special programs at the Franklin Institute Museum. Additionally, the company supports the Philadelphia Eagles. No grant guidelines or application procedures are found on this Web site.

Giving Category (ies): education, environment, social services

◆ Perkins Family Restaurants

http://www.perkinsrestaurants.com/

Perkins focuses its support on the Give Kids the World organization, which gives children with life-threatening illnesses and their families cost-free vacations to Florida's Disney World. Perkins Restaurant and Bakery also provides free meals to guests of Give Kids the World Village and is helping to build another dining area for this facility.

Giving Category (ies): youth

◆ Pfizer

http://www.pfizer.com/pfizerinc/philanthropy/

The Pfizer Foundation's mission is to promote access to quality healthcare and education, to nurture innovation and to support the community involvement of Pfizer people. The company supports programs and services designed to improve the health of children and works to eliminate debilitating diseases around the world. One of Pfizer's educational programs takes science "on the road" to children whose schools don't have needed equipment. The company strives to create new opportunities in neighborhoods struggling to recover from urban decay. They also support zoos, botanical gardens, museums, performing arts centers and other cultural and civic organizations. Several of the Pfizer Foundations programs are highlighted such as an animal care center at the Folsom Children's Zoo in Lincoln, NE, and the company's Trachoma Initiative.

Giving Category (ies): education, health

◆ Phillips Petroleum Company-Our Citizenship

http://www.phillips66.com/citizen.html

This corporate giver's Web site provides grantseekers with information on its philanthropic priorities, community action projects, employee volunteerism initiative, funding guidelines and restrictions. Most of the company's programs are oriented toward education and the environment. Grantseekers can view an online version of the company's 1998 Health, Environmental and Safety Report, which contains a comprehensive review of their programs. Phillips Petroleum's corporate home page offers visitors information on its products, services and financial and investor data.

Giving Category (ies): education, environment, health, social services

◆ Pillsbury Company

http://www.pillsbury.com/about/foundation.asp

The primary goal of the Pillsbury Company Foundation is to help provide caring adult mentors and role models who will prepare and empower economically disadvantaged young people, ages six to 12, to become self-sufficient and contributing members of our community. The foundation's secondary focus is youth empowerment organizations and programs that offer educational, employment and life skills young people need to achieve self-sufficiency. The Web site offers contact information, grant guidelines and restrictions.

Giving Category (ies): education, youth

◆ Proctor & Gamble Community Center

http://www.pg.com/community/

The Proctor & Gamble Community Center home page briefly describes the funder's priorities by program area. Grantseekers can find a summary of 1998-99 Proctor & Gamble contributions. Employees can find volunteer activities that fit with their interests. Guidelines and restrictions are not provided.

Giving Category (ies): arts, civic, education, environment, health, social services

◆ Prudential Foundation

http://www.prudential.com/community/cmfzz1000.html

Grantseekers will find a description of the Prudential Foundation's grantmaking programs on this Web site. The Prudential Foundation provides support to direct service programs that address the needs of the communities they serve in three areas, "Ready to Learn, Ready to Work, Ready to Live." There is a listing of some of the recent grants made by the foundation. A link to a larger list of grants, by geographical location, is also available. Foundation policies, guidelines and restrictions are provided. Grantseekers can download a copy of the Prudential Foundation application form. A link to the company home page provides information on Prudential services and financials, such as a 1998 annual report.

Giving Category (ies): arts, education, health, social services

◆ Quad/Graphics

http://www.qg.com/

The Quad/Graphics Community Fund has disbursed funds to help fight disease, further medical research, stock food pantries, support services at senior centers, supplement literacy and educational programs and assist in disaster relief. Quad/Graphics also matches employee contributions dollar for dollar, thereby doubling the amount. Employees can contribute in the form of cash, check or payroll deduction.

Giving Category (ies): health, social services

◆ Quaker Oats Foundation

http://www.quakeroats.com/about/community.html

The Quaker Oats Foundation funds education, healthcare, social services and strives to fight hunger. Contact information is provided, as is a list of organizations receiving funding. The Quaker Oats Foundation has supported the National Hispanic Scholarship Fund, the Greater Chicago Food Depository, the Boys and Girls Clubs of America and Chicago, various marathons that support research efforts on behalf of AIDS, cancer, diabetes and heart disease and Literacy Plus.

Giving Category (ies): education, health, social services

◆ Quantum Corporation

http://www.quantum.com/quantum/corporate/community/community.htm

Quantum makes grants to qualified nonprofit and public organizations in areas where it has facilities and its employees live, including: the greater Santa Clara Valley in California; Shrewsbury, MA, and nearby communities; Colorado Springs and Boulder, CO; as well as certain localities in Europe and Asia. Quantum grants focus on K-12 education, specifically teacher/professional development. Quantum also offers Capacity for Caring grants which include general support for the arts, health and human service and environmental organizations. Grant guidelines and instructions for submitting a grant proposal can be found on this Web site.

Giving Category (ies): arts, education, environment, social services

◆ Ralston Purina Company

http://www.ralston.com/corpinfo/communit.htm

The Ralston Purina Company supports a broad range of charitable organizations, including those which assist the disadvantaged, those which provide arts and cultural programs and those which support improvements in educational systems. Two of the company's current programs are, Purina Pets For People program and Change Your Clock, Change Your Battery program. These programs involve donations to humane shelters and encourage people to change the batteries in their smoke detectors.

Giving Category (ies): arts, education, social services

◆ Rand Merchant Bank Social Responsibility

http://www.rmb.co.za/company/social.html

Rand Merchant Bank is committed to contributing to the transformation of South Africa. The Rand Merchant Bank Social Responsibility Web site offers grantseekers a basic overview of this South African company's giving priorities that include a reconstruction and development program and education initiatives. The Andrew Mapheto Memorial is awarded annually to a deserving scholar from a disadvantaged background. The bank played a major role in the establishment and funding of the Nelson Mandela Children's Fund. It also provides financial assistance to aspiring black accountants, supports teacher training, funds international scholarships for candidates at U.S. banks and supports extracurricular holiday programs for disadvantaged youths. Grantseekers also can link to the corporate home page for details on services, financials and career opportunities.

Giving Category (ies): civic, education

◆ Reebok

http://www.reebok.com/humanrights/home.html

Grantseekers will find detailed information on the Reebok Human Rights Program on this site. A history of the program is provided along with a list of human rights award recipients and a description of the Witness project. A brief overview of Reebok's Human Rights Foundation guidelines is available, along with a contact phone number for additional information.

Giving Category (ies): civic, international, social services

◆ Rhone-Poulenc Foundation

http://www.rhone-poulenc.com/framu/prms1000.htm

This Web site contains information on the company's history, its corporate foundation and the foundation management committee. The site also describes the foundation's giving priorities: research and scientific partnerships, arts and culture, education and sponsorship of Institute de France. Grantseekers also can link to the company's home page for information on its products, services and financials.

Giving Category (ies): arts, education, science

◆ Rite Aid

http://www.riteaid.com/company_info/citizen_ra/citizen_frameset.html

Rite Aid is currently supporting two healthcare programs, Mother's Day Mammograms and the Children's Miracle Network. Information is provided on both of these programs, including a FAQs section and a listing of all the children's hospitals that have received funding.

Giving Category (ies): health

◆ Rohm and Haas and the Community

http://www.rohmhaas.com/company/CSI/index.html

Rohm and Haas' Internet site contains information on its philanthropic program, along with the company's funding criteria. Grantseekers also will find giving guidelines; application procedures; links to corporate data, including a company overview; lists of products and services; and financial information.

Giving Category (ies): arts, civic, education, health, social services

◆ Rolex Awards for Enterprise

http://www.rolexawards.com/

Rolex offers awards to men and women forging new ground in areas that advance human knowledge and well-being. The Web site provides information on the Rolex Awards for Enterprise, including history, guidelines and restrictions. Recent and past winners may be viewed, the selection committee is listed and contact information is provided.

Giving Category (ies): civic

◆ Samsung Group Social Activities

http://www.samsung.com/community/index.html

The Samsung Group Social Activities Web site lists its four major funding areas: social welfare, academic and education programs, culture and art and environmental preservation. Grantseekers can link to each giving category for a sample list of company-sponsored projects and organizations. Much corporate community relations information is available. Information also is provided on the volunteer service program. Grantseekers can learn more about Samsung's products and services via a link to the corporate Web site.

Giving Category (ies): arts, education, environment, social services, youth

◆ Sears, Roebuck and Company

http://www.sears.com/
(No direct link-Click "About Sears"-Click "For the Public"-Click "Community")

Sears includes some limited corporate contributions on its Web site, including a link to Gilda's Club, a favorite charity of the retailer. Sears is backing Gilda's Club with storewide programs to generate awareness and raise funds which will enable Gilda's Club to open more clubhouses around the country. The Web site discusses how the company promotes employee volunteerism. One such volunteer program is retired General Colin L. Powell's America's Promise campaign, where the company's 300,000 associates contributed more than 160,000 hours volunteering at local nonprofit agencies last year. Sears, Roebuck and company joined forces with Youth Service America (YSA) to honor outstanding young people with the Sears/YSA Larger Than Life Awards. Although some giving totals are included, the site does not detail specific policies or grantmaking guidelines.

Giving Category (ies): health, social services

◆ Sega Foundation

http://www.sega.com/foundation/

Since 1992 the Sega Foundation has been committed to supporting youth education and health organizations. Organizations supported by Sega are providing access to healthcare and services for those affected by HIV/AIDS. In 1997, the Sega Foundation aligned its giving with the organizational values of America's Promise so as to ensure that all American children and youth have access to a mentor, a safe place after school hours, a healthy start, marketable skills through education and an opportunity to serve their communities. There is a link to America's Promise. There are links to sample education and health programs. Grantseekers will find a list of funding guidelines and product donations. Users will be able to view a list of grant recipients, broken down by giving category, for the years 1992 through 1998. Grantseekers also can link to the sponsoring company's home page for information on its product and services.

Giving Category (ies): education, health, social services

◆ SmithKline Beecham Community Partnership

http://www.sb.com/company/community

This corporate giver's Web site provides a brief overview of the healthcare projects it supports, including its broad product donation program. The foundation's range of giving is both national and international in scope. The Community Partnership program focuses on programs that complement the company's core business of providing healthcare. In January 1998, SmithKline Beecham announced a very large global disease elimination program, where SmithKline Beecham will be collaborating with the World Health Organization (WHO) to eliminate lymphatic filariasis. Grantseekers will find application procedures and guidelines at the site, as well as e-mail addresses for giving officers. A link to the corporate home page describes the company's products and services and lists employment opportunities.

Giving Category (ies): health, international, social services

◆ Sonoco Foundation

http://www.sonoco.com/sonoco_foundation.htm

The Sonoco Foundation site provides basic information on its funding policy and program areas and includes application procedures and restrictions on giving. The vast majority of the company's funds support United State institutions with a local, rather than a national, perspective. A grants guidelines/considerations link gives a brief description of what types of programs are funded for each of the different giving categories. Grantseekers can link to the sponsoring company's Web site for information on its products and services, financial data, list of operating locations and employment opportunities.

Giving Category (ies): arts, education, environment, health, social services

◆ Southwire Company-Our Work in the Community

http://www.southwire.com/community/

Southwire's Web site provides information on its education initiatives and environmental awards and projects. Education grant request and environmental awards forms are available online, along with speakers bureau request and Southwire tour request forms. The company's home page lists information on its products and services.

Giving Category (ies): civic, education, environment

◆ Sprint Corporation

http://www.sprint.com/sprint/overview/commun.html

On this corporate giver's Web page, grantseekers will find information on employee volunteerism, corporate sponsorships and the company-sponsored Sprint Foundation. The site also contains information on the foundation's philanthropic interests and application guidelines. Users are able to view the company's 1998 annual report, which contains details of all grants made in that year. Grantseekers also can link to the company's Web site to learn more about its products and services.

Giving Category (ies): arts, civic, education, social services

◆ Starbucks Corporation

http://www.starbucks.com/company/community.asp?nav=3

The Starbucks Corporation founded the Starbucks Foundation and is involved in community giving and the environment. The Starbucks Foundation focuses on literacy. Grant information and past recipients are reviewed. Starbucks provides cash and product donations and participates in Earth Day clean-ups, regional AIDS walks and local literacy organizations. Environmental programs are also reviewed.

Giving Category (ies): education, environment, social services

◆ Stolichnaya

http://www.stoli.com/foe/charities/index.cgi

On this Web site, grantseekers will find a list of charities and events. The company donates advertising space to deserving nonprofits, primarily supporting health, environmental and welfare organizations. Grantseekers also will find more information on the company on its home page.

Giving Category (ies): environment, health, social services

◆ Stonyfield Farm

http://www.stonyfield.com/earth/action.htm

The company gives 10 percent of its profits to efforts that help protect or restore the earth. Some recipients of the company's Profits for the Planet program include Project Life Lab, the Conservation Law Foundation, the Northeast Organic Farming Association and Earth College. Stonyfield Farm has also created EcoAdventures for kids, which includes audio lessons that teach kids about Earth and what they can do to be Planet Protectors. This tape and a companion guide are available to parents and teachers. A telephone number is available for further questions about these programs. Many links are available to other aspects of the company.

Giving Category (ies): environment

◆ Stride Rite Foundation

http://www.strideritecorp.com/philanthropy_index.html

Stride Rite's charitable giving directs funds and manpower towards youth-oriented organizations and groups that positively impact a child's skill development, health, education and sense of self. Grant guidelines, contact information, past recipients, financial information and an online application are all provided on this Web site.

Giving Category (ies): education, health, youth

◆ Sun Microsystems

http://www.sun.com/aboutsun/comm_invest/foundation.html

The Sun Microsystems' Web page contains information on the company's foundation, its funding criteria, application procedures, deadlines and funding cycle dates. The Sun Microsystems Foundation funds grants made through the following worldwide corporate affairs programs: education and employment training grants program; Open Gateways program; employee matching gifts program; and community partnership program. There is a list of foundation staff contacts. Grantseekers also can find information on the company's employee volunteer program or link to the company's home page to learn more about its products and services.

Giving Category (ies): civic, education

◆ Tandy Corporation

http://www.tandy.com/scholars/

The Tandy Corporation sponsors the Radio Shack National Teacher Awards program. Awards are presented to outstanding mathematics, science and technology teachers. Program description and history, application procedures, deadlines and eligibility requirements, a list of the National Advisory Council, contact information, past recipients and an events calendar are all provided to grantseekers.

Giving Category (ies): education

◆ Target Stores

http://target.com/company/community/

Target supports communities locally, through scholarships, grants and Target volunteers. On a national scale, they support the Washington Monument, the Red Cross, the United Way and St. Jude Children's Research Hospital. Locally, the company supports three areas: the arts, education and families. A grant guidelines brochure for Target Arts in Education Grants may be obtained at any Target store. Eligibility requirements and application procedures are offered through this Web site.

Giving Category (ies): arts, education, health, social services

◆ Tesoro Hawaii Foundation

http://www.energypeople.com/community/index.htm

The Tesoro Petroleum Company's Foundation Web site, formerly known as the BHP Hawaii Foundation Web page, provides only minimal information on the company's giving program. It focuses primarily on environmental and education concerns. The site includes a list of nonprofits that have received funding along with program descriptions. A brief set of guidelines also is provided.

Giving Category (ies): education, environment, social services

◆ Texaco Foundation

http://www.texaco.com/corporate/foundation/foundation_main.htm

This Web site contains information on the company; its various products, services and programs; and its foundation. This Internet site contains detailed corporate data as well as information on its sponsorship activities in the arts. Grant guidelines are included, with information on how grant applications are evaluated.

Giving Category (ies): arts, civic, education

◆ Texas Instruments Corporate Citizenship

http://www.ti.com/corp/docs/community/community.html

This Web page contains detailed information on the company's funding priorities, which have a major emphasis on education. Grantseekers also will find information about the TI Foundation, including information on application procedures and giving guidelines. It also provides some links to major grant recipients and links back to the company's home page for information on its products, services and financials.

Giving Category (ies): arts, education, health, science

◆ Think Quest

http://www.thinkquest.org/index.shtml

The Think Quest Web page provides information on its various competitions, such as: Internet Challenge; Junior; and Tomorrow's Teachers. There are links to each of these contests, complete with descriptions. There are five award categories: science and mathematics; arts and literature; social sciences; sports and health; and interdisciplinary. The Internet site contains step-by-step contest instructions. Grantseekers also can link to 1999 judging feedback, with sample judge's scores and comments.

Giving Category (ies): education, international, science

◆ Thomson Financial Services Community Spirit

http://www.tfn.com/THOMSON/community/index.html

The company focuses on two major areas of giving: community groups and initiatives providing innovative services that focus on child and youth development, learning and leadership development; and public primary and secondary schools. Thomson Financial Services Community Spirit Web site offers grantseekers basic information on its school partnerships, employee matching gifts program and volunteer advocacy program. The company also makes used computer donations. A link to the corporate home page informs users of the company's products and services, latest news and employment opportunities.

Giving Category (ies): civic, education

◆ Tom's of Maine

http://www.tomsofmaine.com/mission/grants.htm

Tom's of Maine sets aside at least 10 percent of every year's pre-tax profits and awards this money to nonprofits that are doing work to support the arts, education, the environment and indigenous peoples. Typical grants range from $500 to $5,000, but larger grants are sometimes awarded. Recent and past grants can be viewed. Giving guidelines, eligibility requirements, application procedures, submission dates and contact information are provided.

Giving Category (ies): arts, education, environment, social services

◆ Toshiba America Foundation

http://www.toshiba.com/about/taf.html

Toshiba America's Web site provides an overview of the workings of the Toshiba America Foundation. The foundation supports middle and high school science and mathematics education programs, projects and activities throughout the United States. Detailed application guidelines, restrictions and deadlines for the foundation are provided, as well as examples of recent grants. The foundation's total annual grants budget is approximately $500,000. Users can e-mail the foundation directly from the Web site, with any questions or comments.

Giving Category (ies): education, science

◆ Toyota USA Foundation

http://www.toyota.com/welcome/index.html

The Toyota USA Foundation, which focuses giving on K-12 education, pays special attention to math and science. Grantseekers will find information on foundation news and guidelines, as well as the foundation's application process. There are also links to current and past grant recipients. A link to the corporate home page provides information on products and services.

Giving Category (ies): education, science

◆ Trillium Foundation

http://www.trilliumfoundation.org/

The Trillium Foundation was established in 1982 to ensure that a portion of the proceeds of the Ontario Lottery Corporation is directed toward social issues in Ontario. The foundation Internet site contains general background information; detailed giving program descriptions; financial statements; list of board members, staff and advisors; funding guidelines and restrictions; application procedures; recent grants list; and an online version of its annual report.

Giving Category (ies): civic, education, social services

◆ Union Carbide

http://www.unioncarbide.com/general/gencomm.html

Union Carbide's site notes that the company has organized community advisory panels at all of their major U.S. sites. These panels meet regularly with company representatives to discuss topics ranging from emergency response to environmental issues. Recycling is an important concern of the company. One of the Union Carbide Foundation's programs sponsors teachers from targeted communities to attend the Keystone Science School where they learn the best ways to teach environmental science to middle and high school students.

Giving Category (ies): arts, education, environment

◆ Unisys Social Responsibility

http://www.unisys.com/Unisys/sponsorships/

The Unisys sponsorship program Web site provides a short overview of this corporation's sponsorship program. Unisys primarily focuses its giving on math, science and technology literacy as well as on the arts and human services. The company also is a corporate underwriter of the Science and Learning Project, an Internet project spearheaded by the National Science Foundation. Brief giving guidelines are provided.

Giving Category (ies): arts, civic, education, social services

◆ United Parcel Service

http://www.community.ups.com/community/leading/foundation.html

The United Parcel Service's UPS Foundation has provided financial support for programs that support family and workplace literacy, food distribution and increased nationwide volunteerism. Overviews of the company's many programs are offered, such as the Region/District Grant program, Volunteer Impact initiative and the Prepared and Perishable Food Rescue Program.

Giving Category (ies): education, social services

◆ United Technologies Community Involvement

http://www.utc.com/commun/index.htm

The United Technologies Community Involvement Internet site lists the funding priorities of this corporate giver and gives brief descriptions of programs it has supported. Grantseekers also will find information on United Technologies matching gifts program, application guidelines and restrictions and a graphic display of funding totals by program area. A link to the corporate home page provides information on company products, services and financial data.

Giving Category (ies): arts, education, environment, international, social services

◆ US West

http://www.uswest.com/about/communities/

A listing of major initiatives, description of funding areas, recent grants list and application guidelines can be found on the US West Internet site. Projects of the US West Foundation are detailed, as is the RFP process. E-mail addresses of the program officers are provided and corporate sponsorship and volunteer efforts are reviewed.

Giving Category (ies): arts, civic, education, social services

◆ USG Corporation

http://www.usg.com/careers/involvement.html

USG's tradition of community involvement focuses on their corporate home of Chicago. The USG Foundation matches employee's contributions to colleges, hospitals and cultural institutions. The foundation focuses on helping the disadvantaged and the homelessness. Recent projects include the funding of a job training center on Chicago's south side and a grant to the Child Welfare League of the United States for parenting training for families living in shelters where USG's plants are located. Grantseekers are given the opportunity to apply online.

Giving Category (ies): arts, education, social services

◆ Valero Energy Corporation

http://www.valero.com/community/index.htm

Valero Energy Corporation's philanthropy includes its organized Valero volunteer councils, as well as the company's corporate financial support of many charitable organizations. Valero's contributions focus on such areas as health and social services; education; the environment; and culture and the arts. A few examples of recent Valero volunteer council projects are: adopt-a-school programs and mentoring; neighborhood beautification projects; building playgrounds in low-income neighborhoods; hosting Christmas dinner for low-income residents in the company's headquarters cafeteria; and the United Way.

Giving Category (ies): arts, education, environment, health, social services

◆ Vastar Resources, Inc.

http://www.vastar.com/fi/direct-charitables.html

Vastar's contributions priorities are education, community and health services, arts and humanities, environment and public information. Each area of funding is clearly defined. Application procedures and grant guidelines are offered. Grantseekers can view all of this information through Adobe Acrobat.

Giving Category (ies): arts and humanities, civic, education, environment, health, social services

◆ Vision Service Plan

http://www.vsp.com/corp/html/Comunity.htm

Vision Service Plan (VSP) focuses its funding on children and youth, human services and healthcare. One of the company's largest programs is Sight for Students, in which VSP provides eye exams and eyeglasses to children of the working poor. VSP and its employees have often come to the aid of their local communities after natural disasters, such as replacing lost or damaged eyeglasses of victims of Hurricane Hugo.

Giving Category (ies): health, social services, youth

◆ Vulcan Inc.

http://www.vulcaninc.com/plt0p04.htm

Vulcan Scholarships is Vulcan's company-sponsored foundation. Vulcan Scholarships provides financial support to engineering students. Forty-two scholarships have been awarded since 1985 and currently the foundation has 12 Vulcan Scholars who are engineering majors at colleges and universities across the nation. Current and past scholarship recipients are shown. Details about the Vulcan Scholarships are given, including award requirements, application procedures and contact information.

Giving Category (ies): education

◆ Walgreens

http://www.walgreens.com/about/community/default.jhtml

While a substantial amount of Walgreens' corporate donations go to health-related causes, the company also supports education and provides aid in the wake of disasters. A sample of recent charities that Walgreens has donated to is provided, including: Jackie Joyner-Kersee Youth Center Foundation; Children's Hospital of Southwest Florida; Turkish Consul General Earthquake Relief Fund; Multiple Sclerosis Society MS Walk; Zoological Society of Milwaukee County; and Houston Ebony Music Society, Inc.

Giving Category (ies): education, health, social services

◆ Wal-Mart Foundation

http://www.walmartfoundation.org

The Wal-Mart Foundation Web site offers information on the programs that Wal-Mart provides to the community. The foundation offers funding in the areas of education, the environment, health and human services and economic involvement. The Web site offers some general giving guidelines and funding restrictions. Grantseekers can see a list of how funds were dispersed for the year of 1998. The site reviews the company's work in the community, describes support to national organizations like the United Way and the Children's Miracle Network and offers information on scholarships and education initiatives. The Wal-Mart Foundation also responds to communities during natural disasters by contributing to the local Salvation Army and Red Cross. This site also connects to the Wal-Mart corporate home page that offers company, store and community information, including specific store department promotions.

Giving Category (ies): education, environment, health, social services

◆ Wendy's International, Inc.

http://www.wendys.com/community/community_frame.html

The Dave Thomas Foundation for Adoption was established in 1992. Its sole purpose is to help children throughout the United States find permanent homes and loving families. Many important links are available, which deal with adoption information, such as adoption agencies and support groups. The Wendy's High School Heisman Awards, Wendy's Three-Tour Challenge and Wendy's Classic Achiever are other programs that the company sponsors. They are all reviewed in this Web site.

Giving Category (ies): education, youth

◆ Whirlpool Foundation

http://www.whirlpoolcorp.com/whr/ics/foundation/

Through the Whirlpool Foundation, the company seeks to improve the quality of family life primarily in the communities where their businesses are. The foundation focuses on organizations that target family life issues. The Whirlpool Foundation site provides a description of its strategic grants program; citizenship grants program; employee-directed grant programs, including its matching gifts and dollar for doers; and scholarships for dependents of employees. The company also offers product donations. Grantseekers can e-mail the contact person for the foundation directly from the Web site. The foundation has a historic commitment that focuses on women's issues and the site offers a link to the women's studies section of the foundation. Users can view the company's report of corporate citizenship. The site also contains links to the sponsoring company's home page for information on its products, services and financials.

Giving Category (ies): civic, education, health, social services

◆ Windermere Foundation

http://63.224.45.138/about/comservindex.html

The Windermere Foundation, which makes grants to nonprofit organizations assisting the homeless in the Northwest, provides only basic information on its Web site. Grantseekers will find a copy of the foundation's mission, as well as some information about the corporation's volunteer efforts. The company sponsors a community service day, where employees volunteer their time to complete neighborhood improvement projects. The foundation also sponsors the University of Washington rowing program. The event is referred to as the Windermere Cup. A portion of each associate's commission helps fund the foundation, therefore, the agents themselves determine fund distribution.

Giving Category (ies): social services

◆ WRQ

http://www.wrq.com/aboutwrq/commun.htm

WRQ's philanthropy focuses on children and the environment. WRQ supports the Nature Conservancy with donations and volunteer labor. WRQ's other major commitment to the community is to Childhaven, providing child care, support services and education to help children and their families heal from the trauma of abuse and break its cycle.

Giving Category (ies): environment, youth

◆ Yahoo! Inc.

http://www.yahoo.com/info/community/

Yahoo! offers limited sponsorships of online media exposure to qualified nonprofit organizations. Yahoo! does not provide cash grants or financial sponsorships. Guidelines, contact information and application procedures are provided. This Web site also offers a listing of the company's current community Partners.

Giving Category (ies): civic, health, social services

◆ Yorkshire Electricity

http://www.yeg.co.uk/community/welcome.html

Yorkshire Electricity is committed to supporting community projects and is equally as committed to protecting the environment. Projects and sponsorships include: Yorkshire Wildlife Trust; Dyslexia Institute; and South Yorkshire People United. These projects, as well as the others that the company sponsors, are fully explained in their accompanying links.

Giving Category (ies): environment

◆ ZDNet

http://www.zdnet.com/familypc/schoolpc/

ZDNet's FamilyPC Teachers' Technology Foundation awards grants to teachers who have innovative ideas on how to integrate technology into their classrooms. The FamilyPC Teachers' Technology Foundation is the product of a collaboration between FamilyPC and their advertisers. The foundation's current board of advisors is provided, along with a short biography on each advisor. An overview of past winners is available. In addition, this Web site offers many, many links to educational resources and sites for children and parents to explore. Educational products for children are reviewed and then given an overall score.

Giving Category (ies): education

◆ AARP Andrus Foundation

http://www.andrus.org/

The AARP Andrus Foundation works to enhance the lives of older persons by expanding our understanding of aging. Its site offers users press releases, contact information, funding guidelines, information on the grant making process and types of grant programs available.

Giving Category (ies): health, social services

◆ Abelard Foundation

http://www.commoncounsel.org/foundation.html

Abelard is a family foundation with a history of progressive funding. The foundation is committed to supporting social change organizations. Its site offers users a list of past and present grantees, application deadlines, general grant information and a mailing address.

Giving Category (ies): social services

◆ Abell Foundation

http://www.abell.org/abell/

The Abell Foundation's mission is to effect positive change on societal problems in the Baltimore area, with a strong focus on programs promoting educational reform, job creation and tourism; strengthening families; reducing drug addiction; and alleviating hunger and homelessness. The foundation makes grants exclusively to organizations located in the state of Maryland. The Abell Foundation Internet site offers grantseekers information on its history, funding areas, guidelines, restrictions, application procedures and deadlines for submitting proposals. Users can download a copy of the application form. Links to several other related nonprofit and philanthropic organizations are provided.

Giving Category (ies): civic, education, health, social services

◆ Able Trust

http://www.abletrust.org/

The Able Trust, also known as the Florida Governor's Alliance for the Employment of Citizens with Disabilities, was established to provide Floridians with disabilities fair employment opportunities. The site offers information on endowments, special programs, grants, board members and how to contact the staff.

Giving Category (ies): health, social services

◆ Achelis Foundation

http://fdncenter.org/grantmaker/achelis/index.html

The Achelis Foundation focuses funding on biomedical research, arts and culture, education, social services and youth organizations. The site offers users a biennial report, grants list, foundation history, president's message, application guidelines and a list of trustees, officers and staff.

Giving Category (ies): arts, education, health, science, social services, youth

◆ Ahmanson Foundation

http://www.cerritos.edu/cerritos/development/funders_ahmanson.html

The Ahmanson Foundation focuses on arts/culture, disadvantaged (homeless, low-income), education (collegiate, pre-collegiate), environment, library (specialized collections) and medicine/healthcare (services). The site offers users a mailing address, general application/grant guidelines such as how to apply, deadlines, limitations and average dollar amounts donated.

Giving Category (ies): arts and humanities, education, environment, health, social services

◆ Aid to Artisans

http://www.aid2artisans.org/

Aid to Artisans (ATA) offers practical assistance to artisans worldwide, working in partnerships to foster artistic traditions, cultural vitality and community well-being. This Web site provides users with contact information including e-mail address, an online newsletter, a list of officers, directors and staff, an events calendar, a listing of job opportunities within the organization, past ATA programs and some very general information about grantmaking. Grantseekers may e-mail the ATA directly from the Web site for more specific information.

Giving Category (ies): arts

◆ Akron Community Foundation

http://www.ohio.com/nonprofit/acf/foundation_faq.html

Akron Community Foundation (ACF) links community resources with community needs by building a permanent endowment fund from donors in the community. From these funds, ACF distributes grants to qualified local nonprofit organizations and institutions which are actively working to improve the quality of life in Greater Akron. This site offers grantseekers contact information, an online information request form, a listing of staff and trustees, a calendar of events, press releases, grant application procedures and application deadlines.

Giving Category (ies): civic, education, social services, youth

◆ Alaska Conservation Foundation

http://www.akcf.org/

Alaska Conservation Foundation (ACF), is a community foundation for the environment that receives and awards grants throughout the state to protect the integrity of Alaska's ecosystems; and promote sustainable livelihoods for Alaska's communities and people. This Web site offers grantseekers contact information, grant guidelines, ACF publications for viewing, such as an annual report and newsletters, a list of recent grants and an in depth look at the foundation's programs and initiatives.

Giving Category (ies): environment

◆ Alaska Science and Technology Foundation

http://www.astf.org/

Established in 1988, the Alaska Science and Technology Foundation (ASTF), is operated as a state agency for the purpose of investing money towards the improvement of Alaska's economy, as well as for the advancement of the state's science and engineering capabilities. This Web site provides users with annual reports from the years 1995-1998, recent newsletters and press releases, a foundation history, an overview of grants and proposals, an online application and contact information, including e-mail links for the entire staff, as well as the mailing address, phone and fax numbers for the foundation's headquarters.

Giving Category (ies): science

◆ Alberta Foundation for the Arts

http://www.affta.ab.ca/

The mission of the Alberta Foundation for the Arts (AFA), is to help all Albertans to fully participate in and appreciate the cultural life of this province. The Web site offers users a listing of the foundation's board members, issues of the AFA Bulletin, information on the grants process, foundation and grants programs, advice on writing a proposal and toll free phone numbers to contact each staff member.

Giving Category (ies): arts

◆ J. A. and Kathryn Albertson Foundation

http://www.jkaf.org/fon.html

The J. A. and Kathryn Albertson Foundation is committed to "positive educational change, reform and improvement in the state of Idaho." The Web site offers the following information to grantseekers: foundation history; publications; FAQs; an overview of the foundation's programs and giving; and report forms for grantees. There is also a list of the foundation's staff and contacts, with corresponding e-mail addresses.

Giving Category (ies): education

◆ Albion Community Foundation

http://www.albionfoundation.org/

The Albion Community Foundation seeks to enhance the quality of life in the greater Albion area, for today's generation as well as future generations to come. The Web site contains grant information, application deadlines, application cover sheet and recent grants awarded by the foundation. There is a list of the foundation staff including the 1999 board of trustees. Grantseekers may contact the foundation directly from this Web site, via e-mail.

Giving Category (ies): arts, civic, education, health, social services

◆ Alcoholic Beverage Medical Research Foundation

http://www.abmrf.org/

The Alcoholic Beverage Medical Research Foundation (ABMRF) describes itself as being, "the largest, independent, nonprofit foundation in North America devoted solely to supporting research on the effects of alcohol on health, behavior and prevention of alcohol-related problems." The Web site gives contact information including mailing address, fax number and an e-mail address. Grantseekers are able to download the application and guidelines applicable to pursuing a grant from ABMRF. Application deadlines and a listing of 1998 grant recipients is also available.

Giving Category (ies): health

◆ Alger Regional Community Foundation

http://www.cmif.org/algerabout.htm

This foundation's focus is in improving the quality of life in Alger County. The Web site provides a list of the board of directors, foundation contact information and grant application information, including eligibility, guidelines and how to apply. There is even an online grant application.

Giving Category (ies): civic, education, health, social services

◆ Allegheny Foundation

http://www.scaife.com/allegheny.html

The Allegheny Foundation concentrates its giving in the Western Pennsylvania area and confines most of its grant awards to programs for historic preservation, civic development and education. A 1998 annual report is available for viewing. A very brief overview of how to apply for a grant, can also be found. Grantseekers may contact the foundation's president through the foundation's mailing address only.

Giving Category (ies): civic, education, social services

◆ Paul G. Allen Charitable Foundation

http://www.paulallen.com/foundations/

The foundation's goal is, "to promote the health and development of vulnerable populations and to strengthen families and communities in the Pacific Northwest." Priority is given to projects and programs that address social challenges and promote positive change. Grantseekers will find a list of past grant recipients, an overview of funding priorities and an online submission form that acts as a grant application. As for contact information, only a mailing address is available for the foundation's executive director.

Giving Category (ies): health, science, social services

◆ Allen Foundation

http://www.tamu.edu/baum/allen.html

Visitors to the Allen Foundation site will find a description of its funding program, which focuses on the field of human nutrition and the funding of relevant nutritional research anywhere in the world; information on its founder, William Webster Allen; list of trustees; basic guidelines and application procedures, including an application form title page that may be downloaded; and online annual reports for the past six years (1993-1998). The site also provides links to nutrition-related nonprofits and programs.

Giving Category (ies): education, health, international

◆ Allen Foundation for the Arts

http://www.paulallen.com/foundations/

The mission of the Allen Foundation of the Arts is to "strengthen the Pacific Northwest's cultural community and its services by supporting organizational and artistic excellence, innovation, diversity and access." Users will find a list of past grant recipients, an overview of funding priorities and an online submission form that acts as a grant application. As for contact information, only a mailing address is available for the foundation's executive director.

Giving Category (ies): arts

◆ Alliance Healthcare Foundation

http://www.alliancehf.org

The Alliance Healthcare Foundation, whose mission is to "promote quality healthcare for the medically indigent and underserved, primarily in San Diego County, through proactive grantmaking, fundraising, advocacy and education," lists on its Web site its giving priorities, giving guidelines and restrictions and recent grants. Application guidelines are provided for submitting both letters of intent and formal proposals.

Giving Category (ies): health

◆ Herb Alpert Foundation

http://www.almosounds.com/herbalpert/secondwind/found.html

The Herb Alpert Foundation makes annual contributions to the fields of education, the arts and the environment. The site offers a list of 1999 recipients of the Alpert Award in Arts. These awards are presented in conjunction with the California Institute of the Arts. The Web site offers information on the nomination process; and e-mail addresses and names of the foundation's program director and program assistant.

Giving Category (ies): arts, education, environment

◆ Jenifer Altman Foundation

http://www.jaf.org/

The Jenifer Altman Foundation describes itself as, "dedicated to the vision of a socially just and ecologically sustainable future through program interests in environmental health, mind-body health and improved child care." A description is given of each of the foundation's main programs. Grant application guidelines and instructions are reviewed, a foundation grant application cover sheet is provided, as is contact information.

Giving Category (ies): environment, health

◆ Amateur Athletic Foundation of Los Angeles

http://www.aafla.org

The Amateur Athletic Foundation of Los Angeles (AAF), created with a surplus of funds from the 1984 Olympic Games, was established to enhance the role that sports plays in the lives of Southern California residents and makes grants to organizations devoted to amateur sports. On the foundation's Web page grantseekers will find application criteria, an explanation of how the foundation administers grants, suggestions for grant applications, foundation history, board of directors and AAF publications.

Giving Category (ies): social services, youth

◆ American Association of Museums

http://www.aam-us.org/map.htm

The American Association of Museums' Institutional Assessment Program reviews a museum's entire operation, including mission and planning, governance, administration, finance, collections stewardship, interpretation and presentation, marketing, public relations, membership and community support. On the Web site, the assessment process is reviewed, as are funding options. Users of this Web site can also find out eligibility information, deadlines and application schedules. An application may be printed from the site. Phone and fax numbers are provided, as is an e-mail address.

Giving Category (ies): arts

◆ American Association of Physics Teachers

http://www.aapt.org/

The American Association of Physics Teachers (AAPT), continues its mission to "support the advancement of the physics education profession and the quality and effectiveness of physics education in the U.S. and throughout the World." Users will find information on events, meetings and committees. AAPT programs and publications may be viewed. The association can be contacted by e-mail.

Giving Category (ies): education, science

◆ American Association of School Libraries

http://www.ala.org/aasl/

The mission of the American Association of School Librarians (AASL) is, "to advocate excellence, facilitate change and develop leaders in the school library media field." Grantseekers will find AASL news, conferences and events on its site. Staff and contact information is provided, as are links to professional resources.

Giving Category (ies): arts and humanities, education

◆ American Association of University Women

http://www.aauw.org/

The American Association of University Women (AAUW) site includes information on the AAUW Educational Foundation, which funds pioneering research on girls and education, community action projects and fellowships and grants for outstanding women around the globe; and the AAUW Legal Advocacy Fund, which provides funds and a support system for women seeking judicial redress for sex discrimination in higher education. The site contains information on AAUW fellowships, grants and awards; research; membership features; publications; and related resources.

Giving Category (ies): civic, education, social services

◆ American Brain Tumor Association

http://neurosurgery.mgh.harvard.edu/abta/flwships.htm

The basic intent of the American Brain Tumor Association fellowship program is to encourage talented, junior investigators to enter or remain in, the field of brain tumor research. Foundation fellowships are reviewed. Application information, such as where to obtain an application form is provided. Contact information including an e-mail address is listed.

Giving Category (ies): health, science

◆ American Federation for Aging Research

http://www.afar.org/

The American Federation for Aging Research (AFAR), has helped scientists begin and further careers in aging research and geriatric medicine. 2000 AFAR award programs are listed. A mailing address is given for those interested in receiving an application. The federation's board of directors and executive staff are also listed. AFAR publications and press releases are available.

Giving Category (ies): health, science

◆ American Foundation for AIDS Research

http://www.amfar.org/index.html

The American Foundation for AIDS Research supports AIDS research, prevention and related public policy. The Web site provides daily news updates, press releases, publications, information on conferences and special events and contacts in each of the foundation's many departments. Grant information is available, such as deadlines and an RFP that may be downloaded from the Web site. Key foundation programs are reviewed.

Giving Category (ies): health, science

◆ American Foundation for the Blind

http://www.afb.org/afb/

The American Foundation for the Blind (AFB) is a leading national resource for people who are blind or visually impaired, the organizations that serve them and the general public. Foundation contact information is provided to all of the AFB's offices in the United States, including its headquarters located in New York. The Journal of Visual Impairment and Blindness is available to users in an online subscription format. AFB news, press releases, year 2000 scholarships and a 1998 annual report are all provided. Detailed information about all the different scholarships available, as well as instructions on how to apply for each of them, can also be found on this Web site.

Giving Category (ies): health, science, social services

◆ American Health Assistance Foundation

http://www.ahaf.org

The American Health Assistance Foundation is dedicated to funding research on age-related and degenerative diseases, educating the public about these diseases and providing emergency financial assistance to Alzheimer's disease patients and their caregivers. Contact information including an e-mail address is provided to grantseekers searching for grants in the areas of research and education. Those in need of financial assistance may also use the same contact information. The Web site offers links to many foundation related publications. An annual report may be ordered. Detailed descriptions are given about the foundation's major programs.

Giving Category (ies): health, science

◆ American Historical Association

http://www.theaha.org/

The American Historical Association's (AHA) Web site contains general information about the AHA, such as information on grants, prizes, fellowships, staff information, AHA's charter and mission statements, AHA's Constitution and bylaws and features how the AHA serves the K-12 teaching community through outreach programs, partnerships and other programs. Included is a list of 1999 grant and fellowship winners.

Giving Category (ies): arts, civic

◆ American Legion Child Welfare Foundation

http://www.legion.org/cwf.htm

The American Legion Child Welfare Foundation Web page highlights the foundation's purpose, application procedures, administrative process and lists information about donating to the foundation. The foundation supports organizations working to disseminate knowledge to improve the physical, mental, emotional and spiritual welfare of children and youth.

Giving Category (ies): education, health, social services, youth

◆ American Medical Association

http://www.ama-assn.org/med-sci/npsf/main.htm

The American Medical Association's National Patient Safety Foundation's Web page offers basic information about the foundation and its mission, patient safety literature from the American Medical Association, RFPs and related sites. The foundation's annual report can be viewed in Adobe Acrobat.

Giving Category (ies): health

◆ American Music Center

http://www.amc.net

The American Music Center Web page provides information on the center's grant programs, including the Aaron Copland Fund for Music Recording Program, the Aaron Copland Fund for Music Support for Performing Ensembles, the Mary Flagler Cary Charitable Trust/Live Music for Dance Program and the Margaret Fairbank Jory Copying Assistance Program. Information on the site includes the foundation's past, present and future, application deadlines, eligibility requirements, board of directors and directions for submitting applications. Also available on this Web site is the foundation's award winning "New Musicbox" monthly Web magazine.

Giving Category (ies): arts and humanities

◆ Amy Foundation

http://www.amyfound.org/index.html

The Amy Foundation is best known for its Amy Writing Awards, which the foundation refers to as, "a call to present biblical truth reinforced with scripture in secular, non-religious publications." These awards are considered to be one of the most popular journalism contests in the nation. Grantseekers can e-mail the foundation directly from the Web site. Information given about the Amy Writing Awards include: prize amounts; rules; eligibility; content; judging; and submission. Users can read past award winning articles.

Giving Category (ies): education, religion

◆ Annenberg Foundation

http://www.whannenberg.org/

The foundation's current grantmaking focus is on pre-collegiate education with a special interest in public school restructuring and reform involving grades K through 12. The Web site offers users information on the foundation's history and donor, the foundation's finances and how to apply for a grant. Sample grants are included, as are grant guidelines, eligibility requirements, the review process and contact information.

Giving Category (ies): education, youth

◆ Appalachian Community Fund

http://www.fex.org/applach/acfdesc.html

The Appalachian Community Fund only offers support to projects that are directly tied to grassroots organizations working for social change. A listing of 1998 grant recipients is available. Grant guidelines are briefly reviewed, the board of directors and staff is listed and an application deadline is stated. A request proposal package may be requested by grantseekers by e-mail.

Giving Category (ies): civic

◆ Arca Foundation

http://fdncenter.org/grantmaker/arca/index.html

The Arca Foundation focuses on empowering citizens to help shape public policy, environmental issues, U.S. foreign policy toward Central America and Cuba and the urgent need to curb corporate domination of our politics through genuine campaign finance reform. This Web site offers financial information, a 1998 grants list, a listing of the board of directors, the history behind the foundation, grantmaking guidelines and deadlines. Contact information is provided in the form of a mailing address and a phone number. However, no e-mail address is given.

Giving Category (ies): civic

◆ Arizona Commission on the Arts

http://az.arts.asu.edu/artscomm/

The foundation's self described mission is "to assure that broader and more diverse segments of the Arizona public will value and embrace the arts as a vital part of their lives." The Web site offers grantseekers foundation history, goals and vision, contact information and a listing of the staff with accompanying links to each members e-mail address. The Web site has a link to ArtShare, Arizona's arts endowment fund. At this site, grant and giving information is outlined and a list of recent recipients is provided.

Giving Category (ies): arts

◆ Arizona Community Foundation

http://www.azfoundation.com

The Arizona Community Foundation is "a charitable organization that acts as a vehicle for facilitating personalized and endowed individual and family philanthropy." The foundation aims to improve the lives of children, families and the elderly by improving living conditions in neighborhoods, communities and the environment across the state. The Web site offers contact information, a foundation fact sheet, affiliate locations, foundation publications and a list of the board of directors. General grantmaking is reviewed, as is the application process. Program descriptions and special areas of interest are discussed.

Giving Category (ies): civic, environment, social services, youth

◆ Art Council of Northwest Florida

http://www.artsnwfl.org/programs.htm

The Art Council of Northwest Florida describes itself as a combination United Way and Chamber of Commerce for artists and arts groups. Grant programs are detailed along with the names of past recipients. Specific grant guidelines, contact information and a staff listing are not found on this Web site.

Giving Category (ies): arts

◆ Arthritis Foundation

http://www.arthritis.org/

The Arthritis Foundation is behind today's arthritis research programs and has supported its growth in both the private and public sectors. The Web site contains the following information for grantseekers: annual reports; foundation history; contact information; a calendar of events; a free trial issue of one of the foundation's latest publications; and information about volunteer and giving opportunities. There is also a link to the Juvenile Arthritis Organization.

Giving Category (ies): health, science

◆ ASM International Foundation

http://www.asmintl.org/member/scolar.htm

The ASM International Foundation awards more than 40 scholarships annually in the field of education. An application is available online, several of the scholarships are described, eligibility and application requirements are reviewed, deadlines are stated and contact information is provided.

Giving Category (ies): education

◆ Atkinson Charitable Foundation

http://atkinsonfdn.on.ca/

The Atkinson Charitable Foundation provides grants for innovative, Ontario-based projects that focus on either: early childhood education and development and/or economic justice. Grantseekers will find a foundation directory, complete with a list of board members and staff, foundation publications and up-to-date foundation news. Application guidelines are provided including general projects, funding areas, how to apply, writing a proposal, deadlines and past winners.

Giving Category (ies): civic, education

◆ Atlanta Women's Foundation

http://www.atlantawomen.org/index2.html

The Atlanta Women's Foundation's mission is to cause positive change in the lives of women and girls. The Web site has a section on recent grants. Contact information and foundation history are provided. There is also a list of the foundation's board of directors. The Web site tells how and when to apply for a grant. Grantmaking policies are reviewed.

Giving Category (ies): civic, social services

◆ Aurora Foundation

http://fdncenter.org/grantmaker/aurora/index.html

The Aurora Foundation is a collection of individual funds and resources given by local citizens to enhance and support the quality of life in the greater Aurora area. Financial information is given, though it is several years old. There is a listing of the foundation's governing board and administration. A list of grant recipients along with actual dollar amounts is provided, though it is also several years old.

Giving Category (ies): arts, education, health, social services, youth

◆ Mary Reynolds Babcock Foundation

http://fdncenter.org/grantmaker/babcock/index.html

The Mary Reynolds Babcock Foundation focuses on assisting people in the Southeast to build communities that "nurture people, spur enterprise, bridge differences, foster fairness and promote civility." Grantseekers will find a listing of the foundation's board of directors and staff, as well as contact information. Each of the foundation's programs are explained, as are application procedures and deadlines.

Giving Category (ies): civic, youth

◆ Helen Bader Foundation

http://www.bader.org/

The Web site offers potential grantseekers an information section on each of the foundation's priority areas. General foundation information, recent grants and an online grant application also are available. The Helen Bader Foundation supports innovative programs that are making an impact on the lives of people throughout Wisconsin, the United States and Israel. The foundation focuses on five areas: Alzheimer's Disease and dementia, children and youth in Israel, economic development, Jewish life and learning and education. Grant guidelines and foundation staff are listed. Links are available to contact the foundation and to find out about current foundation news.

Giving Category (ies): civic, education, health, social services, youth

◆ Francois-Xavier Bagnoud Foundation

http://www.fxb.org/ffxb/fxb.htm

This foundation's Web site provides background and history, donor and contact information, news and events and giving priorities. A major focus area for the foundation is children and HIV. The foundation also funds five aerospace fellowships, including the Francois-Xavier Bagnoud Aerospace Prize.

Giving Category (ies): health, science, social services, youth

◆ Baptist Community Ministries

http://www.bcm.org/

Baptist Community Ministries is committed to the development of a healthy community offering a wholesome quality of life to its residents and to improving the physical, mental and spiritual health of the individuals they serve. The Web site offers users a history of the foundation and contact information. Grant application procedures are provided, areas of interest are clearly defined, dates for applying, application deadlines, eligibility requirements and a listing of approved grants for the year 1998 all can be found on this site.

Giving Category (ies): civic, health, religion, social services

◆ Baraga County Community Foundation

http://www.cmif.org/baraga.htm

The Baraga County Community Foundation makes grants in the fields of cultural arts, community service, education, the environment and conservation, health and human services, youth and scholarships. This Web site offers grantseekers the foundation's mission and role, location and contact information, news releases and a current foundation newsletter. Grantseekers will also find grant application information including eligibility, guidelines, application procedures, a grant application form and a listing of 1999 award recipients.

Giving Category (ies): arts, civic, education, environment, health, social services, youth

◆ Battle Creek Community Foundation

http://www.willard.lib.mi.us/npa/bccf/bccfindx.html

The Battle Creek Community Foundation provides resources to address specific community needs in order to create positive change within their local community. The grantmaking process is reviewed including how to apply, where to get an application, deadlines, eligibility and restrictions. The board of trustees and foundation staff are both listed. Grantseekers will also find a listing of the grants distributed through March 1998. The only contact information provided is a telephone number.

Giving Category (ies): civic, social services

◆ Bauman Foundation

http://ombwatch.org/www/ombw/info/bauman.html

The Bauman Foundation supports education, the arts, social justice and civil rights. The foundation supports whatever activities are needed to achieve results within its areas of interest, including public education, publications, conferences, organizing and policy research. Current programs are reviewed. Grantseekers may contact the foundation by telephone for additional information.

Giving Category (ies): arts, civic, education, environment

◆ Benton Foundation

http://www.benton.org/

The Benton Foundation mission is to realize the social benefits made possible by the public interest use of communications. The Benton Foundation Web site provides descriptions of foundation's programs and history, along with links to its publications. The Web site provides a list of officers and directors, but no real information on giving guidelines or application procedures. Grantseekers also can receive foundation news and program updates via e-mail. To subscribe to the foundation's mailing list, grantseekers must fill out an online form on the foundation's Web page.

Giving Category (ies): arts, civic, education

◆ H. N. and Frances C. Berger Foundation

http://www.hnberger.org/

The goal of the H. N. and Frances C. Berger Foundation is to "help people help themselves." While a variety of civic, educational and community projects are supported by the foundation, children and youth projects are of special interest. The foundation does not solicit funds, nor does it solicit grant proposals. However, a mailing address to submit requests for consideration is provided.

Giving Category (ies): civic, education, social services

◆ Bernardine Franciscan Sisters Foundation

http://www.bfranfound.org/

The Bernardine Franciscan Sisters Foundation works to promote, support, conduct and/or participate in charitable, scientific and educational activities related to the works of the Bernardine Sisters of the Third Order of Saint Francis, such as, care of the sick or injured, the promotion of health and the prevention of disease. Grantseekers are provided with contact information, a listing of the board of directors and administrative staff, an overview of recent grants made and grantmaking policies. The grantmaking process is briefly reviewed, but the foundation itself must be contacted for specifics and to obtain an official grant application.

Giving Category (ies): health, social services

◆ Frank Stanley Beveridge Foundation

http://www.beveridge.org/

Grantseekers visiting the Frank Stanley Beveridge Foundation Internet site will find a description of its mission and purpose, biographical information on the founder, program funding areas, list of directors, recent grants, eligibility requirements and restrictions. Recent grant distributions also are broken down by funding category.

Giving Category (ies): arts, civic, education, environment, health, religion, social services

◆ Big Ben Foundation, Inc.

http://www.lehigh.edu/~inifc/bbf/bbf.html

The purpose of the Big Ben Foundation is to raise and distribute funds to other nonprofit community-based organizations or individuals with specific economic hardships. Some information about the foundation is provided, as is a list of officers. The Web site also provides an address and phone number for the foundation.

Giving Category (ies): social services

◆ Amy Biehl Foundation

http://www.amybiehl.org/

The Amy Biehl Foundation was founded to continue the legacy of its namesake, Amy Biehl. The foundation focuses on South African issues, such as equality and the rights of women. The Web site gives a brief history on Amy Biehl and the work that she did. Contact and support information are provided. Users will find a foundation newsletter and links to news related articles.

Giving Category (ies): international

◆ William Bingham Foundation

http://fdncenter.org/grantmaker/bingham/index.html

The William Bingham Foundation focuses on the areas of education, health and human services, science and the arts. Grantseekers will find foundation history and its mission, trustees, officers and staff, 1999 approved grants and financial statements. Grantmaking procedures are reviewed, including how to apply, important dates and foundation contact information.

Giving Category (ies): arts, education, health, science, social services

◆ Blakemore Foundation

http://www.blakemorefoundation.org/

The Blakemore Foundation was established to "encourage the study of Asian languages at an advanced level and to increase the understanding of Asian art in the United States." Grantseekers are provided with foundation history, contact information and a listing of board members and founders. Language and art grants are available. Grant information provided includes: eligibility and selection criteria; grant guidelines; application instructions; and past grants awarded. An application form may be printed from this Web site.

Giving Category (ies): arts and humanities

◆ Blandin Foundation

http://www.blandinfoundation.org/

The Blandin Foundation Web site contains some basic historical information on the foundation, its mission statement, funding guidelines and restrictions, application procedures, proposal deadlines and review process. The site also contains information on the foundation's seven program focus areas: education, cultural opportunities, community leadership training, environmental stewardship, safe communities, economic opportunity and convening. Users will find individual contacts and their e-mail addresses for each of the foundation's focus areas. Grantseekers also are kept abreast of current news and information about the foundation. Additionally, the site provides links to the Council on Foundations and the Foundation Center.

Giving Category (ies): arts, civic, education, environment

◆ Arthur M. Blank Family Foundation

http://www.blankfoundation.org/

The Arthur M. Blank Family Foundation is committed to supporting programs and organizations that create opportunity, enhance self-esteem and increase awareness about cultural and community issues among young men and women. Funding priorities are detailed, as are the foundation's geographical areas of focus. Information about the grant application process, important dates and deadlines, how to apply and what attachments are required can all be found on this Web site. Grantseekers can print an application from the site. A mailing address is provided.

Giving Category (ies): arts, civic, environment, social services, youth

◆ Blowitz-Ridgeway Foundation

http://fdncenter.org/grantmaker/blowitz/index.html

The Blowitz-Ridgeway Foundation's Internet site lists its mission statement, funding guidelines, restrictions and application procedures. Grantseekers will find a list of 1998-1999 grant recipients along with dollar amounts. One of the foundation's primary funding areas is the support of nonprofit agencies that provide medical, psychiatric and psychological care to economically disadvantaged children and youth. Grantseekers may contact the foundation, via e-mail or telephone, for application forms or a copy of its latest annual report.

Giving Category (ies): health, social services, youth

◆ Bodman Foundation

http://fdncenter.org/grantmaker/bodman/index.html

The Bodman Foundation distributes funds in the religious, educational and charitable fields "for the moral, ethical and physical well-being and progress of mankind." Users will find a foundation history, trustees, officers and staff, application guidelines and a recent grants list.

Giving Category (ies): education, environment, social services, youth

◆ Corella and Bertram F. Bonner Foundation

http://www.bonner.org/

The foundation focuses on two major areas of giving: The Bonner Scholars Program, a community service scholarship program supporting 1500 students at 24 colleges and universities; and the Crisis Ministry Program, which supports faith-based anti-hunger initiatives. The Web site provides contact information, including an e-mail address, foundation news, a calendar of events, a listing of the board of trustees and staff, program descriptions and the foundation's history. Information is available on how to apply for a Bonner Scholarship, as is a list of universities currently participating in the Bonner Scholars Program.

Giving Category (ies): education, religion

◆ Booth Ferris Foundation

http://ats.edu/faculty/spons/B0000401.HTM

The Booth Ferris Foundation's primary interest is in the field of education, including smaller colleges, independent secondary schools and theological schools. All that grantseekers will find on this Web site is the foundation's mailing address and phone number, as well as a very brief description of some of the things that the foundation does and doesn't fund.

Giving Category (ies): education

◆ Mary Owen Borden Foundation

http://fdncenter.org/grantmaker/borden/index.html

The Mary Owen Borden Foundation limits its funding to New Jersey's Mercer and Monmouth counties. The primary focus on current giving is to address the needs of disadvantaged youth and their families and much of the foundation's grants go to nonprofit entities in Trenton, Asbury Park and Long Branch. This Web site offers a listing of officers and trustees, a summary of past grants awarded, contact information, funding guidelines, deadlines, typical amount and frequency of grants and the foundation's other areas of interest. The site also tells grantseekers how to prepare a grant application for submission.

Giving Category (ies): education, health, social services, youth

◆ Boston Foundation

http://www.tbf.org/

The Boston Foundation is greater Boston's community foundation, which "seeks to nurture a sense of community among the people of greater Boston." Foundation initiatives are described, recent news and publications are available. The Web site advises grantseekers on how to apply for funding. A list of the foundation's board of directors and staff, as well as contact and financial information is also provided.

Giving Category (ies): civic, social services

◆ Robert Bowne Foundation

http://fdncenter.org/grantmaker/bowne/index.html

The Robert Bowne Foundation makes grants to a wide variety of New York City organizations serving disadvantaged groups. Young people have been a special interest of the foundation and are the focus of giving at the present time. In addition, the foundation has also supported a number of major cultural institutions in New York City. The Web site offers a list of trustees and staff, the history of the foundation, past grants, a description of the foundation's grantmaking focus, contact information and application procedures.

Giving Category (ies): education, youth

◆ Lynde and Harry Bradley Foundation

http://www.townhall.com/bradley/

The Bradley Foundation Web site offers grantseekers detailed information on the foundation's mission, purpose, history, grant policies, guidelines and a list of its board of directors. At present, the foundation aims to encourage projects that focus on cultivating a renewed, healthier and more vigorous sense of citizenship among the American people and among peoples of other nations. The foundation supports scholarly studies and academic achievement.

Giving Category (ies): civic, education

◆ Joe Brain Foundation

http://www.mts.net/~jmbfdn/index.html

The Joe Brain Foundation is a private Canadian foundation that provides funding to Manitoba based registered charitable organizations, with some emphasis on Northern Manitoba. The foundation's mission is "to advance education, with particular emphasis on mining research and education, medical research and relief of poverty." The Web site offers contact information, a foundation profile and application procedures.

Giving Category (ies): education, health, social services

◆ Brainerd Foundation

http://www.brainerd.org/

The Brainerd Foundation is dedicated to protecting the environmental quality of the Pacific Northwest. Its Web site offers grantseekers a foundation mission statement, list of staff members and board of directors, program descriptions, grants lists for the past three years, funding guidelines and restrictions, application procedures and links to other related philanthropic sites. Users also will find a list of frequently asked questions and can send their comments to the foundation via e-mail. A 1998 financial statement is included on the site.

Giving Category (ies): environment

◆ Bread and Roses Community Fund

http://www.fex.org/bread/bread.html

Bread and Roses Community Fund describes itself as "a unique partnership of donors and activists committed to building a permanent base for social change in the Delaware Valley." Staff members are listed, contact information is provided and grant guidelines are reviewed. A list of 1998 general fund grants is available to grantseekers. Scholarships are explained and an application form can be printed.

Giving Category (ies): civic

◆ Otto Bremer Foundation

http://fdncenter.org/grantmaker/bremer/index.html

The Otto Bremer Foundation site lists its mission statement, a summary of recent grants according to program area, eligibility requirements and application guidelines. The foundation's main program areas are the following: racism, rural poverty, community affairs, education, health, human services, religion, miscellaneous, initiatives and investments.

Giving Category (ies): civic, education, health, religion, social services

◆ Brookdale Foundation Group

http://www.ewol.com/brookdale/

The Brookdale Foundation Group consists of the Brookdale Foundation, the Glendale Foundation and Ramapo Trust. The Brookdale Foundation focuses on the needs and challenges of America's elderly population. Major funding initiatives are clearly outlined and contact information is provided.

Giving Category (ies): health, social services

◆ Brother's Brother Foundation

http://www.brothersbrother.com/

The Brother's Brother Foundation (BBF) Web site includes descriptions of supported programs and contact information, as well as the history of the foundation's founder. No grant guidelines are available. An application form for International Recipient Organizations is available. The foundation is a 501(c)(3) charity that distributes donated medical, educational and agricultural resources throughout the world without regard to race, creed or politics. The Web site does include information on volunteer opportunities and how to donate to the foundation. Grantseekers will also find the foundation's Fall 1999 newsletter online.

Giving Category (ies): education, health, international, social services

◆ James Graham Brown Foundation

http://www.brownfoundation.com/

The mission of the James Graham Brown Foundation is "to foster the well-being, quality of life and image of Louisville and Kentucky." The foundation does this by actively supporting and funding projects in the fields of civic affairs, economic development, education, health and general welfare. Funding priorities and restrictions are explained and contact information is provided. The Web site gives deadlines and directions on how to apply for funding. 1998 grants highlights and recipients can also be found on this site.

Giving Category (ies): civic, education, health, social services

◆ Bullitt Foundation

http://www.bullitt.org/

The Bullitt Foundation is committed to the protection and restoration of the environment of the Pacific Northwest including environmental problems that disproportionately impact lower-economic people in both urban and rural communities. The Web site offers contact information, application procedures, Bullitt Foundation news and past grant recipients.

Giving Category (ies): environment

◆ Burroughs Wellcome Fund

http://www.bwfund.org

The Burroughs Wellcome Fund Internet site provides information on the fund's philanthropic programs. Grantseekers will find listings of awardees, giving guidelines, applications deadlines, list of its board (with brief biographical data) and staff and online versions of its program brochures, newsletters and news releases. The foundation gives grantseekers information on their new headquarters.

Giving Category (ies): education, science

◆ Edyth Bush Charitable Foundation

http://fdncenter.org/grantmaker/bush/index.html

The Edyth Bush Charitable Foundation Web site provides grantseekers with historical information on the foundation, funding policies and procedures, restrictions on giving, application requirements and a list of recent grants for the years 1997 through 1999. The foundation typically supports the arts, education, healthcare and human services, as well as other areas of support such as the Michigan State Humane Society.

Giving Category (ies): arts, education, health, social services

◆ Barbara Bush Foundation for Family Literacy

http://www.barbarabushfoundation.com/

The focus of the Barbara Bush Foundation is to promote family literacy programs and to end the cycle of intergenerational illiteracy. The Web site offers users contact information, press releases, foundation publications and information on state literacy initiatives and the national grant program. Descriptions of these programs are available, as are application procedures. Grantseekers can print grant applications from this Web site.

Giving Category (ies): education

◆ Cadillac Area Community Foundation

http://users.netonecom.net/~cavb/CACF.htm

The Cadillac Area Community Foundation is available to those who reside in the Cadillac, MI, area. The foundation provides opportunities for grantseekers in the areas of arts and culture, education, healthcare, environment, human service, economic development, youth and recreation. The Web site provides contact information, a list of trustees and a listing of current areas of funding.

Giving Category (ies): arts, civic, education, environment, health, social services, youth

◆ California Community Foundation

http://www.calfund.org/

The California Community Foundation Web site tells of its mission and history. Grantseekers can access the foundation's recent grants and press releases, giving guidelines, application forms, board of governors (with biographical data) and staff and its calendar of events. The site also allows users to view the foundation's 1999 annual report. Users may receive other publications from the foundation by completing and submitting an online form.

Giving Category (ies): arts, civic, education, environment, health, social sciences

◆ California Endowment

http://www.calendow.org/

The mission of the California Endowment is "to expand access to affordable, quality healthcare for underserved individuals and communities and to promote fundamental improvements in the health status of all Californians." Grantseekers will find listings of the foundation's staff and board, an annual report, contact information, funding initiatives and a list of grantees.

Giving Category (ies): health

◆ California HealthCare Foundation

http://www.chcf.org/

The California HealthCare Foundation's mission is "to expand access to affordable, quality healthcare for underserved individuals and communities and to promote fundamental improvements in the health status of the people of California." Grantseekers can sign up to be on the foundation's mailing list to receive information on specific areas of interest. Contact information is provided and foundation program areas are defined.

Giving Category (ies): health

◆ California Wellness Foundation

http://www.tcwf.org/

The California Wellness Foundation is an independent, private grantmaker, funded in 1992 by an endowment from Health Net, one of California's largest health maintenance organizations, to improve the health and well-being of the people of California. Its Internet site contains the foundation's mission statement, a description of its strategic initiatives, eligibility criteria and restrictions on giving, application guidelines, a recent grants list and its most recent newsletter that may be downloaded using Adobe Acrobat. Grantseekers also can link to "What's New" to find out the most recent foundation events and news.

Giving Category (ies): civic, health, social services

◆ Cancer Treatment Research Foundation

http://www.ctrf.org/

The goal of this foundation is to support clinical research, offer options and hopefully find a cure to this disease. The Web site offers news and events, contact information and research highlights.

Giving Category (ies): health, science

◆ Canyon Research

http://www.canyonresearch.org/

Canyon Research is a San Diego-based private, operating foundation which supports research and education projects that focus on innovative computer-related communications technology, public communications policy and domestic communications regulatory issues. Financial and contact information can be found on this site. Application procedures, grant-making guidelines and areas of exclusion also can be found.

Giving Category (ies): education

◆ Captain Planet Foundation

http://www.turner.com/cpf/

The Captain Planet Foundation promotes environmental activities for young people. Grant policies and guidelines are reviewed. Visitors to this site will find a listing of the foundation's board of trustees, along with biographical information on each. Users can chose to look up past grant recipients from a U.S. map that is divided by region and state. The foundation can be e-mailed directly from the Web site. There is also a link to grant highlights. Grantseekers will find an online proposal form.

Giving Category (ies): environment, youth

◆ CarEth Foundation

http://www.funder.org/careth

The CarEth Foundation's mission is to promote a world of enduring peace, with justice and with social, economic and political equality. Its Web site provides all the information grantseekers require to apply for funding. Visitors will find the foundation's mission, funding priorities, giving guidelines, restrictions and recent grants for 1998 and 1999. The foundation also allows users to e-mail them directly from their Web site.

Giving Category (ies): civic

◆ CARLISLE Foundation

http://www.carlislefoundation.org/

The CARLISLE Foundation describes itself as being a private, operating foundation which "attempts to promote creative problem solving and interventions through effective grant-making." Contact information, a listing of past grants awarded and a list of trustees and staff are provided. The Web site offers an overview of the two types of grants that the foundation awards: long term and annual.

Giving Category (ies): social services, youth

◆ Carnegie Corporation of New York

http://www.carnegie.org/

The Carnegie Corporation of New York Web site contains history and general information about the foundation's philanthropy, detailed program descriptions including a list of new initiatives, program guidelines and priorities, application procedures, grant restrictions, a directory of its staff and trustees and a list of 1999 grants. Online copies of foundation publications, such as their 1998 annual report, are also available.

Giving Category (ies): civic, education, international

◆ Carnegie Endowment for International Peace

http://www.ceip.org/

The Carnegie Endowment for International Peace conducts programs of research, discussion, publication and education in international affairs and U.S. foreign policy. The latest edition of the endowment's quarterly magazine may be viewed from this Web site. The site offers recent news, publications, a list of the staff and board, contact information and a large listing of all the projects that are supported.

Giving Category (ies): civic, international

◆ Carthage Foundation

http://www.scaife.com/carthage.html

The Carthage Foundation confines most of its grant awards to programs that will address public policy questions concerned with national and international issues. The Web site contains some very general guidelines for applying for a grant. Contact information, with the exception of an e-mail address and a 1998 annual report are available.

Giving Category (ies): civic

◆ Roy J. Carver Charitable Trust

http://www.carvertrust.org/

Scientific research, scholarships, general education and other issues related to the needs of youth are the program areas of greatest interest to the Roy J. Carver Charitable Trust. A history of the trust's founder can be found on this Web site. Grantseekers will also find an illustrated and comprehensive explanation of the trust's general distribution of grants. Each of the trust's areas of interest are explained in great detail and grantseekers may view past grants awarded in each category. Users of this site will be able to learn of the trust's grant policies and guidelines, application procedures and submission deadlines. Grantseekers may contact the trust via e-mail for general questions, but applications must be submitted through the U.S. mail. Application cover sheets can be printed from this Web site.

Giving Category (ies): education, science, youth

◆ Annie E. Casey Foundation

http://www.aecf.org/

The Annie E. Casey (AEC) Foundation is a private charitable organization dedicated to helping build better futures for disadvantaged children in the United States. Its Web site contains a mission statement, description of major national program initiatives, an overview of its Kids Count project, basic guidelines and restrictions, application procedures and a list of publications. Grantseekers also can find a list of recent grants by following the AEC publications link and then looking in the AEC Focus report.

Giving Category (ies): civic, social services, youth

◆ Samuel N. and Mary Castle Foundation

http://fdncenter.org/grantmaker/castle/index.html

The Castle Foundation serves the state of Hawaii. The foundation has provided leadership in funding for building projects, children's programs, improvements in health facilities, environmental causes, emergency relief, Protestant-related causes and educational needs from preschool through graduate school. The Web site offers a listing of the foundation's officers and trustees, the history behind the foundation, grantmaking policies and procedures, past grantees, how to make a proposal to the foundation and contact information.

Giving Category (ies): education, environment, health, religion, youth

◆ Catholic Campaign for Human Development

http://www.nccbuscc.org/cchd/grant.htm

The Catholic Campaign for Human Development (CCHD) funds two categories of projects in their fight against poverty: organizing and economic development. The Web site offers visitors foundation publications, press releases, news and events. A summary of criteria and guidelines for funding is also available to grantseekers. Both areas of funding are outlined along with funding limitations and a pre-application process. CCHD may be contacted through the mail or by telephone.

Giving Category (ies): civic, religion, social services

◆ Center for Theology and the Natural Sciences

http://www.ctns.org/

The self-described mission of the Center for Theology and the Natural Sciences is "to promote the creative mutual interaction between contemporary theology and the natural sciences." The history of the foundation is outlined, as are the strong beliefs of its founder, Robert John Russell. Visitors will find foundation news items, contact information and a staff directory complete with e-mail addresses. Past grant recipients are highlighted and major programs are reviewed.

Giving Category (ies): education, religion, science

◆ Central Indiana Community Foundation

http://www.cicf.org/

The Central Indiana Community Foundation (CICF) is a collaborative effort between community foundations serving Marion County and Hamilton County. The Web site contains an annual report, a list of the foundation's board members and senior staff and an overview of the foundation's special initiatives. Grantseekers may contact the CICF by e-mail or by phone. Grantseekers can find out the specifics on the foundation's initiatives, such as specific areas of interest, guidelines and restrictions, application procedures, grant proposal instructions and an online application form.

Giving Category (ies): civic, social services

◆ Century Foundation

http://www.tcf.org

Formerly known as the Twentieth Century Fund, the Century Foundation offers information about the fund, its publications and activities on its Web site. Although the fund does not award grants, fellowships or scholarships, it does encourage proposals that develop policy arguments concerning four major public challenges: improving living standards, restoring civil society, reinvigorating the media and identifying new foundations for American foreign policy. The Web site also contains detailed information about the fund's publications and includes a calendar of events.

Giving Category (ies): civic

◆ Champlin Foundations

http://fdncenter.org/grantmaker/champlin/index.html

The Champlin Foundations provide "hands-on" equipment or facilities for those who are served by tax-exempt organizations — athletic, educational, hospital, etc., in the state of Rhode Island. The Web site clearly details the foundations' funding criteria and restrictions. Contact information is supplied, as is a list of recent grants awarded. Grant guidelines are also reviewed.

Giving Category (ies): education, health

◆ Chesapeake Bay Trust

http://www2.ari.net/home/cbt/

The Chesapeake Bay Trust Web site contains giving information, grant guidelines and application forms for civic and community organizations, schools and volunteer groups seeking funding for Chesapeake Bay education and restoration projects in Maryland. It also provides a list of 10 ways to help clean up the bay.

Giving Category (ies): education, environment, youth

◆ Chi Chi Rodriguez Youth Foundation

http://www.chichi.org/

The Chi Chi Rodriguez Youth Foundation's mission is "to serve inner city youths who are at risk of dropping out of school by improving their self-esteem, character, work ethic, social adjustment and academic performance." This Web site offers news and events, a searchable database of golf courses, a foundation yearbook and a list of the foundation's staff, along with a biography on each staff member. The foundation may be contacted about specific information via an online e-mail form.

Giving Category (ies): youth

◆ Chiang Ching-kuo Foundation for International Scholarly Exchange

http://www.cckf.org/

The foundation's purpose is to promote the study of Chinese culture and society. The site contains contact information, a listing of directors, staff and past grantees. The Web site provides grantseekers with a brief overview of each program, including the application procedure. This Web site may also be viewed in Chinese.

Giving Category (ies): education, international

◆ Chinook Fund

http://www.fex.org/chinook/chinook.html

The Chinook Fund supports the work of organizations in Colorado that are working to address the root causes of social problems such as racism, sexism, homophobia and discrimination against people with disabilities. The Web site provides contact information, an online newsletter, upcoming events and a list of staff, board and committee members. A list of groups that the fund supports is also available. Funding guidelines and programs are reviewed.

Giving Category (ies): civic

◆ CJ Foundation for SIDS

http://www.cjsids.com/

The CJ Foundation for Sudden Infant Death Syndrome (SIDS) is a nationwide voluntary health organization dedicated to recognizing the special needs of the SIDS community through funding SIDS research and support services. Grant opportunities for the upcoming year are reviewed. Information available includes: timelines and deadlines for applying; funding limitations; and current funding priority areas. Contact information, research updates, a foundation newsletter, SIDS information and resources are also provided.

Giving Category (ies): health, youth

◆ Edna McConnell Clark Foundation

http://fdncenter.org/grantmaker/emclark/index.html

The Web site offers a history of the Edna McConnell Clark Foundation and its founders. The areas of interest of this foundation include child and youth development, tropical disease research, New York neighborhoods, student achievement and justice. Each area of funding is clearly defined and past grants may be viewed. Grant guidelines and contact information are also included on the Web site.

Giving Category (ies): civic, education, health, youth

◆ Robert Sterling Clark Foundation

http://fdncenter.org/grantmaker/rsclark/index.html

The foundation has three main areas of funding: arts and culture including projects that strengthen the management of cultural institutions in New York City; government accountability including projects that improve the performance and accountability of government agencies responsible for the delivery of human services in New York City; and family planning including projects that ensure access to family planning services and protect reproductive freedom nationally. The Web site offers the following: contact information; staff list; application procedures; and program guidelines.

Giving Category (ies): arts, civic

◆ Cleveland Foundation

http://www.clevelandfoundation.org/

The Cleveland Foundation seeks to "enhance the quality of life for all citizens of Greater Cleveland, now and for generations to come." Contact information is provided, as is a list of officers and trustees. Grantmaking priorities are defined, as are grantmaking restrictions. Grantseekers will find guidelines, deadlines and other important dates. Applications can also be found on this Web site.

Giving Category (ies): arts, civic, education, social services

◆ Clipper Ship Foundation

http://www.agmconnect.org/clipper1.html

The foundation makes grants to nonprofit operating organizations serving the Greater Boston community and the residents of Lawrence, MA. Priority is given to those organizations devoted to helping the homeless and ill-housed, the destitute, the handicapped, children and the aged or supplying the needs of new immigrant and other needy communities and neighborhoods. Some general information is provided, such as how to apply and the range of grants awarded. Contact information is given to obtain specific guidelines. A grants list, divided by category is available, as is an annual report for the foundation.

Giving Category (ies): social services

◆ Coleman Foundation

http://www.colemanfoundation.org/

The Coleman Foundation provides funding for cancer research, education programs for the disabled and training programs associated with poverty and unemployment. The Web site offers grantseekers information on how to contact the foundation and offers a listing of staff, directors and officers. Grant application guidelines are reviewed, a past grant listing is available and financial information may be reviewed.

Giving Category (ies): civic, education, health

◆ Commonwealth Fund

http://www.cmwf.org

The Commonwealth Fund Web site provides grantseekers with all the information they need to apply for a grant. Information on the fund's site includes its mission statement, history, giving guidelines, list of its officers and directors, ongoing programs, fellowships and details on its publications. A list of recent grants also is provided. Annual reports from 1997 to 1999 are available.

Giving Category (ies): health, social services

◆ Community Foundation of Sarasota County

http://www.sarasota-foundation.org/

The Community Foundation of Sarasota County's site offers grantseekers a statement of its mission, purpose and grantmaking priorities (arts and humanities, community development, education, environment, health and human services), funding guidelines and restrictions, application procedures, evaluation process and donor information. The site also provides an overview of the foundation's scholarship program. Users must contact the foundation for scholarship application forms. There is also a link to frequently asked questions.

Giving Category (ies): arts and humanities, civic, education, environment, health, social services

◆ Cooper Foundation

http://www.cooperfoundation.org/

Visitors to the Cooper Foundation Internet site will find a statement of its mission, historical background, funding priorities (education, human services and the arts and humanities), application guidelines and a description of the application process. A recent grants list is not provided.

Giving Category (ies): arts, education, social services

◆ Cottonwood Foundation

http://www.pressenter.com/~cottonwd

The foundation is dedicated to promoting empowerment of people, protection of the environment and respect for cultural diversity. This site provides the foundation's mission statement, background, application guidelines, 1998 annual report, Fall 1998 newsletter and a summary of 1998 grant recipients. There is also a link for online contributions to the foundation.

Giving Category (ies): arts, environment, social services

◆ Crail-Johnson Foundation

http://www.crail-johnson.org/

The Crail-Johnson Foundation Web site provides information on its mission statement, programs and special projects, list of board members and staff, application guidelines and recent grants. The foundation focuses primarily on child welfare causes. Users also will find an online version of its annual report and links to other private and corporate foundations and associations of grantmakers.

Giving Category (ies): education, health, social services, youth

◆ Nathan Cummings Foundation

http://www.ncf.org/

The Nathan Cummings Foundation site contains background information, including a mission statement; program area descriptions, including current issues and initiatives; a list of trustees and staff; guidelines and application procedures; grants lists for 1990 through 1999, with links to grantee Web sites; reports and publications, with an online version of its 1997 annual report; links to other philanthropic sites; and contact information for each specific program area. A new link called the "Grantee Gallery" has been added to the Web site. The foundation focuses its philanthropy on five core areas: arts; environment; health; Jewish life; and interprogram, with initiatives aimed at democratic values and contemplative practice. Two secondary program areas are community grants and presidential grants.

Giving Category (ies): arts, civic, environment, health, religion, social services

◆ D.C. Commission on the Arts and Humanities

http://www.capaccess.org/ane/dccah/

The D.C. Commission on the Arts and Humanities (DCCAH) is the official arts agency of the District of Columbia. The DCCAH develops and promotes local artists, arts organizations and arts activities as part of its mission to enrich the quality of life for the people of Washington, DC. Foundation commissioners and staff are listed, as are current and past grantees. All of the many grants available are reviewed and applications can be downloaded.

Giving Category (ies): arts

◆ Daiwa Anglo-Japanese Foundation

http://www.daiwa-foundation.org.uk/

The foundation's main aims are: to enhance the United Kingdom's and Japan's understanding of each other's people and cultures; and to enable British and Japanese students and academics to further their education by visiting each other's countries. Contact information, a listing of trustees, foundation publications, related events and foundation activities can all be found on this Web site. Information is available on general grants, scholarships and prizes. There is a question and answer section that contains valuable application information. The entire Web site may also be viewed in Japanese.

Giving Category (ies): education, international

◆ Charles A. Dana Foundation

http://www.dana.org

The Charles A. Dana Foundation Web page contains information on the foundation's grantmaking policies and procedures, a list of its officers and directors and data on its publications. This site also provides information on the Charles A. Dana Awards for Pioneering Achievement in Health and Education and the Dana Alliance for Brain Initiatives.

Giving Category (ies): education, health, science

◆ Arthur Vining Davis Foundations

http://www.jvm.com/davis/

The Arthur Vining Davis Foundations Web site contains background information on the foundations and their donor, detailed program descriptions, application guidelines and giving restrictions, 1998 and 1999 grants, a list of common questions and updates on new activities at the foundations. The foundations focus giving on private higher education, secondary education, religion (graduate theological education), healthcare (caring attitudes) and public television.

Giving Category (ies): arts, education, health, religion

◆ Gladys Krieble Delmas Foundation

http://www.delmas.org

The Gladys Krieble Delmas Foundation "promotes the advancement and perpetuation of humanistic inquiry and artistic creativity by encouraging excellence in scholarship and in the performing arts, and by supporting research libraries and other institutions that preserve the resources which transmit this cultural heritage." The foundation's Internet site provides a brief history and donor information, program descriptions, recent grants lists, eligibility requirements and restrictions, application procedures and a list of trustees and staff. The foundation's programs include the humanities program; performing arts program; research library program; and Venetian research program. Grantseekers can request via e-mail copies of the foundation's annual report, informational brochure, giving guidelines and application forms.

Giving Category (ies): arts and humanities, education, international

◆ DJ&T Foundation

http://www.djtfoundation.org/

The DJ&T Foundation's goal is to fund low cost or free spay/neuter clinics as a way to help relieve animal over population. While its mission is to assist all qualified spay/neuter clinics, the foundation is most committed to making grants at the grassroots level to underfunded clinics that provide free and or low cost spay/neuter services. Grantseekers may download applications from this Web site. Contact information is available. There is a FAQs section for grantseekers to review, to determine eligibility. The Web site offers a step-by-step application process.

Giving Category (ies): social services

◆ Do Right Foundation

http://www.doright.org/

The Do Right Foundation Web site offers general foundation information and history, a mission statement, contact information, preliminary inquiry form, application guidelines, funding restrictions, formal application form and a listing of recent grants. The Do Right Foundation supports pilot programs that address "current obstacles to a more joyful and rewarding society," particularly efforts to reduce crime and joblessness, increase productivity of the legal system, promote the welfare to work transition, improve the integrity and efficiencies of government and develop children through the education of parents. The foundation has recently added three new funding areas: homelessness, fire safety/prevention and quality management.

Giving Category (ies): civic, education, social services

◆ Geraldine R. Dodge Foundation

http://www.grdodge.org/

The foundation's site includes the mission, history, grant areas, guidelines, summary of giving, current initiatives and contact information. The Geraldine R. Dodge Foundation offers grants to support elementary and secondary education, the arts, welfare of animals, public issues and local projects in New Jersey. The foundation also funds the Geraldine R. Dodge Poetry Festival.

Giving Category (ies): arts, civic, education, social services

◆ J.C. Downing Foundation

http://www.jcdowning.org/

The J.C. Downing Foundation makes project grants in five areas: science and technology, sports and athletics, education and child development, wildlife research and preservation and environmental research and economics. The Web site includes the foundation's mission, application procedures, guidelines, restrictions, previous grant awards and foundation publications. The site also offers resources for recommended reading, nonprofit organizations and foundation links.

Giving Category (ies): civic, education, environment, science, social services, youth

◆ Camille and Henry Dreyfus Foundation

http://www.dreyfus.org/

The Camille and Henry Dreyfus Foundation's purpose is "to advance the science of chemistry, chemical engineering and related sciences as a means of improving human relations and circumstances around the world." Its Web site offers grantseekers a brief history and details of its seven major programs, as well as a list of its board of directors and staff. Each program area contains an overview, eligibility requirements, award nomination procedures, deadlines for nomination forms, program assessment, award expenditure information, deadlines for submitting necessary reports or publications and a list of award recipients. A new initiative called Senior Scientist Mentors has been added to the foundation's list of programs. Applicants can request nomination forms by e-mail.

Giving Category (ies): education, science

◆ Peter F. Drucker Foundation for Nonprofit Management

http://www.pfdf.org

The Peter F. Drucker Foundation for Nonprofit Management Web site offers general information on the foundation and the Peter Drucker Award Competition. The site also contains information on the Frances Hasselbein Community Innovation Fellows Program, including application procedures, deadlines and an application that can be downloaded in either Word or PDF form. Users can also download issues of the Drucker Foundation News in PDF format.

Giving Category (ies): civic

◆ Dunn Foundation

http://www.dunnfoundation.org/grants1.htm

The Dunn Foundation's mission is to "increase public understanding of the contribution community appearance makes to our quality of life" and to link people to the tools they need to make positive aesthetic changes in their environment. The foundation believes that America's natural beauty is being lost to mass commercialism, poorly designed, out-of-character buildings, barren asphalt parking lots and creeping suburbia. The foundation offers public outreach and training projects to educate on this subject. Grantseekers will find the following information: how and where to contact the foundation; and funding guidelines and priorities. Grantseekers can obtain an application through this Web site and can view several featured grants.

Giving Category (ies): environment, youth

◆ Echoing Green Foundation

http://www.echoinggreen.org/

Echoing Green is a nonprofit foundation that offers full-time fellowships to emerging social entrepreneurs. The site offers background information on the foundation, news and events, a resource center and a FAQS section. Application information is not currently available, as the next application cycle for the Fellowship 2001 will begin in June. At that time, application procedures will be posted.

Giving Category (ies): education

◆ Electronic Frontier Foundation

http://www.eff.org/

The Electronic Frontier Foundation has been established to help civilize the electronic frontier and to make it available to everyone. These sites contain many articles, newsletters, action alerts, legislation information, organizational materials and lists of related publications. Additionally, they offer links to information on federal funding opportunities. Information is available on joining the foundation.

Giving Category (ies): civic, education

◆ Energy Foundation

http://www.ef.org/

The Energy Foundation provides on its Web site a copy of its mission statement, descriptions of its philanthropic programs, a list of grant recipients, giving guidelines and application procedures. Grantseekers also can link to a number of energy-related sites.

Giving Category (ies): science

◆ Epilepsy Foundation

http://www.efa.org/what/research/overview.htm

The Epilepsy Foundation Web page contains information on its fellowships and research grants. Grantseekers will find descriptions of funding opportunities along with deadline information. Application brochures can be downloaded.

Giving Category (ies): education, health, science

◆ Eurasia Foundation

http://www.eurasia.org/

The Eurasia Foundation Web site provides information on the foundation's history and mission, philanthropic programs, application procedures and other non-grantmaking activities. Grantseekers also will find sample grants, giving guidelines and a list of the staff and office locations. The site offers grant success stories, press releases and job openings within the foundation. The foundation is dedicated to funding programs that build democratic and free market institutions in the twelve New Independent States (NIS) of the former Soviet Union — Armenia, Azerbaijan, Belarus, Georgia, Kazakstan, the Kyrgyz Republic, Moldova, Russia, Tajikistan, Turkmenistan, Ukraine and Uzbekistan.

Giving Category (ies): civic, international

◆ Lettie Pate Evans Foundation

http://www.lpevans.org/

Grants of the Lettie Pate Evans Foundation are limited to specified public charities in Georgia and Virginia. The grant program of the Lettie Pate Evans Foundation reflects a strong emphasis in the following areas: private secondary and higher education; arts and culture; and museums and historic preservation. Contact, financial, background and board information are provided. Grantseekers will find an analysis of the foundation's most recent grants, as well as grant application guidelines.

Giving Category (ies): arts, education

◆ Fargo-Moorhead Area Foundation

http://rrnet.com/~pepp1/fmaf/index.html

The Fargo-Moorhead Area Foundation makes grants in these program areas: arts and culture, civic improvements, education, health, recreation and youth and human service. The foundation gives preference to projects that seek to contribute to the welfare of the people of the Fargo-Moorhead area. The Web site offers contact information, application deadlines, eligibility requirements and grant application instructions.

Giving Category (ies): arts, civic, education, health, social services, youth

◆ Samuel S. Fels Fund

http://www.dvg.org/Fels/index.html

The Samuel S. Fels Fund is a private independent foundation with broad interests in community programs, education and the arts. The Web site contains foundation history, staff and trustees, contact information, recent grants, grant guidelines and applications.

Giving Category (ies): arts, civic, education

◆ Feinstein Foundation

http://www.feinsteinfoundation.com/

The Feinstein Foundation is dedicated to philanthropic endeavors focusing on the advancement of public service and the alleviation of hunger. The Web site offers contact information, foundation history, press releases, information on scholarships and educational programs.

Giving Category (ies): civic, social services

◆ Fetzer Institute

http://www.fetzer.org/

The Fetzer Institute supports research, education and service programs exploring the integral relationships among body, mind and spirit. The Web site offers contact information, foundation history, news releases and selected programs of interest. Specific funding opportunities that are currently available are listed and include eligibility, deadline and application information.

Giving Category (ies): education, health, religion

◆ Flinn Foundation

http://www.flinn.org

The Flinn Foundation site contains brief biographical information on the foundation's donors (Dr. Robert S. Flinn and Irene P. Flinn), its mission statement, its funding priorities, grantmaking procedures and a list of the its officers and directors. Also found on the Web site is the foundation's newsletter with all the foundation's latest news. An annual report, as well as many other foundation related reports may be ordered online.

Giving Category (ies): arts, education, health

◆ Ford Foundation

http://www.fordfound.org/

Included on the Ford Foundation Internet site are the following: the foundation's mission statement; program descriptions; list of trustees, officers and staff; guidelines and application procedures; grants search for 1997 through 1999; online annual reports; Ford Foundation Reports; frequently asked questions; addresses and e-mail links to the headquarters office and overseas branch offices; news and press releases; a catalog of publications, films and videos; information on ordering free publications online; and links to other philanthropic sites. Grantseekers should visit the site map to navigate through the wealth of information. A handy search engine also is available.

Giving Category (ies): arts, civic, education, environment, health, international, social services, youth

◆ Foundation for Anesthesia Education and Research

http://www.faer.org/

The foundation's self described mission is "to raise the standards of the specialty by fostering and encouraging education, research and scientific progress in anesthesiology." The Web site provides a 1998 annual report; monthly reports; a list of the board of directors, complete with photos and contact information; and a description of the resident scholar program. The Web site offers information on its awards and grants including general award information, a grant application form, a list of award and grant recipients and an overview of the review process.

Giving Category (ies): education, science

◆ Foundation for Exceptional Children

http://www.cec.sped.org/fd-menu.htm

The Foundation for Exceptional Children is a national organization committed to improving the lives of children and youth with disabilities. Contact information is provided, as is a foundation history. Grantseekers can view a list of award recipients. Scholarship requirements and guidelines are reviewed and an application may be printed from the Web site.

Giving Category (ies): education, youth

◆ Foundation for Microbiology

http://www.tiac.net/users/waksman/

The foundation's mission is "to promote, encourage and aid scientific research in microbiology; to provide and assist in providing the funds and facilities by which scientific discoveries, inventions and processes in microbiology may be developed...all to the end that the science of microbiology shall progress in the service of mankind." The Foundation for Microbiology supports lectureships, prizes or courses related to the field of microbiology, as well as publications or other activities in this field. The Web site includes contact information, financial information, the foundation's purpose and activities, its fields of interest, grant types, restrictions, application guidelines, publications, 1998 grants and a listing of officers and trustees.

Giving Category (ies): science

◆ Foundation for Seacoast Health

http://www.nh.ultranet.com/~ffsh/

The Foundation for Seacoast Health's mission is "to support and promote healthcare in any one or more of the cities and towns in the New Hampshire/Maine Seacoast area." Its Web site contains background information on the foundation; program descriptions, including an overview of its scholarship program; giving guidelines and restrictions; application procedures; deadlines; and a description of the review process. A recent grants list is not provided, however. Users can e-mail the foundation.

Giving Category (ies): education, health

◆ Foundation for the Carolinas

http://www.fftc.org/

The foundation serves the Carolinas area and has been doing so for the past forty years. They are the largest community foundation in the Carolinas. The Web site offers an annual report, publications, foundation history and an e-mail address. Some general financial information is given. The site offers a special section for grantseekers with information on deadlines, guidelines, specialized grant programs and available scholarships.

Giving Category (ies): civic, social services

◆ Freedom Forum

http://www.freedomforum.org/

The Freedom Forum Web site is a valuable source of information on the organization's resources, programs and activities. The forum is the largest foundation in the United States focused on fostering First Amendment rights and freedoms, journalism education, professional development of journalists, media studies and international journalism programs. Included on the Web site is a list of foundation trustees and staff, job openings, contact information and foundation history.

Giving Category (ies): arts, civic, education

◆ Friends of the Environment Foundation

http://www.fef.ca/

The site of the Friends of the Environment Foundation, established in 1990 by the Canadian Trust, provides information on the foundation's history, its mission and grants program. Grantseekers also will find press releases, grant guidelines and an online application form.

Giving Category (ies): civic, environment

◆ Fund for the City of New York

http://www.fcny.org/

The Fund for the City of New York's mandate is "to respond to the opportunities and problems of New York City; to improve the performance of the city's government and the quality of life of its citizens." The fund's Web page provides information on its main funding areas: technology and information, government management, youth development and assistance to nonprofits. Under the nonprofit assistance area, giving is allocated for three major programs: general grants, cash flow loan program and an incubator program. Programs funded by the foundation include the Sloan Public Service Awards, the Union Square Awards and the Organizational Assistance Program. Unfortunately, grantseekers will not find giving guidelines, application procedures or sample grants on this site. Grantseekers will find a list of the foundation's board of directors and executive staff, contact information and job opportunities.

Giving Category (ies): civic, health, science, social services, youth

◆ Bill and Melinda Gates Foundation

http://www.gatesfoundation.org

The Bill and Melinda Gates Foundation's detailed Web site offers grantseekers information on recent grantees, guidelines, application information, FAQs, a recent annual report, eligibility information, news, foundation background and a listing of staff. The Bill and Melinda Gates Foundation places a major focus on helping to improve people's lives through health and learning. The foundation works with public libraries in low-income areas to provide the computer equipment required for community access to digital information. Grants also offer training and technical assistance to library staff. Grantseekers should use the site map to navigate through all of the important and useful information contained within this Web site.

Giving Category (ies): education, health, international, youth

◆ Wallace Alexander Gerbode Foundation

http://fdncenter.org/grantmaker/gerbode/index.html

Grantseekers visiting the Wallace Alexander Gerbode Foundation Web site will find information on its mission, giving guidelines, deadlines and restrictions, list of trustees and staff and financial statement for 1998. A list of grants for each funding area from the years 1995 through 1998 is also available. The foundation generally supports organizations that fall within the following categories: arts and culture, environment, population, reproductive rights, citizen participation/building communities/inclusiveness, philanthropic process and special projects.

Giving Category (ies): arts, civic, environment

◆ J. Paul Getty Trust

http://www.getty.edu/grant/

The J. Paul Getty Trust funds a diverse range of projects that promote researching the history of art and related fields, advancement of the understanding of art and conservation of cultural heritage. This Web site offers background and financial information, the Getty grant program staff, the board of trustees, foundation publications, a calendar of events, application information and recent grants awarded. Areas of support and grant guidelines are also reviewed.

Giving Category (ies): arts and humanities

◆ Gill Foundation

http://www.gillfoundation.org/

The Gill Foundation serves as a catalyst and provides resources for communities in pursuit of justice and equality, while building awareness of the contributions gay men and lesbians make to American society. Foundation history, contact information, a staff listing, foundation related news and publications, FAQs, past grants, proposal tips and grant guidelines can all be found on this Web site.

Giving Category (ies): civic, social services

◆ Glenn Foundation for Medical Research

http://www.glenn.deco.net/

The Glenn Foundation for Medical Research Web site provides information on its donor and foundation programs, including workshops, conferences and awards. The site also provides links to sites with information on aging research. Since the foundation neither solicits nor accepts applications for grants, the site serves primarily as a gateway for organizations or individuals interested in aging research.

Giving Category (ies): health, science

◆ Global Fund for Women

http://www.globalfundforwomen.org/

The Global Fund for Women Web site provides an overview of the fund's support for women's rights organizations in developing countries. The site includes information on grant criteria, eligibility requirements and an online grant request form. The Web page also provides links to other related women's issues sites.

Giving Category (ies): civic, international, social services

◆ Arnold P. Gold Foundation

http://www.humanism-in-medicine.org/cgi-bin/start.cgi/AB/missionframe3.htm

The mission of the Arnold P. Gold Foundation is to foster humanism in medicine. Grantseekers will find contact information, a listing of the foundation's board of trustees, newsletters and a searchable resource database.

Giving Category (ies): health

◆ Richard and Rhoda Goldman Fund

http://www.goldmanfund.org/index2.html

The Richard and Rhoda Goldman Fund supports the Bay area in the fields of environment, population, Jewish affairs (domestic and Israel), violence prevention, the elderly, children and youth, social and human services, health, education and the arts. Financial and contact information,FAQs, application procedures and program and geographical limitations can all be found on this Web site. Program highlights are also offered.

Giving Category (ies): arts, education, health, religion, social services, youth

◆ Green Bay Packers Foundation

http://www.packers.com/community/foundation.html

The Green Bay Packers Web site includes brief information on the foundation, including grant guidelines, contact information, a total grant figure and a listing of recent grants. The site also offers links to the Packers Pro Shop and team news. The Green Bay Packers Foundation supports Wisconsin organizations in the areas of education, youth related services, civic issues, healthcare and human services.

Giving Category (ies): civic, education, health, social services, youth

◆ Harry Frank Guggenheim Foundation

http://www.hfg.org/

The Harry Frank Guggenheim Foundation "sponsors scholarly research on problems of violence, aggression and dominance." The foundation provides both research grants to established scholars and dissertation fellowships to graduate students. This foundation Internet site contains information on research priorities, guidelines and restrictions, application procedures, deadlines and a list of recent grant and fellowship recipients. Grantseekers also can request application forms via e-mail and browse through the Spring 1999 issue of The HFG Review, the foundation's semi-annual journal.

Giving Category (ies): education

◆ John Simon Guggenheim Memorial Foundation

http://www.gf.org/

The John Simon Guggenheim Memorial Foundation Web site provides individuals interested in applying for its fellowships with nearly all the information they will need. The foundation only supports individuals. It does not make grants to institutions or organizations. The site includes information on eligibility, deadlines, applications, competitions and a list of fellows from 1992 through 1999. The site also provides answers to a list of frequently asked questions, links to other unrelated Guggenheim institutes and a list of its trustees. The Web site may also be viewed in Spanish.

Giving Category (ies): arts, international, social services

◆ George Gund Foundation

http://www.gundfdn.org/

The foundation's site includes details on the foundation's background and donor, program areas, applications, restrictions, approved grants from the years 1997 through 1999, general financial information for the year 1999, recent press releases and a listing of related Web sites. The George Gund Foundation awards grants for education, economic development and community revitalization, human services, arts, environment and civic affairs.

Giving Category (ies): arts, civic, education, environment, social services

◆ Gunk Foundation

http://www.gunk.org

The GunkWeb Internet site contains information about the Gunk Foundation's Public Arts Grants and Critical Press' publications and projects. The Web site is easy to use and well structured. An application form may be printed from this Web site. Selected grants from 1995 through 1998 are listed. The Gunk Tourist Project is reviewed.

Giving Category (ies): arts

◆ Walter and Elise Haas Fund

http://www.haassr.org/welcome.htm

The Walter and Elise Haas Fund contributes to the following areas: art; citizenship and civic education; education; environment; human services; humanities; Jewish life; and professional ethics. This Web site offers a history of the foundation, contact information (with the exclusion of an e-mail address), a listing of officers, trustees and staff, an overview of recent and past grants, grant guidelines and application procedures.

Giving Category (ies): arts, civic, education, environment, religion, social services

◆ Harmony Foundation

http://www.harmonyfoundation.org/

The Harmony Foundation was incorporated as a charitable subsidiary of the Society for the Preservation and Encouragement of Barber Shop Quartet Singing in America, Inc. Contact and staff information, news features and newsletters are provided. Grant guidelines and deadlines are available to grantseekers, who may also print an application from this Web site.

Giving Category (ies): arts

◆ Hartford Foundation for Public Giving

http://www.hfpg.org/

The Hartford Foundation for Public Giving Web site contains information on the community foundation, including a description of its programs, geographical area served, list of board of directors and staff, updated grant guidelines and detailed application procedures. A categorical giving breakdown is provided, along with a list of recent grant recipients. Users may view the Winter 1999 issue of the foundation's newsletter. A graph illustrates the 1998 assets by type of fund.

Giving Category (ies): arts, education, health, social services, youth

◆ John A. Hartford Foundation

http://www.jhartfound.org/

The John A. Hartford Foundation makes grants in the areas of aging and healthcare. The Web site includes basic grant proposal submission guidelines and financial information. Detailed information is available on the foundation's areas of interest.

Giving Category (ies): health

◆ John Randolph Haynes and Dora Haynes Foundation

http://www.haynesfoundation.org/index.html

The John Randolph Haynes and Dora Haynes Foundation makes grants for research in the political and social sciences, including economics, public policy, history, social psychology and sociology, favoring projects with specific application to the Los Angeles area. The foundation Web site provides information on specific research and fellowship programs and it contains guidelines and restrictions on giving, application procedures and a list of trustees. Users also can browse through a bibliography of publications and reports produced as a result of Haynes Foundation research and grants to outside organizations.

Giving Category (ies): civic, education

◆ Healthcare Foundation of New Jersey

http://fdncenter.org/grantmaker/hfnj/index.html

Formerly known as the NBI Healthcare Foundation, the Healthcare Foundation of New Jersey's mission is to alleviate the suffering of the most vulnerable members of the community. The goal is to identify and strengthen existing healthcare programs and to seed innovative projects that address unmet healthcare needs. The Web page contains a brief history of the foundation, funding priorities, 1998 grants list, restrictions on giving, application procedures and an outline of the review process. The foundation focuses on healthcare needs of the Jewish community; healthcare needs of the vulnerable population of the South Ward of Newark, NJ, and the general community; healthcare education; and clinical medical research. There is a list of the foundation's board of trustees and administrative staff. Financial data for the foundation is also available for viewing.

Giving Category (ies): health, social services

◆ William Randolph Hearst Foundations

http://fdncenter.org/grantmaker/hearst/index.html

The William Randolph Hearst Foundations are two legal entities — the William Randolph Hearst Foundation and The Hearst Foundation, Inc. The William Randolph Hearst Foundations Internet site offers grantseekers information on their funding priorities: education, health, social service and culture. The site also contains information on foundations' guidelines and restrictions on giving, application procedures and staff members. The site describes two programs administered by the foundations: Hearst Journalism Awards Program and the United States Senate Youth Program. Users will not find a list of recent grants on the Web site.

Giving Category (ies): arts, education, health, social services

◆ Heinz Endowments

http://www.heinz.org

The Heinz Endowments are really two entities — the Howard Heinz Endowment and the Vira I. Heinz Endowment. In addition to employing a joint management and program team, the foundations share a commitment to supporting programs in Southwestern Pennsylvania in arts and culture, education, economic opportunity, children, youth, families and the environment. The Heinz Endowments Web page contains detailed information about the endowments' mission, history, funding priorities, recent grants and application guidelines. The Internet site also contains lists of the endowments' board of directors and staff, foundation headlines and commentaries and contact information.

Giving Category (ies): arts, civic, education, environment, social services, youth

◆ Jim Henson Foundation

http://www.henson.com/index.html

Muppet creator Jim Henson created the Jim Henson Foundation in 1982 to promote and develop the art of puppetry in this country. Grantseekers can be added to the Jim Henson Foundation mailing list by e-mailing the foundation directly from this Web site. The Jim Henson Foundation awards grants for the development and creation of new works of puppet theater by American artists. Seed and project grants range from $1,000 - $5,000. Grantseekers can print an application form from this Web site. Application procedures and important dates and deadlines are provided. Contact information is available, as is company information.

Giving Category (ies): arts

◆ William and Flora Hewlett Foundation

http://www.hewlett.org

The William and Flora Hewlett Foundation focuses its grantmaking on education, the performing arts, population, environment, conflict resolution, family and community development and U.S.-Latin American relations. The Web site lists detailed program descriptions, advice for applicants, board of directors and staff, recent grant awards and authorized grants.

Giving Category (ies): arts, civic, education, environment, international, social services

◆ Hogg Foundation for Mental Health

http://hogg1.lac.utexas.edu/

An administrative unit of the University of Texas at Austin, the Hogg Foundation is comprised of both the Will C. Hogg Fund, which supports new mental health projects throughout the state of Texas and the Ima Hogg Endowment, which only supports direct mental health services for children and their families in the Houston area. Priority is given to projects in the areas of: children and their families; youth development; and minority mental health. During the 1998-99 fiscal year, the Hogg Foundation awarded 70 grants and three fellowships totaling $2,608,072 from its funds and endowments. The Hogg Foundation for Mental Health Web site contains information on the foundation, its regional library, giving guidelines and funding restrictions. The Web site provides a 1998-1999 grants listing, information on each of the specific funding areas and contact information.

Giving Category (ies): health, social services, youth

◆ Houston Endowment

http://www.hou-endow.org/

The Houston Endowment contributes to a broad range of programs in education, healthcare, human services, cultural arts and other areas. The endowment's Internet site contains information on its donors and the organization's purpose; board members, officers and staff; its high school scholarship program; eligibility criteria and deadlines; application procedures; recent grants lists; and online annual reports.

Giving Category (ies): arts, civic, education, health, social services

◆ Howard Hughes Medical Institute

http://www.hhmi.org/grants/

Howard Hughes Medical Institute (HHMI) Web site contains information on all the institute's initiatives, as well as specific information on each of its grant programs: precollege, undergraduate, graduate and international. The site also contains detailed information on giving priorities and an awards database that can be searched for recent and past grant recipients. An online version of its annual report and a list of current foundation events is available.

Giving Category (ies): education, science

◆ Humboldt Area Foundation

http://www.northcoast.com/~hafound

The Humboldt Area Foundation Web site contains general information on the community foundation. Information contained on the site includes descriptions of its donor services, application procedures and links to other philanthropic sites. Grantseekers also will find a link to the William T. Rooney Resource Center that provides information on additional grant opportunities in the Humboldt area. A link is also provided for the Union Labor Health Foundation, which serves Humboldt County.

Giving Category (ies): civic

◆ I Have a Dream Foundation

http://www.ihad.org/

The I Have a Dream Foundation (IHAD) is a nationally recognized program that helps children stay in school, graduate and go on to college or meaningful employment. The Web site offers foundation history, stories from IHAD participants, a listing of participating schools throughout the country (including contact information), FAQs and related resources.

Giving Category (ies): education, youth

◆ Irvine Health Foundation

http://www.ihf.org/

Grantseekers will find on this Web site a brief history of the foundation, a list of frequently asked questions, recent grants and application procedures. The foundation's site also contains a lists of the foundation's publications and board of directors, its press releases and links to other related sites. Grantseekers can request a free CD-Rom of the foundation's 1996-1997 annual report. There is also a link to the foundation's lecture series.

Giving Category (ies): health

◆ Ittleson Foundation

http://www.ittlesonfoundation.org/

The Ittleson Foundation serves the needs of the underprivileged and provides resources for organizations. Contact information and an annual report that contains a list of the foundation's board of directors and a list of grants, are both found on this Web site. Current programs of interest include AIDS, mental health and the environment. Application guidelines and restrictions are provided.

Giving Category (ies): environment, health, science

◆ Japan Foundation

http://www.jpf.go.jp/

The Japan Foundation's home page contains general information about the foundation, its aims, programs, finances and application guidelines. The Web site also can be viewed in Japanese. The site provides related links, including a link to the Japan Foundation's Center for Global Partnership. Grantseekers also can view the foundation's publications online.

Giving Category (ies): arts, education, international

◆ Elton John AIDS Foundation

http://www.ejaf.org/

The Elton John AIDS Foundation's mission is "to provide funding for educational programs targeted at HIV/AIDS prevention and/or the elimination of prejudice and discrimination against HIV/AIDS affected individuals and for programs that provide services to people living with HIV/AIDS." The Web site provides background, contact and board information. A calendar of upcoming fundraising events and merchandise, press releases and links to AIDS information can all be found on this Web site. A grant request must be mailed directly to the foundation to receive information and/or consideration.

Giving Category (ies): education, health

◆ Magic Johnson Foundation

http://www.magicjohnson.org/

In the beginning, the foundation was established to raise funds for community-based organizations that deal with HIV/AIDS educational and prevention programs. Now, the foundation awards grants to community-based organizations that deal with educational, health and social programs for America's youth. Visitors can contact the foundation through this Web site. A brief history of Magic Johnson may also be of some interest to users of this site. The Web site offers information about foundation news, events, staff and directors. Grantseekers will be able to find out how to apply for a grant, where to send their application and when.

Giving Category (ies): education, health, social services, youth

◆ Robert Wood Johnson Foundation

http://www.rwjf.org/

The Robert Wood Johnson Foundation's mission is to improve the health and healthcare of all Americans. This healthcare funder's Web site contains information on the foundation's goals, programs, officers and staff, statistics, grant winners and guidelines. The site provides grantseekers with a list of answers to frequently asked questions about its proposal-review process, information on current requests for proposals (RFPs), press releases, contact information and a brief history of the foundation and its founder. Grantseekers also will find copies of the funder's 1998 annual report and other publications. There is a link to "What's New" within the foundation, as well as a link to current events regarding the foundation.

Giving Category (ies): health

◆ Walter S. Johnson Foundation

http://www.wsjf.org/

The Walter S. Johnson Foundation Internet site provides general information on the foundation and its founder; funding priorities; new initiatives; a list of trustees, officers and staff; giving guidelines and restrictions; application procedures; and a recent grants list from 1999. This family foundation focuses its funding on three major areas: promoting the well being of children and youth, strengthening public education and assisting young people in the transition to adulthood.

Giving Category (ies): civic, education, social services, youth

◆ W. Alton Jones Foundation

http://www.wajones.org/

The W. Alton Jones Foundation is a private grantmaking foundation focusing on global environmental protection and the prevention of nuclear war or other massive release of radioactive material. The W. Alton Jones Foundation site contains information on the foundation's grantmaking programs, application procedures, a 1994-1998 grants lists, current initiatives and publications. A list of foundation officers and directors is offered as well. Grantseekers may request a copy of the foundation's annual reports from 1994 through 1998. The site also offers links to organizations supported by the foundation, other foundations and philanthropic resources.

Giving Category (ies): civic, environment

◆ Juvenile Diabetes Foundation International

http://www.jdf.org/index.html

The Juvenile Diabetes Foundation International (JDF) Web site offers information on the foundation's research grant, fellowship and award opportunities and application information. The site also contains information on local chapters, 1999 annual report and diabetes information and publications. Recent news and events concerning the foundation are highlighted, including a new partnership between JDF and National Institutes of Health.

Giving Category (ies): health, science

◆ Henry J. Kaiser Family Foundation

http://www.kff.org/

This healthcare funder's Web site provides grantseekers with only basic information, including mission statement, contact information, a list of the board of trustees and a list of its publications. For copies of the foundation's annual report, giving guidelines or recent grants, grantseekers must call the foundation. The site also offers links to other health resources. The site provides medical information on a variety of topics.

Giving Category (ies): health

◆ Kansas Health Foundation

http://www.kansashealth.org/

The Kansas Health Foundation provides grants to organizations throughout the state that share the foundation's mission to improve the quality of healthcare in Kansas. The foundation's three primary funding categories are children's health, leadership and public health. Its Internet site contains historical information on the foundation, funding program descriptions, general giving guidelines and a list of staff. Information is given about the foundation's recognition grants, including guidelines, restrictions, deadlines and an application form that can be downloaded using Adobe Acrobat.

Giving Category (ies): health, youth

◆ Ewing Marion Kauffman Foundation

http://www.emkf.org/

The Ewing Marion Kauffman Foundation Web site contains detailed information on the foundation and its programs: youth development; elementary, secondary and higher education; and entrepreneurial leadership. Grantseekers also will find application procedures and program brochures, press releases, 1999 grantmaking report, funding guidelines and a list of publications.

Giving Category (ies): civic, education, social services, youth

◆ Calvin K. Kazanjian Economics Foundation

http://www.kazanjian.org/

This foundation seeks to "help bring greater happiness and prosperity to all through a better understanding of economics." Contact information, a brief biography of the foundation's founder, recent projects, grant guidelines and application instructions are all available on this Web site.

Giving Category (ies): education

◆ W. K. Kellogg Foundation

http://www.wkkf.org/

The W. K. Kellogg Foundation's Web site contains a mission statement; historical data on the foundation and its founder; list of trustees and staff; detailed descriptions of U.S. programs and programs in South Africa, Latin America and the Caribbean; program guidelines and restrictions; application procedures; list of resources related to the foundation's program interests; a searchable database of all current foundation grants; press releases; contact information; and an online 1998-1999 annual report. Grantseekers also can submit a short preproposal letter to the foundation online and browse through Online Journal, an electronic version of the International Journal of the W. K. Kellogg Foundation.

Giving Category (ies): civic, education, health, international

◆ Kennedy Center Fund for New American Plays

http://www.kennedy-center.org/programs/theater/fnap/

The fund's mission is to help ensure the continued vitality of American theater by supporting its emerging playwrights. Contact information, background history, past recipients, guidelines for application and the fund's honorary committee can all be found on this Web site.

Giving Category (ies): arts

◆ Joseph P. Kennedy, Jr. Foundation

http://www.familyvillage.wisc.edu/jpkf/

The Joseph P. Kennedy, Jr. Foundation's mission is "to provide leadership in the field of mental retardation and service to persons with mental retardation, both those born and unborn and their families." The foundation's site provides general background information on the foundation and its donor, program descriptions, guidelines and restrictions on giving, application procedures, an overview of the Public Policy Fellowship Program and links to other sites related to mental retardation, such as the Special Olympics International home page. Grantseekers will not find a recent grants list on this site. There is a new link to the Kennedy 2000 International Awards in Mental Retardation that gives information about the awards and the nomination process.

Giving Category (ies): health, international, social services

◆ Kentucky Foundation for Women

http://www.kfw.org/

The Kentucky Foundation for Women's goal is "to change the lives of women by supporting feminist expression in the arts in Kentucky; by publishing *The American Voice*, a literary journal; and by operating Hopscotch House, a rural retreat for women near Louisville." The foundation's Web site offers grantseekers information on its giving program, eligibility requirements and restrictions, deadlines, list of 1998 and 1999 grant recipients and details on its literary journal and retreat house. Users must contact the foundation for application forms and may request general information forms online.

Giving Category (ies): arts

◆ Kettering Foundation

http://www.kettering.org/

The Kettering Foundation Web site contains general information about the foundation and its research focus. The foundation produces books for forums that encourage policy debates, promote journalism and facilitate international government. The Kettering Foundation does not make grants; instead it seeks to make joint ventures with organizations with similar interests.

Giving Category (ies): civic

◆ John S. and James L. Knight Foundation

http://www.knightfdn.org/

The Knight Foundation's site includes a statement of purpose, a brief history, FAQs, the foundation's annual report and listings of staff and trustees. The John S. and James L. Knight Foundation supports community initiatives, journalism, education, the arts and culture. Program descriptions, application guidelines, list of eligible communities, proposal cover sheet and sample application are all available on the site. The Web site also features news releases and an online newsletter.

Giving Category (ies): arts, civic, education

◆ Emily Davie and Joseph S. Kornfeld Foundation

http://fdncenter.org/grantmaker/kornfeld/

Visitors to the Emily Davie and Joseph S. Kornfeld Foundation Web site will find information on giving priorities and contact information. The foundation primarily supports "programs in medical ethics, care of the dying and relief of pain; and programs that teach reading, writing, math, science and the arts to students who attend the New York City public schools." Applications for programs in medical ethics, care of the dying and relief of pain are no longer accepted. Instead, the foundation runs the Kornfeld Fellows program in which grants are made to individuals to study medical ethics or palliative care. Grantseekers can call, fax, write or e-mail the foundation to request a recent annual report or to find out specific details about the foundation's programs.

Giving Category (ies): education, health, social services, youth

◆ LEF Foundation

http://www.agmconnect.org/lef.html

The LEF Foundation funds projects, programs and services that encourage "a positive interchange between the arts and the natural and urban environment." The Web site offers grantseekers contact information, eligibility and application information, a list of past recipients and general grant guidelines.

Giving Category (ies): arts, environment

◆ Charles A. and Anne Morrow Lindbergh Foundation

http://www.lindberghfoundation.org/

The Charles A. and Anne Morrow Lindbergh Foundation Web site contains information about the foundation and its philanthropic programs. The foundation sponsors the Lindbergh Grants competition, the Lindbergh Award, as well as educational programs and publications. The foundation makes grants to individuals who seek to further the balance between technology and environmental preservation. The Web site also contains a grant application along with frequently asked questions about the process; a list of past recipients; a list of officers, directors and staff; and links to other relevant sites. Grantseekers can order the foundation's publications online and view its annual report.

Giving Category (ies): education, environment, health

◆ Long Island Community Foundation

http://www.licf.org/

The Long Island Community Foundation serves as the Long Island arm of the New York Community Trust for the 3 million citizens of Nassau and Suffolk Counties. The Web site offers contact information, a list of the board of advisors, foundation publications, current grantmaking guidelines and an overview of past grants awarded.

Giving Category (ies): civic, social services

◆ Edward Lowe Foundation

http://www.lowe.org/

This foundation's mission is "to champion the entrepreneurial spirit by providing information, research and educational experiences for growing companies." The Web site offers information on the foundation's history and its founder. The foundation, which exists to encourage entrepreneurship, sponsors the Edward Lowe Digital Library database, a collection of approximately 4,000 full text documents compiled to help small businesses. Grantseekers will find grant guidelines, as well as application procedures.

Giving Category (ies): civic

◆ George Lucas Educational Foundation

http://www.glef.org/

The George Lucas Educational Foundation Web site provides information on the foundation's mission and history and contains current and past issues of the foundation's newsletter *Edutopia*. The foundation promotes efforts to improve education, primarily by integrating technology with teaching and learning. The areas of focus are K-12 public education. The George Lucas Educational Foundation is a nonprofit operating foundation and is not a grantmaking organization. However, the Web site does offer a list of resources and other links for those seeking grants. Users also can access video, audio and texts of interviews with George Lucas. One of the foundation's current projects is the "Learn & Live" documentary hosted by Robin Williams, which will be broadcast on public television stations nationwide in 2000. The Web site provides a calendar of foundation related events, as well as contact information.

Giving Category (ies): education

◆ Ludwick Family Foundation

http://www.ludwick.org/

The Ludwick Family Foundation is a California nonprofit public benefit corporation established exclusively for charitable, scientific, literary and educational purposes. Areas of interest include children and youth, education and social services. An extensive listing of past recipients includes links to the various organizations who received funding. Application guidelines including a grant procedure and timetable, geographic restrictions and eligibility rules are provided to grantseekers.

Giving Category (ies): education, social services, youth

◆ John D. and Catherine T. MacArthur Foundation

http://www.macfdn.org/

The John D. and Catherine T. MacArthur Foundation site provides information on the foundation's programs, special grant competitions, MacArthur Fellows Program, staff, board and its initiatives. The site also contains application information, giving restrictions guidelines and deadlines, summary of authorized grants, as well as a list of grants awarded by program area and links to other resources. The foundation's annual report is available by mail.

Giving Category (ies): civic, education, health, international

◆ Maddie's Fund

http://www.maddies.org/

Maddie's Fund is an independent, private foundation devoted to the welfare of companion animals. Grantseekers can download an application from this Web site. The Web site offers lots of funding information and guidelines to potential grantseekers, who will find all they need to know to apply. Advice on how to write a successful proposal is also available, as is contact information.

Giving Category (ies): social services

◆ A. L. Mailman Family Foundation

http://www.mailman.org/

The A. L. Mailman Family Foundation's primary funding priority is children and families, with special emphasis on early childhood. The foundation's Web site contains specific program descriptions; a list of officers, directors and advisors; giving guidelines and restrictions; application procedures and deadlines; and a listing of 1999 grants.

Giving Category (ies): civic, education, social services, youth

◆ Manitou Foundation

http://www.manitou.org/mf_homepage.html

The Manitou Foundation's primary focus is to offer land grants in Crestone/Baca, CO, to qualified organizations in the following categories: religious organizations and spiritual projects, ecological and environmental sustainability projects and related education endeavors (youth and adult). Beginning in 1995, the foundation shifted its focus to the research and development of a comprehensive habitat conservation plan, to place most of its remaining land holdings into permanent conservation. The foundation's Internet site offers grantseekers program objectives, land grant criteria, application procedures and a description of the Solitary Retreat Hermitage building project and land preservation program.

Giving Category (ies): civic, education, environment, religion

◆ Marin Community Foundation

http://marin.org/npo/mcf/

The Marin Community Foundation site contains information on the foundation's mission, its history and its primary donor — the Buck Trust. The foundation offers competitive and non-competitive grants, as well as loans. The Web site also contains information on the foundation's programs, services, board of directors and recent grants. Grantseekers are able to contact the foundation electronically to order its publications. Detailed guidelines and application procedures also are provided.

Giving Category (ies): arts, civic, education, environment, social services

◆ John and Mary R. Markle Foundation

http://www.markle.org/

The John and Mary R. Markle Foundation's current goal is "to develop and use the technologies of communication and information to enhance lifelong learning and to promote an informed citizenry." The foundation focuses its programs on three main priorities: media and political participation, interactive communications technologies and communications policy. The foundation's Web site offers grantseekers an extensive history of the foundation and its donors; program descriptions; list of board members and staff; approved expenditures; application procedures and giving restrictions; financial information; articles and press releases; and a list of publications and products resulting from foundation support. Users also can link to grantee Internet sites.

Giving Category (ies): civic, education

◆ Massachusetts Environmental Trust

http://www.agmconnect.org/maenvtr1.html

The trust takes a positive, activist approach to promoting increased awareness, understanding and protection of the waterways of the Commonwealth — all Massachusetts bays, rivers, streams, ponds and lakes. Recent grants awarded, contact information, grant guidelines and funding programs of specific interest can all be found on this Web site.

Giving Category (ies): environment

◆ Mayday Fund

http://fdncenter.org/grantmaker/mayday/

The Mayday Fund's sole purpose is "the reduction of the physical and psychological toll of pain and its consequences." Its Web site contains a description of the fund's giving program, a list of trustees and advisors, a recent grants list and application guidelines. Grantseekers can request a 1998 annual report by contacting the foundation.

Giving Category (ies): health

◆ McCarthy Family Foundation

http://fdncenter.org/grantmaker/mccarthy/

Visitors to the McCarthy Family Foundation Internet site will find a brief description of its funding priorities, application procedures, restrictions on giving, proposal deadlines and a recent grants list. The foundation makes grants in five major areas: secondary school science education; AIDS research, education and support; assistance to the homeless; support for children and families in need; and environmental protection. A listing of all 1999 paid grants is available, by giving category, with dollar amounts included. A geographical distribution of grants is also provided.

Giving Category (ies): education, environment, health, science, social services, youth

◆ Robert R. McCormick Tribune Foundation

http://www.rrmtf.org

The Robert R. McCormick Tribune Foundation Web site contains general background information on the foundation, detailed program descriptions and funding priorities, a list of board members and staff, giving guidelines and restrictions, proposal deadlines, application procedures, recent grants lists, summary of grants from 1996-1998, links to other grantmaking resources and a description of the foundation's support of Catigny, a park that is open to the public for the "education, instruction and welfare of the people of Illinois." The foundation focuses on four main programming areas: communities, journalism, education and citizenship.

Giving Category (ies): civic, education, health, social services

◆ James S. McDonnell Foundation

http://www.jsmf.org/

The James S. McDonnell Foundation Web site contains detailed program information, application guidelines, a listing of grants and awards made by the foundation, as well as the most current financial reports. In particular, the site expands on the foundation's three main funding areas: biomedical and behavioral sciences, research and innovation in education and global understanding. Grantseekers also will find a list of officers and directors and frequently asked questions about the proposal process.

Giving Category (ies): health, international, science

◆ McGregor Fund

http://www.mcgregorfund.org/

The McGregor Fund's mission is "to relieve the misfortunes and promote the well-being of mankind." To this end, the fund concentrates on the following program areas: human services, education, healthcare, arts and culture and public benefit. Its Web site provides background information on the fund's founders; a list of trustees, officers and staff; financial data; giving guidelines and restrictions; application procedures; and a 1999 grants distribution graph.

Giving Category (ies): arts, civic, education, health, social services

◆ Meadows Foundation

http://www.mfi.org

The Meadows Foundation exists "to assist people and institutions of Texas improve the quality and circumstances of life for themselves and future generations." On the foundation's Web site, grantseekers will find it's vision statement; history and background on the founders; program funding areas; list of officers, directors and staff; financial statements; funding guidelines and restrictions; application procedures and deadlines; a recent grants list; and links to other related sites. Users also can learn more about the foundation's Wilson Historic District Project.

Giving Category (ies): arts, civic, education, health, social services, youth

◆ Medina Foundation

http://www.medinafoundation.org/

The Medina Foundation Web site contains all the information grantseekers need to know about the foundation to apply for funding. Information provided on the Web page includes giving guidelines, application procedures, a list of frequently asked questions and links to other resources.

Giving Category (ies): civic, social services

◆ Andrew W. Mellon Foundation

http://www.mellon.org/

The Andrew W. Mellon Foundation Web page provides information on the foundation's history, trustees, staff and detailed descriptions of its philanthropic programs. Grantseekers also can access a number of foundation publications. Application procedures are provided, as are financial reports for the foundation dating back to 1979. The foundation's most recent summary of grants and contributions for last year is also included.

Giving Category (ies): arts, civic, education, environment

◆ Joyce Mertz-Gilmore Foundation

http://www.jmgf.org/

The foundation focuses on the areas of energy, Israel and Palestine, human rights and New York City. In 1997, the Joyce Mertz-Gilmore Foundation became a partner in the joint initiative that supports the work of the Energy Foundation and has transferred responsibility for much of its U.S. energy grantmaking to that undertaking. A link to the Energy Foundation can be found on this Web site. The foundation's site also offers visitors a history of the organization, financial data, program descriptions, a list of directors and staff, giving guidelines and restrictions, basic application procedures and sample grants. Grantseekers can download the foundation's biennial report and 1999 grants in Adobe Acrobat format.

Giving Category (ies): arts, civic, environment, international

◆ Meyer Memorial Trust

http://www.mmt.org/

The Meyer Memorial Trust operates three grantmaking programs: general purpose grants, small grants and support for teacher initiatives. Its Web site offers grantseekers information on the trust's history and founder, Fred G. Meyer; descriptions of funding programs; list of trustees and staff; giving guidelines and restrictions; application procedures; recent grants list; frequently asked questions; and links to other related resources. Users also can download application cover sheets.

Giving Category (ies): arts, civic, education, environment, health, social services

◆ Mid Atlantic Arts Foundation

http://www.charm.net/~midarts/

The Mid Atlantic Arts Foundation Web site outlines the foundation's programs of financial support, including direct grants and fellowships, technical assistance and services to artists and arts organizations in Delaware, the District of Columbia, Maryland, New Jersey, New York, Pennsylvania, the U.S. Virgin Islands, Virginia and West Virginia. Grantseekers also can view selected articles from the foundation's newsletter, ArtsInk. A listing of the staff and board is provided.

Giving Category (ies): arts

◆ Milbank Memorial Fund

http://www.med.harvard.edu/publications/Milbank/fund.html

The Milbank Memorial Fund supports nonpartisan analysis, study and research on significant issues in health policy. The fund publishes the results of its work in pamphlets, books and the Milbank Quarterly. Users can browse the quarterly online newsletter. The fund's Web site only contains a list of publications and a brief description of its priorities. It emphasizes programs in clinical policy, organizing and financing policy and public health policy. The fund's projects are not supported by grants, but rather by individuals and partner institutions who join the fund in contributing time and other resources.

Giving Category (ies): health

◆ Milken Family Foundation

http://www.mff.org

The Milken Family Foundation Internet site provides grantseekers with a background on its founders, a list of directors and staff, grant guidelines and descriptions of its funding programs, which focus on education, medical research and healthcare and community welfare. Unfortunately, guidelines, application procedures and sample grants are not provided.

Giving Category (ies): education, health, science, social services

◆ Montana Community Foundation

http://www.mtcf.org/

The Montana Community Foundation seeks "to protect and enhance the unique resources of Montana, its people and their needs, its diversity of culture, its richness of artistic creation and appreciation and the beauty and quality of its land, air and water, so that these resources may be enjoyed now and in the future." The foundation Web site offers grantseekers general background information, a listing of staff and board, facts on donating to the foundation, a sample of organizations endowed by the foundation with links to their sites and a message from the chairman.

Giving Category (ies): arts, civic, education, environment, social services

◆ Charles Stewart Mott Foundation

http://www.mott.org/

Users accessing the Charles Stewart Mott Foundation Internet site will find general background information on the foundation and its founder; foundation philosophy; detailed program descriptions, with graphical displays of allocated funds; giving guidelines and restrictions; application procedures and deadlines; searchable database of recent grants; list of publications, including an online order form; press releases; and an online version of the foundation's newsletter, Mott Exchange. The foundation concentrates on four main funding areas: civil society; poverty; the Flint, MI, area; and the environment. Approximately 20 percent of its grants go to international causes.

Giving Category (ies): arts, civic, education, environment, international, social services, youth

◆ Ms. Foundation for Women

http://www.ms.foundation.org/

The Ms. Foundation for Women "funds and assists women's self-help organizing efforts and pursues changes in public consciousness, law, philanthropy and social policy." The foundation's Web site provides detailed descriptions of its funding programs including the Collaborative Fund for Women's Economic Development, Health and Safety; Women's Economic Security; and the Healthy Girls/Healthy Women Collaborative Fund. Sample grants for the Collaborative Fund for Women's Economic Development are included. Users will not find guidelines or application procedures on the site. Take Our Daughters to Work Day is one of the highlighted programs on this site. The foundation's mission and history is reviewed. There is a link to the Top 10 Role Models of the Year. Users may view foundation reports and newsletters in Adobe Acrobat.

Giving Category (ies): civic, health, social services

◆ Museum Loan Network

http://loanet.mit.edu/Grants/gi_desc.htm

The Museum Loan Network (MLN) was launched to promote collection sharing among museums in the United States. The Web site offers a history of the MLN, a list of its advisory committee, news and press releases, recent and previous grant awards, grants descriptions, deadlines, guidelines and forms.

Giving Category (ies): arts

◆ National Council for Social Studies Online

http://www.ncss.org/awards/home.html

The National Council for Social Studies (NCSS) home page provides grantseekers with information about the organization, including councils, conferences, news and announcements, awards and grants. The awards section describes all of the NCSS recognition programs, criteria and submission guidelines. Other attributes of this Web site include links to other sites, such as the *Federal Register* and a listing of grant providers for technology in the classroom. There is also a listing of 1999 award and grant recipients.

Giving Category (ies): education

◆ National Foundation for the Improvement of Education

http://www.nfie.org/

The National Foundation for the Improvement of Education's (NFIE) mission is to promote excellence in teaching and learning. NFIE carries out its mission by providing teachers, other school employees and higher education faculty and staff with opportunities to develop and test solutions to the challenges facing American public education. The NFIE Web site contains general background information on the foundation; a list of staff; funding opportunities, including its Change of Course, Learning Tomorrow, Road Ahead and Leadership Grants programs; giving guidelines and restrictions; application procedures and deadlines; and an online version of the On the Road Ahead newsletter. A new program called the Jordan Fundamentals partners the foundation with Michael Jordan to provide grants to secondary school teachers. Users also can view NFIE's annual report.

Giving Category (ies): education

◆ National Geographic Society Education Foundation

http://www.nationalgeographic.com/society/ngo/foundation/

The National Geographic Society Education Foundation's mission is "to revitalize the teaching and learning of geography in the nation's K-12 classrooms." Its Web site contains a history of the foundation, program descriptions for grantmaking in four major areas (geographic network alliance, teacher grants, urban initiatives and restricted state endowments), guidelines and restrictions, application procedures and deadlines, sample grants and information on donating to the foundation. An application cover sheet is available for teacher grants. Grantseekers also are provided with a nationwide list of contacts in the geographic network alliance.

Giving Category (ies): education

◆ National Rivers Coalition

http://www.amrivers.org/nr-coalition.html

The National Rivers Coalition, a group of national conservation/recreation organizations focusing on conserving and restoring rivers and watersheds, strives each year to provide seed grants to the grassroots river community. An application form may be printed from this Web site. General information is provided about what types of programs are considered for funding. Contact information is also provided.

Giving Category (ies): environment

◆ National Science Teachers Association Awards Programs

http://www.nsta.org/programs/

The National Science Teachers Association Awards Programs Web page provides information on more than $1 million in award programs for students and teachers. The Internet site contains program descriptions, eligibility requirements and deadlines for each of the awards. A list of recent award winners is also provided. Grantseekers can view a variety of foundation related journals, press releases and publications.

Giving Category (ies): education, science

◆ National Trust for Historic Preservation

http://www.nthp.org/main/frontline/departments/urban.htm

The National Trust for Historic Preservation seeks to promote the use of historic preservation as a tool for revitalizing America's historic urban neighborhoods. Grantseekers will find a listing of the types of funding available. Foundation news and a calendar of events are also offered. Contact information including a mailing address, fax number and phone number are provided as well.

Giving Category (ies): arts and humanities

◆ New Israel Fund

http://www.nif.org/

The New Israel Fund works "to safeguard civil and human rights, promote Jewish-Arab coexistence, advance the status of women, foster tolerance and religious pluralism, bridge social and economic gaps, pursue environmental justice and encourage government accountability." On its Internet site, grantseekers will find a statement of the fund's mission and goals; general overview of its funding programs; list of officers and directors; recent grants list and links to grantees; press releases; information on volunteering in Israel; and an online annual report and newsletter. No real giving guidelines or application procedures are included. However, the general criteria for core grants is explained. Links to news, study tours, a library, events and speakers are provided.

Giving Category (ies): civic, environment, international, religion, social services

◆ Norman Foundation

http://www.normanfdn.org/

The Norman Foundation Web site offers grantseekers financial information on the foundation, recent grants awarded, a list of officers and directors, application procedures, guidelines and restrictions. The foundation supports civil rights/individual liberties, economic justice and environmental justice. Due to a generational change, the Norman Foundation is restructuring. Until June 1, 2000, the foundation will not consider grant applications or new proposals.

Giving Category (ies): civic, environment

◆ Laird Norton Endowment Foundation

http://www.lairdnorton.org/

The Laird Norton Endowment Foundation funds distinctive programs in conservation and forestry education. Recent and past grants are available for viewing. Users of this site can read up on the foundation's history. The Web site has an overview of the foundation's current funding focus, sustainable forestry. Contact and application information, as well as application guidelines and procedures are offered to grantseekers.

Giving Category (ies): environment

◆ Olfactory Research Fund

http://www.olfactory.org/

The Olfactory Research Fund awards grants for scientific and psychological research at universities and hospitals around the world on the sense of smell and the psychological benefits of fragrance. The Web site provides a description of the fund and its mission, board of directors, sponsored research, press releases, prominent studies, other fund activities and a listing of corporate sponsors. The fund was established by the Fragrance Foundation (http://www.fragrance.org) in 1982. The Fragrance Foundation does not include any grantmaking information on its site other than a link to the Olfactory Research Fund. There is an online order form for ordering the foundation's books and journals.

Giving Category (ies): science

◆ Open Society Institute

http://www.soros.org/usprograms/

The Open Society Institute's self described mission is "to strengthen public discourse in areas where one of an issue dominates all others, precluding alternative approaches." Grantseekers will find a listing, as well as corresponding links to the institute's current funding programs including: urban initiatives; death in America; and welfare reform. Publications from the institute and background information about this organization are provided. An application guidelines page is currently under construction for this Web site.

Giving Category (ies): arts, social services

◆ Orchard Foundation

http://home.maine.rr.com/orchard/

The Orchard Foundation is a private charitable foundation that makes grants to nonprofit organizations concerned with the environment and children, youth and families in the New York and New England states. The foundation also supports, on an invitation-only basis, organizations concerned with campaign finance reform at the state and national levels. This Web site offers contact information, application guidelines and an overview of the three main areas of funding, including a list of past grant recipients.

Giving Category (ies): civic, environment, youth

◆ Orthopaedic Research and Education Foundation

http://www.oref.org/

The goal of the foundation is the advancement of knowledge concerning the prevention and treatment of conditions affecting the musculoskeletal and related systems and the maintenance of the general physical well being of the individual. The Web site includes contact information, foundation news and history, staff directory, grant and award recipients, application information and current grants and awards available to grantseekers.

Giving Category (ies): education, health

◆ Ottinger Foundation

http://www.funder.org/ottinger

This private family foundation's Web site provides the grantseeker with basic information including application procedures, giving guidelines, deadlines, restrictions and a list of recent grants.

Giving Category (ies): civic

◆ David and Lucile Packard Foundation

http://www.packfound.org/

The Web site for California's David and Lucile Packard Foundation provides grantseekers with basic information and history about the foundation, an electronic copy of its guidelines with information on each of Packard's priority areas, tips on how to apply for funds, deadlines, contact names and information on what the proposals should include. Grantseekers will find a 1999 listing of grant recipients, the 1998 annual report and current news about the foundation.

Giving Category (ies): arts, civic, education, environment, health, science, youth

◆ Pet Life Foundation

http://www.petlifefoundation.org/plf_home.html

The Pet Life Foundation provides for the support of the many groups dedicated to the preservation of the quality of life and the prevention of homelessness for companion pets worldwide. Foundation objectives are clearly defined for grantseekers. Grant criteria is reviewed, including deadlines, proposal submission, grant procedures and application forms. A listing of the foundation's board and personnel is also available. Some general financial information is supplied, as is an e-mail contact form.

Giving Category (ies): social services

◆ Pew Charitable Trusts

http://www.pewtrusts.com/

This user-friendly site provides grantseekers with information on the Pew Charitable Trusts' history, detailed descriptions of its philanthropic programs, application procedures and guidelines, lists of publications, recent grants and links to program and administrative staff.

Giving Category (ies): arts, civic, education, environment, health, religion, social services

◆ Philadelphia Foundation

http://www.philafound.org/

The Philadelphia Foundation Web site provides information on the community foundation's history and mission, grantmaking, fund management and community services. Grantseekers also will find the foundation's application guidelines, a list of its officers and directors and sample grants.

Giving Category (ies): civic, education, social services

◆ Points of Light Foundation

http://www.pointsoflight.org

The Points of Light Foundation Web site offers the mission, history and grantmaking goals of the foundation. The foundation's mission is to engage more people more effectively in volunteer community service to help solve serious social problems. The foundation's 1998 annual report is accessible, as well as program summaries, descriptions of awards, a list of board members and contact information. The Web site offers a link to Daily Points of Light.

Giving Category (ies): civic, social services

◆ Pollock-Krasner Foundation

http://www.pkf.org/

The Pollock-Krasner Foundation's mission is "to aid, internationally, those individuals who have worked as professional artists over a significant period of time." Its Web site provides general information on the foundation along with a history of its grantmaking, list of officers and staff, application guidelines and restrictions, description of the selection process, application procedures and a list of 1998-1999 grant recipients. Grantseekers may download a grant application form in Adobe Acrobat.

Giving Category (ies): arts, international

◆ Princess Grace Foundation - USA

http://www.pgfusa.com/

The foundation's program is dedicated to identifying and assisting young talent in theater, dance and film through grants in the form of scholarships, apprenticeships and fellowships. This Web site offers foundation history, past recipients, the board of trustees, contact information, a fact sheet and grant guidelines.

Giving Category (ies): arts, education

◆ Puerto Rico Community Foundation

http://www.fcpr.org/

The Puerto Rico Community Foundation is "a philanthropic instrument created for the purpose of applying the necessary energies and resources to confront the principal socio-economic problems facing the people of Puerto Rico." The foundation's Internet site provides the mission and a brief history of the organization; list of directors and staff; description of its giving programs, including permanent fund for the arts, community housing development organizations program, middle school renewal initiative and Institute for the Development of Philanthropy; and links to related sites. Grantseekers will not find guidelines, application procedures or a recent grants list. The Web site can also be viewed in Spanish.

Giving Category (ies): arts, civic, education, health, social services

◆ Puffin Foundation

http://www.angelfire.com/nj/PuffinFoundation/

The Puffin Foundation seeks to open the doors of artistic expression to those who are often excluded because of their race, gender or social philosophy. The Web site offers contact information, application procedures and proposal deadlines.

Giving Category (ies): arts

◆ Quantum Foundation

http://www.quantumfoundation.com/

The mission of the Quantum Foundation is "to advance the health, education and community betterment for the residents of Palm Beach County." Visitors to this site will find listings of board and staff members, grant criteria, focus areas and a listing of current grant programs for healthcare, education and community betterment. An annual report may be ordered from this Web site.

Giving Category (ies): civic, education, health

◆ Retirement Research Foundation

http://fdncenter.org/grantmaker/rrf/index.html

The Retirement Research Foundation is the nation's largest private foundation exclusively devoted to aging and retirement issues. The Retirement Research Foundation operates a general grants program and an award program called Congregation Connection Program. In addition, the foundation has recently announced a new initiative called the Organizational Capacity Building Initiative. Its Internet site contains a description of funding programs, including special programs and awards; giving guidelines and restrictions; application procedures and deadlines; an overview of the National Media Owl Awards program; a frequently asked questions link; and a recent grants list.

Giving Category (ies): civic, health, social services

◆ Z. Smith Reynolds Foundation

http://www.zsr.org/

Grantseekers will find a brief foundation history; lists of officers, trustees and staff; program descriptions; detailed grant application procedures; lists of frequently asked questions; and publications.

Giving Category (ies): civic, education

◆ Kelly and Cal Ripken, Jr. Foundation

http://ww1.sportsline.com/u/fans/celebrity/ripken/outofu/foundation.html

The foundation is currently focusing its support on adult and family literacy through the Baltimore Reads Ripken Learning Center and youth recreation programs in the greater Baltimore area. In addition, the foundation has recently provided funding for the establishment of the Kelly G. Ripken Program, a resource for thyroid education and patient care at Johns Hopkins. Contact information is provided, as are links to information about Cal Ripken, Jr. and his baseball career.

Giving Category (ies): education, health, social services

◆ Fannie E. Rippel Foundation

http://fdncenter.org/grantmaker/rippel/index.html

The Fannie E. Rippel Foundation Web site contains information on the foundation's history; program objectives; list of trustees, officers and staff; financial data; application guidelines and restrictions; and lists of both appropriated and paid grants for 1999. Foundation funding is directed toward the "relief and care of aged women," the construction and maintenance of hospitals, the treatment of and/or research concerning heart disease and the treatment of and/or research concerning cancer.

Giving Category (ies): health, social services

◆ Jackie Robinson Foundation

http://www.jackierobinson.org/

The Jackie Robinson Foundation perpetuates the legacy of Jackie Robinson by providing college scholarships for minority youths. News features, contact information and information on the foundation's sponsorship board are all found on this Web site. Information about the foundation's scholarship program is reviewed, including eligibility requirements, key dates and an application form.

Giving Category (ies): education

◆ Rockefeller Brothers Fund

http://www.rbf.org/

The Rockefeller Brothers Fund (RBF) is a philanthropic organization dedicated to improving the well-being of all people in the transition to global interdependence. On July 1, 1999, the RBF and the Charles E. Culpeper Foundation merged. Under the name of the Rockefeller Brothers Fund, the major grantmaking programs of both foundations will be continued. The Web site offers grantseekers information on this newly formed foundation's history including financial data, list of trustees and staff, program guidelines and application procedures, grantmaking process, recent grants listed by program area and links to other foundation and nonprofit sources. The foundation focuses its giving in the following program areas: health, education, arts and culture, the New York City area, South Africa, global security and the administration of justice. Users will find a 1997 RBF annual report and a 1998 Charles E. Culpeper Foundation annual report. Both reports are available for download and in print. Contact information such as address, phone, fax and e-mail are available.

Giving Category (ies): arts, civic, education, health, international

◆ Rockefeller Family Fund

http://www.rffund.org/

The Rockefeller Family Fund makes grants in five program areas: citizen education and participation, economic justice for women, environment, institutional responsiveness and self-sufficiency. The fund's Web site offers grantseekers a list of trustees and staff, detailed program descriptions, application procedures, a recent grants list and links to the Rockefeller Foundation and the Rockefeller Brother's Fund. The site also contains an overview of the Rockefeller Technology Project.

Giving Category (ies): civic, environment

◆ Rockefeller Foundation

http://www.rockfound.org/

The Rockefeller Foundation organizes its funding around the following programs: African initiatives, agricultural sciences, arts and humanities, health sciences, equal opportunity, global environment, population sciences, building democracy, strategic alliance, special interests, international security, special international initiatives and Bellagio, Italy. The foundation maintains the Bellagio Study and Conference Center in northern Italy for conferences of international scope and for residencies for artists, scholars, policymakers and other professionals from around the world. Grantseekers will find a great deal of information on the Rockefeller Foundation Web site including detailed funding program descriptions, financial data, a list of trustees, giving guidelines and restrictions, application procedures and a recent grants list. The site also offers online versions of the foundation's most recent publications.

Giving Category (ies): arts, civic, education, environment, health, international, science

◆ Rosenberg Foundation

http://www.rosenbergfdn.org/

The Rosenberg Foundation makes grants to nonprofits in California to improve the well-being of children and their families, particularly those children who are minority, low-income or immigrant. The foundation's Web site offers information on its three grant priority areas: the changing population of California; children and their families in poverty; and child support reform; as well as applications, foundation history, financial information and a listing of board members.

Giving Category (ies): civic, social services, youth

◆ Judith Rothschild Foundation

http://fdncenter.org/grantmaker/rothschild/

The goal of the Judith Rothschild Foundation is to increase the public understanding of lesser known and insufficiently appreciated artists, thus affording their work the opportunity for public viewing, institutional acquisition and critical reassessment. The Web site offers contact information, history of the foundation's founder and a listing of staff and board. Grantseekers can view recent and past grants lists and grant guidelines.

Giving Category (ies): arts

◆ Russell Sage Foundation

http://www.russellsage.org/

The Russell Sage Foundation is the principal U.S. foundation devoted exclusively to research in the social sciences. It is a research center, a funding source for studies by scholars at other academic and research institutions and an active member of the nation's social science community. The foundation's Internet site contains information on funding priorities, a list of trustees and staff, giving guidelines and application procedures, lists of visiting scholars and recent project awards and a lengthy inventory of publications.

Giving Category (ies): civic, education

◆ San Antonio Area Foundation

http://www.saafdn.org/

The San Antonio Area Foundation Internet site contains information on the community foundation's mission, its history, board of directors and application procedures.

Giving Category (ies): arts, civic, education, health, social services

◆ San Diego Community Foundation

http://www.sdcf.org/

The San Diego Community Foundation focuses its grantmaking on the areas of health and human services, arts and culture, the environment, urban and civic affairs and education. Its Web site contains a list of board members and staff, examples of programs receiving funding, giving guidelines and restrictions, application procedures and deadlines, a 1998 grants list, a list of services provided to donors and an online version of the foundation's newsletter.

Giving Category (ies): arts, civic, education, environment, health, social services

◆ Scaife Family Foundation

http://www.scaife.com/scaife.html

The Scaife Family Foundation supports and develops programs that promote the well-being of the family and traditional values. Grant awards to organizations and projects in Southwestern Pennsylvania are given special consideration. Contact information, an annual report, basic grant guidelines and procedures are provided.

Giving Category (ies): social services

◆ Sarah Scaife Foundation

http://www.scaife.com/sarah.html

The Sarah Scaife Foundation's grant program is primarily directed toward public policy programs that address major domestic and international issues. Contact information, an annual report and basic grant guidelines and procedures are provided.

Giving Category (ies): civic

◆ Sierra Club Foundation

http://www.sierraclub.org/foundation

The mission of the Sierra Club Foundation is to advance the preservation and protection of the natural environment by empowering the citizenry, especially democratically-based grassroots organizations, with charitable resources to further the cause of environmental protection. Users are provided with an overview of the foundation's history, as well as programs and projects being funded, including environmental justice and youth in wilderness. The Web site gives information on how to become a donor. A list of the board of directors and the foundation's staff can also be found on this Web site. Guidelines and application procedures are not available. Grantseekers may view the 1998 annual report in Adobe Acrobat format. A link is provided for the Sierra Club home page.

Giving Category (ies): civic, environment

◆ Alfred P. Sloan Foundation

http://www.sloan.org/

The Alfred P. Sloan Foundation's Internet site contains information on the foundation's mission and a biography of its donor. Grantseekers will find information on the foundation's five primary funding areas: science and technology; economic performance; education and careers in science and technology; selected national issues; and civic projects. The site also contains application procedures and a list of staff and officers. Grantseekers may view the foundation's 1998 annual report. Foundation contact information is also available.

Giving Category (ies): civic, education, science

◆ Sobrato Family Foundation

http://www.sobrato.com/foundation/index.htm

The Sobrato Family Foundation concentrates its giving in four major areas: community building and economic development, education, health and human services and youth development. The foundation's Web site contains its mission statement, list of trustees and officers, program descriptions, funding guidelines and restrictions, application procedures, deadlines and a recent grants list.

Giving Category (ies): civic, education, health, social services, youth

◆ Sonoma County Community Foundation

http://www.sonoma.org/

The Sonoma County Community Foundation Web site contains general background information on the foundation, detailed priorities, giving guidelines, application procedures and deadlines. Grantmaking concentrates on four major areas: health and human services, education, the environment and arts and humanities. Grantseekers should contact the foundation for application forms or they can download them in Adobe Acrobat. There is a recent grants list available.

Giving Category (ies): arts and humanities, education, environment, health, social services

◆ Sonora Area Foundation

http://www.sonora-area.org/

The Sonora Area Foundation "receives and administers donated funds to meet the changing community needs and to serve the charitable interests of donors." Grants have been made in the areas of recreational services, education, social services programs and the arts. The foundation Internet site offers visitors background information on the founder, a mission statement, description of the funds managed by the foundation, list of officers and board members, giving guidelines and restrictions, application procedures and a recent grants list.

Giving Category (ies): arts, civic, education, health, social services

◆ Soros Foundations Network

http://www.soros.org

The numerous nonprofit foundations and organizations created and funded by the philanthropist George Soros are linked together in an network. The Soros Foundations Network Web site provides biographical information on the founder, George Soros, descriptions of funding programs, funding guidelines and application information, frequently asked questions, a worldwide staff directory, lists of its press releases and publications, such as the Open Society News. Some of the foundation's most recent grants are also described.

Giving Category (ies): arts, civic, education, international, science

◆ Southern Poverty Law Center

http://www.splcenter.org/

The Southern Poverty Law Center works to fight back against hate, intolerance and discrimination through education and litigation. Information is available on teaching tolerance, taking legal action and the history behind the center. Those interested in more information can either fill out an online form and e-mail the center or can contact the center through their mailing address.

Giving Category (ies): civic

◆ Spencer Foundation

http://www.spencer.org/

The Spencer Foundation funds "research which contributes to the understanding of education and improvement of its practice." The foundation Web site offers grantseekers general background information; detailed descriptions of research grant and fellowship programs; a list of directors, advisors and staff; giving guidelines and restrictions; application procedures and deadlines; an outline of the proposal review process; and a comprehensive listing of grants, available in the annual report.

Giving Category (ies): education

◆ St. Luke's Charitable Health Trust

http://www.sltrust.com/

The trust's mission is "to invest in the development and support of activities, programs and organizations that improve the health of people and their communities, with emphasis on prevention programs for children, youth and families; the delivery of health services to the underserved and building the capacity of communities to help themselves." Programs are focused primarily in Maricopa County, (the greater Phoenix metropolitan area) although they occasionally fund statewide projects. This Web site contains contact information, grant guidelines, a listing of recent grants awarded, an annual report, news stories and a list of the board of trustees.

Giving Category (ies): health

◆ Stern Family Fund

http://www.essential.org/stern/

The Stern Family Fund is a private foundation that supports policy oriented government and corporate accountability projects. The Stern Family Fund Web site contains an introduction to the foundation, descriptions of its philanthropic programs — Public Interest Pioneers and Strategic Opportunity Grants, a list of its board members and information on recent grants, as well as past ones. There is a link to Stern grant program question and answer page. Also, grantseekers can e-mail the foundation directly from the Web site.

Giving Category (ies): civic

◆ Surdna Foundation

http://www.igc.apc.org/surdna/

The Surdna Foundation site offers general information including the foundation's mission. Recently, programs in effective citizenry and the arts were added. A list of officers and directors, descriptions of grantmaking programs, current priorities, application guidelines and contact information can all be found on this Web site.

Giving Category (ies): arts, civic, environment

◆ TAPPI Foundation

http://www.tappi.org/public/foundation/foundation_main.asp

The TAPPI Foundation, sponsored by the Technical Association of the Pulp and Paper Industry, provides on its Internet site information on the foundation's philanthropic programs, scholarships and awards, application guidelines and restrictions for the Research Funding Program and recent grant recipients. Some of the foundation's programs include the Gunnar Nicholson Gold Medalist Award and William L. Cullison Scholarship.

Giving Category (ies): education, science

◆ John Templeton Foundation

http://www.templeton.org/

The Web site has a specific grant opportunities link that lists current grantmaking initiatives. The John Templeton Foundation awards grants in the areas of spiritual information through science, spirituality and health, free enterprise education, character development and the Templeton Prize for Progress in Religion.

Giving Category (ies): education, health, religion

◆ Toynbee Prize Foundation

http://www.toynbeefoundation.org/

The Toynbee Prize Foundation contributes to the advancement of the social sciences. The Toynbee Prize was created to recognize and honor individuals who have made an outstanding contribution to the theory and/or implementation of the social sciences. The Web site offers: contact information; the foundation's board of trustees; past recipients; and foundation activities. General grant guidelines are available, as is application deadlines.

Giving Category (ies): civic, social services

◆ Triangle Community Foundation

http://www.trianglecf.org/

The Triangle Community Foundation's mission "is to expand private philanthropy in the communities of the greater Triangle area including Wake, Chatham, Durham and Orange Counties." Grants support cultural affairs and the arts, community development, education, environmental issues, health, social services and other areas. The foundation Web sites provides an overview of its grantmaking programs and finances, information on donating to the foundation and creating funds, giving guidelines and restrictions, application procedures and deadlines, recent grants list and an online version of its newsletter. Grantseekers can download a sample discretionary grant application in Microsoft Word format.

Giving Category (ies): arts, civic, education, environment, health, social services

◆ Trinity Grants Program

http://www.trinitywallstreet.org/Programs/grants.html

The Trinity Grants Program seeks "to accomplish four objectives: to meet needs of metropolitan New York; to strengthen the Church in the global south (including Africa, Asia and other economically challenged areas); to strengthen telecommunications in the Anglican Communion; and to strengthen spiritual formation in the Episcopal Church of the United States." Its Web site offers a description of its grantmaking program, funding guidelines and restrictions and application procedures. Users can request a copy of the Trinity Church annual report as well as link to its home page. The site provides an extensive history of Trinity Church.

Giving Category (ies): civic, international, religion, social services

◆ Trust Fund for Children with Special Health Care Needs

http://www.mdch.state.mi.us/msa/cshcs/

The Trust Fund helps pay for services and projects for children with special healthcare needs not provided by other healthcare funds. A history of the trust is given. Eligibility requirements are reviewed and the trust funds committee is listed. A phone number is supplied for application information.

Giving Category (ies): health, youth

◆ Turner Foundation

http://www.turnerfoundation.org/

The Turner Foundation's Web page provides a description of the foundation's mission and goals, detailed program guidelines, giving priorities and application outlines and grant listings. Grants are listed by giving category for the years 1996 through 1998. The four major areas of support are energy, water/toxins, forests/habitats and population. Grantseekers also will find deadline and contact information.

Giving Category (ies): civic, environment

◆ U.S.-Japan Foundation

http://www.japanese.com/nonprofit/foundation.html

The principal mission of the foundation is to promote greater mutual knowledge between the United States and Japan and to contribute to a strengthened understanding of important public policy issues of interest to both countries. The U.S.-Japan Foundation Web site contains information on its two main giving priorities — precollege education and policy studies. Grantseekers also will find information on application procedures and funding restrictions.

Giving Category (ies): civic, education, international

◆ United Hospital Fund of New York

http://www.uhfnyc.org/

The United Hospital Fund, founded in 1879, is a health services research and philanthropic organization that addresses critical issues affecting hospitals and healthcare in New York City. It is the oldest federated charity in the nation. The mission of the United Hospital Fund is to address critical issues affecting voluntary hospitals and healthcare. This site offers contact information, press releases, foundation publications, conferences and events and financial information, including an annual report. The Web site provides a brief description of the fund's grantmaking priorities. Past grants made are listed by giving category.

Giving Category (ies): health

◆ W.E. Upjohn Institute

http://www.upjohninst.org/

The W.E. Upjohn Institute is an independent, nonprofit research organization devoted to finding, evaluating and promoting solutions to employment-related problems. Grantseekers will find a listing of the Institute's senior staff, complete with biographical links and e-mail addresses. Grantseekers will find a wealth of information about the institute's grants program, including: application procedures; deadlines and notification dates; evaluation criteria; mini-grants currently available; and recent grant recipients.

Giving Category (ies): civic, education

◆ Valley Foundation

http://www.valley.org/

The Valley Foundation is a nonprofit organization headquartered in Los Gatos, CA. The foundation seeks to provide funding for nonprofit organizations in Santa Clara County with an emphasis in the medical field. The Web site offers visitors e-mail and mailing addresses, a printable grant application, a financial report and a listing of the foundation's board of trustees. Grant guidelines, application procedures and a grant summary are also available.

Giving Category (ies): health

◆ Victoria Foundation

http://www.reeusda.gov/pavnet/fd/fdvictor.htm

Education, neighborhood development and urban activities in Newark's inner city; youths and families; and statewide environmental issues in New Jersey are all at the heart of the Victoria Foundation's funding. Visitors to this site will find contact information, eligibility requirements, some financial data, application information and important dates.

Giving Category (ies): civic, education, environment, youth

◆ Virginia Environmental Endowment

http://www.cvco.org/vee/

The mission of Virginia Environmental Endowment is to improve the quality of the environment by encouraging all sectors to work together to prevent pollution, conserve natural resources and promote environmental literacy. This Web site offers users contact information, a list of staff, an overview of recent grants and application procedures. Also available is information about the mini-grant program.

Giving Category (ies): environment, youth

◆ Wallace-Reader's Digest Funds

http://www.wallacefunds.org/

In January 2000, the DeWitt Wallace-Reader's Digest Fund and the Lila Wallace-Reader's Digest Fund announced that they combined resources and staffs and will operate as the Wallace-Reader's Digest Funds. The Web site provides details on the merger. The site also offers an overview of the funds' mission, history, principles and strategies, contact and financial information; descriptions of the current grantmaking program; listing of the most recent grants made by the fund; a FAQs section; application guidelines and a listing of fund publications that can be ordered or viewed online.

Giving Category (ies): arts, education, youth

◆ Andy Warhol Foundation for the Visual Arts

http://www.warholfoundation.org/

On the Andy Warhol Foundation for the Visual Arts Web site, grantseekers will find a foundation history, as well as a biography of Andy Warhol. Grant guidelines, FAQs, a calendar of funded projects and recent grants awarded are also available on the site. The site also contains links to the Andy Warhol Museum.

Giving Category (ies): arts

◆ Weeden Foundation

http://www.weedenfdn.org/

The Weeden Foundation Web site contains information on the foundation's mission, giving guidelines, a list of its board and staff and recent grants list. Grant summaries are available for the years 1997 through 2000. Grantseekers also will find a breakdown of the foundation's funding by major category of giving and a 1999 annual report.

Giving Category (ies): civic, environment

◆ Kurt Weill Foundation for Music

http://www.kwf.org/

The Kurt Weill Foundation for Music Web site contains information on the foundation's various activities — the perpetuation and preservation of the legacies of composer Kurt Weill and actress-singer Lotte Lenya. In addition to links to the Weill-Lenya Research Center and the Kurt Weill Edition, the site details information on its grant program and the Kurt Weill Prize, an annual Twentieth Century music theater scholarship. Detailed guidelines and application procedures are provided.

Giving Category (ies): arts

◆ Weingart Foundation

http://www.weingartfnd.org/

The foundation's Web site contains a brief history, online annual reports for 1995 through 1999, financial information, some descriptions of current grantees, grant guidelines and application procedures. The Weingart Foundation's primary area of interest in grantmaking is to assist nonprofits serving children and youth in the Southern California area.

Giving Category (ies): arts, civic, education, health, social services

◆ Wenner-Gren Foundation for Anthropological Research

http://www.wennergren.org

The Wenner-Gren Foundation supports basic research in all branches of anthropology. The foundation's mission is to advance significant and innovative research about humanity's cultural and biological origins, development and variation and to foster the creation of an international community of research scholars in anthropology. The Web site offers contact information, FAQs, foundation programs, board of trustees and advisory council and updated application information. Sample applications are available for viewing.

Giving Category (ies): science

◆ Wheat Ridge Ministries

http://www.wheatridge.org/

Wheat Ridge is a Lutheran organization that strives for health and hope within its ministries. A variety of grant programs assist congregations and agencies who are beginning new health-related ministries. Wheat Ridge also provides and supports activities which equip people for involvement in health ministry. Users of this site will find a questions and answers section, ministry events, press releases and a directory of current grant programs available. Wheat Ridge Ministries provides grantseekers with a contact form that may be e-mailed directly to the foundation.

Giving Category (ies): religion

◆ Whitaker Foundation

http://www.whitaker.org

The Whitaker Foundation is a private, nonprofit foundation dedicated to improving human health through the support of biomedical engineering. The Whitaker Foundation Web page contains a hypertext version of its 1998 annual report as well as information on the foundation's programs, guidelines and trustees. The Internet site also provides application procedures, eligibility criteria, giving restrictions, an application schedule and a list of grants approved in 1998.

Giving Category (ies): health, science

◆ Wilburforce Foundation

http://www.wilburforce.org/

The Wilburforce Foundation provides funding to nonprofit organizations in the U.S. Pacific Northwest and Southwest. The foundation awards grants to nonprofit organizations that have programs operating in Alaska, the Yellowstone to Yukon region, British Columbia, Washington, Oregon, Nevada, Utah, New Mexico or Arizona. The Wilburforce Foundation is dedicated to protecting nature through funding programs that help preserve remaining wild places. The Web site offers information on its funding priorities — environmental and human population issues. The Web site also contains information on recent 1999 grants, giving restrictions and grant guidelines. Grantseekers also can link to other related sites concerning the environment and population, as well as to other foundation and resource sites. Staff and contact information is also provided.

Giving Category (ies): civic, environment

◆ Woods Charitable Fund

http://www.4w.com/woods/index.html

The Woods Charitable Fund Web site offers basic foundation information, grant program specifics, application guidelines, limitations and restrictions, a summary of 1998 grants paid by area of interest and an online letter from the president and executive director of the fund. Grants are made primarily in Lincoln, NE, in the areas of children, youth and families; education; community development and housing; and the arts and humanities.

Giving Category (ies): arts, civic, education, social services

◆ Wray Trust

http://www.wt.org/

The Wray Trust, a small family foundation that funds environmental and art projects in Texas, provides information regarding its philanthropic program on its Web site. Grantseekers can find application guidelines, grant histories and links to other funding sources.

Giving Category (ies): arts, environment

◆ Agency for Healthcare Research and Quality (AHRQ)

http://www.ahcpr.gov

Agency for Healthcare Research and Quality home page advertises current funding opportunities and ongoing program announcements up front in areas of quality improvement and cost. It also provides fact sheets, research summaries and AHRQ newsletters, which discuss research findings and recent awards, often useful in preparing applications. All program descriptions include detailed application guidelines. Users may consult clinical practice guidelines and data and health technology assessment abstracts and brush up on methods for health services and assessment research.

◆ Agriculture Department (USDA)

http://www.usda.gov

A choice site for harvesting information about research and education grants in agriculture-related fields, the USDA Web site has newly organized information on recent grants and recently announced programs. Since funding opportunities appear by organizational unit, it helps to know where to hunt.

• *Cooperative State Research Education and Extension Service (CSREES)*

http://www.reeusda.gov/1700/funding/ourfund.htm

The Cooperative State Research Education and Extension Service home page is a storehouse of more than a score of funding opportunities including USDA's big national research initiative competitive grants, food safety grants, higher education programs, graduate fellowships and the agricultural telecommunications program — not to be confused with USDA's distance learning and telemedicine seed grants, under the Rural Utilities Service (RUS) discussed below. CSREES browsers can dig up program descriptions, guidelines, news of program changes, deadlines and abstracts of previously funded proposals. Users also may subscribe to two mailing lists specific to the national competitive grants initiative and the telecommunications activity for program updates.

• *Food and Nutrition Service (FNS)*

http://www.fns.usda.gov/fns/MENU/CONTRACTS/CONTRACTS.HTM

Increasingly important because of a governmentwide food safety initiative, the Food and Nutrition Service funds mainly by contracts. The FNS primarily contracts for program studies and analyses; food stamp coupon production, storage and distribution; and Federal Information Processing (FIP) resources such as software, hardware, support services and maintenance. Federal assistance is also available through competitive grants and cooperative agreements.

• *Nonprofit Gateway*

http://www.nonprofit.gov/resource/resource.html

This site provides a path for nonprofits to grants and contracts information, technical assistance, publications, databases and other services in other agencies.

• *Rural Utilities Service (RUS)*

http://www.rurdev.usda.gov/rus/index.html

Rural Utilities Service site users will find background and details on education and health-related telecommunications and distance learning project grants, previous project summaries, contacts and rural development discussion groups. The RUS site helps grantseekers quickly identify projects — and colleagues — next door by clicking on a map of recent grantees.

◆ Centers for Disease Control and Prevention (CDC)

http://www.cdc.gov

The Atlanta-based Centers for Disease Control and Prevention Web site remains straightforward as the home page leads right to an up-to-the minute listing of funding opportunities and program announcements published in the *Federal Register*. Grantseekers may view funding information under individual institutes, found under the main menu's "About CDC" option. Users may subscribe for access to application forms and guidance electronically, subscribe to CDC publications and reports electronically, delve into health statistics that may be needed in preparing an application and search CDC databases.

◆ Commerce Department (DoC)

http://www.doc.gov

Commerce provides a wide range of funding opportunities from telecommunications grants for nonprofits to science and technology awards for businesses and universities. Site users will find active solicitations, detailed program descriptions, contacts and answers to common questions.

• *Economic Development Administration (EDA)*

http://www.doc.gov/eda

The Economic Development Administration is the site for community development grants and funding opportunities to localities, planning agencies and universities.

• *International Trade Administration (ITA)*

http://www.ita.doc.gov/

The International Trade Administration funds firms to train interns from the Newly Independent States.

• *National Institute of Standards and Technology (NIST)*

http://www.nist.gov

The National Technology Administration's National Institute of Standards and Technology through its business-oriented Advance Technology Program supports development of enabling technologies. NIST also funds research grants in areas from fire to physics under measurement and standards laboratories and small business innovation research projects.

• *National Oceanic and Atmospheric Administration (NOAA)*

http://www.noaa.gov

The National Oceanic and Atmospheric Administration funds fisheries research and climate studies.

• *National Telecommunications and Information Administration (NTIA)*

http://www.ntia.doc.gov

The National Telecommunications and Information Administration funds telecommunications infrastructure grants to nonprofits to improve delivery of health, education and social services and public telecommunications grants to plan and construct public broadcasting facilities. Focus is on closing the digital divide and NTIA's Technology Opportunities Program (TOP), (formerly the Telecommunications and Information Infrastructure Assistance Program (TIIAP)). Visitors to the Web page can search funded programs, find an online newsletter and valuable outreach information.

◆ Corporation for National Service (CNS)

http://www.cns.gov

The CNS home page leads directly to information about three major program areas: AmeriCorps, the national service corps; Learn and Serve America, which supports service-learning projects in schools; and Senior Corps, which enlists seniors with skills to community service projects. The site provides an online AmeriCorps application and upfront access to several volunteer listservs.

◆ Defense Department (DoD)

http://www.defenselink.mil

Grantseekers can wind through DoD's vast Web site — and still miss important funding information — or head straight for strategic grant targets, which are devoted mainly to research. DoD's home page include sites for an array of centralized research and technology programs and education programs related to DoD interests, including:

• *Air Force Office of Scientific Research (AFOSR)*

http://www.fie.com/fedix/afosr.html

The Air Force Office of Scientific Research funds basic research in areas from chemistry and life sciences to mathematics and space sciences.

• *Army Research Office (ARO)*

http://www.aro.ncren.net/

The Web site for the Army Research Office points grantseekers to an annual omnibus broad agency announcement of funding in areas from biosciences to physics and other opportunities for faculty and small business. ARO also provides a handy phone directory of contacts by program.

• *Defense Department Research and Engineering (DDR&E)*

http://www.dtic.mil/ddre/

The Defense Department Research and Engineering home page leads users to information about DoD's environmental research and the dual use technology initiative, which supports development of technologies that may have defense and commercial applications.

• *Edugate*

http://www.acq.osd.mil/ddre/edugate/

Edugate is a bonus site — it is DoD's gateway to K-12, undergraduate, graduate and teacher preparation efforts funded by DoD and other agencies.

• *National Security Education Program (NSEP)*

http://www.ndu.edu/nsep/

The National Security Education Program provides key support to colleges and universities for language and area studies via institutional grants, scholarships and fellowships to advance international education.

• *Office of Naval Research (ONR)*

http://www.onr.navy.mil

The Office of Naval Research home page is devoted to funding news, including grant and contract information needed to submit a proposal, document shells and forms, research solicitations and information about special initiatives, notice of education and cross-discipline research opportunities for students and faculty and proceedings of recent grants-related conferences.

• *U.S. Army Medical Research and Materiel Command (USAMRMC)*

http://www-usamraa.army.mil

http://cdmrp.army.mil

U.S. Army Medical Research and Materiel Command boasts an active multi-million dollar extramural science program and growing special congressionally directed research initiatives in breast cancer, women's health, prostate cancer and osteoporosis.

◆ Education Department (ED)

http://www.ed.gov/

The Education Department gets high marks for a comprehensive site that guide's grantseekers to more than $1 billion annually in competed grants. ED's "Funding Opportunities" selection, just off the home page, links readers to an increasingly sophisticated grants and contracts page, which opens onto most department sites of use to grantseekers.

• *Grants and Contracts Information (OCFO)*

http://ocfo.ed.gov/

The latest innovation: a grants database — and a contracts counterpart — designed to make grant award data more accessible. Visitors can search the database by award amount, *Catalog of Federal Domestic Assistance* sub-program, state, recipient name and zip code. In addition, the site is replete with links to current grant and contract competitions, ED's annual grants agenda and rules and policies governing grantmaking. Users also can find the Guide to U.S. Department of Education Programs for details of ongoing programs and the primer, "What Should I Know About ED Grants?" The *Federal Register* documents page links directly to current published grant-related announcements. Traveling from ED's main home page, users can peruse ED's budget; look in on staff and offices; browse publications and products; find services, including by state; tap into the world's largest education database — the Educational Resources Information Center; and access the National Center for Education Statistics.

◆ Energy Department (DoE)

http://www.doe.gov

DoE's Internet site is the pipeline for information about the billions of dollars the agency pumps into research, directly and via its network of federal laboratories.

• *Office of Environmental Management*

http://www.em.doe.gov

Tthe Office of Environmental Management provides information on opportunities in restoration, crosscutting programs and the Environmental Management Science grant program which it operates with the Office of Science.

• *Office of Procurement and Assistance Management*

http://www.pr.doe.gov

The Office of Procurement and Assistance Management is a repository of tools, guides and information for contractors. Its site offers a "Doing Business with DoE/Business Communications Center Page," which connects with grant and contract opportunities at DoE field offices and provides information procedures and resources.

• Office of Resource and Management

http://www.er.doe.gov/production/orm

The Office of Resource Management page provides quick access to application guides and forms, a rundown of evaluation criteria and the merit review system by individual program, key grant rules and grant statistics that plot program competitiveness by providing numbers of applications and awards.

• Office of Science (OS)

http://www.sc.doe.gov/

A new Office of Science houses DOE's major research divisions, including the Office for Basic Energy Sciences and the Office of Biological and Environmental Research and the OS Web site provides general grant information. Click on individual office home pages for detailed descriptions of research and fellowship grant programs addressing issues from genome to remediation and climate change, information on how to submit proposals, policy guidelines and merit review procedures.

• Office of Science Grants and Contracts

http://www.sc.doe.gov/production/grants/grants.html

The OS grants and contracts page tells how to apply for grant funding, lists current grant notices inviting applications, provides an explicit grant application guide and downloadable application forms and hot links to grant rules and regulations, including key governmentwide grant circulars from the Office of Management and Budget. The site also provides information on submitting applications to DoE national laboratories.

◆ Environmental Protection Agency (EPA)

http://www.epa.gov

EPA provides grants for research and other activities. Its Web site provides information about grants and opportunities available from EPA headquarters and via centers, laboratories and regions. The main menu's "Money Matters" selection leads to descriptions of community, education and environmental justice programs. Research grant information is available by accessing EPA's National Center for Environmental Research and Quality Assurance, the source of major science funding opportunities for colleges, universities and other organizations.

• *National Center for Environmental Research (NCER)*

http://es.epa.gov/ncerqa

On the NCER home page, grantseekers can join an e-mail mailing list for grant and fellowship announcements as they emerge. The home page also links visitors to other environmentally relevant sites. NCER runs EPA's $100 million extramural STAR grant program (Science To Achieve Results), which funds agency programs in areas such as children's vulnerability to toxic substances and ecological indicators and it participates annually in joint solicitations with the National Science Foundation and other agencies in funding grants in areas such as environmental statistics. In addition to listing current opportunities, NCER enables researchers to look ahead and plan by previewing a partial listing of upcoming topics. NCER visitors also can talk back via its e-mail service.

• *Office of Research and Development (ORD)*

http://www.epa.gov/ORD/

The ORD Web site links to information on laboratories and centers, environmental facts and statistics, scientific and policy reports and final and draft research strategies, which can provide useful background for grantseekers. From the "Grants and Contracts" link, users are taken to NCER's listing of available grant opportunities.

◆ Health and Human Services Department (HHS)

http://www.os.dhhs.gov

The main menu of the biggest federal domestic grantmaker, the Health and Human Services Department, is a terminal for finding general grants information, a path to individual agencies and leads to other health and social services funders and partners. But the home page provides some on-site benefits, too. Via the policy button, grantseekers can access reports on legislation affecting programs, White House Office of Management and Budget grants-related circulars and links to other grants administration sites. The Gateways link leads to the GrantsNet page, which captures information about finding funds, applying for grants and grants information resources. The news site is an archive of press releases and fact sheets, which can provide useful context in which to view HHS grant programs. Visitors also can link to the department's varied funding agencies.

◆ Health Resources and Services Administration (HRSA)

http://www.hrsa.dhhs.gov

Thanks to a major innovation, Health Resources and Services Administration applicants can peruse a year's worth of planned solicitations in its "Preview" of upcoming deadlines, consult detailed program descriptions and grant guidance and learn of the latest policy changes affecting programs. Grantseekers also may download standard and program-specific application kits. A special news room feature, links to relevant, speeches, articles, publications and news releases, many of which provide information about grant awards and recipients under HRSA initiatives. The home page also offers a handy staff telephone directory.

◆ Housing and Urban Development (HUD)

http://www.hud.gov

Grantseekers on the Housing and Urban Development Web site get a reorganized funding opportunities site reflecting a consolidated grant announcement process that HUD has instituted to make applying for HUD grants easier and more efficient. HUD has consolidated most of its grants and their related Notices of Funding Availability (NOFAs) into a SuperNOFA. On the home page, grantseekers may click on "business" then "funding" for current notices of funding opportunities, which link to needed applications, forms and detailed program information; as well as other federal and private funding sources. The business page provides quick references to program descriptions, basic funding information and regulations and policies covering a wide range of programs from neighborhood development and community outreach partnerships to Youthbuild training grants and drug elimination grants.

◆ Institute of Museum and Library Services (IMLS)

http://www.imls.gov/

The Institute of Museum and Library Services site provides all grantseekers need to tap museum and library support grants, including clear concise program descriptions, with deadlines, eligibility requirements and staff contacts. The site also provides numbers of awards and award lists by program category and a calendar of upcoming grant application deadlines for activities ranging from research on learning in museums to conservation and professional services support. Users also can obtain grant applications and examples of successful proposals on the guidelines and forms page.

◆ Justice Department (DoJ)

http://www.usdoj.gov

Grantseekers can track down Justice Department funds two main ways for crime research, law enforcement, youth crime prevention and community safety projects. They can consult the National Criminal Justice Reference Service below or go directly to the agency's recently reorganized official home page. Follow "community support and grants" on the main menu and click on "programs" for an at-a-glance review of funding divisions in the Office of Justice Programs (OJP), the agency's grant center. Descriptions include current budget information and often provide a general forecast of grantmaking activity. The main menu's "organizations" selection or the site map at the top of the page leads to OJP.

• *Justice Information Electronic Newsletter (JUSTINFO)*

http://www.ncjrs.org

• *Juvenile Justice Electronic List (JUVJUST)*

http://ojjdp.ncjrs.org/about/about-4.html

Two handy NCJRS mailing lists speed information to grantseekers: the Justice Information Electronic Newsletter arrives about twice monthly by e-mail; a juvenile justice analog appears sporadically. Information about JUSTINFO is at the bottom of the NCJRS main page; information about JUVJUST is on the Office of Juvenile Justice and Delinquency Prevention home page via NCJRS.

• *National Criminal Justice Reference Service (NCJRS)*

http://www.ncjrs.org

The National Criminal Justice Reference Service is an extensive source of information on criminal and juvenile justice. Clicking on "justice grants" brings up the listings of funding opportunities on DoJ home pages, along with application kits and funding guidelines. In addition to grants information, NCJRS offers a searchable database, a catalog of publications and a schedule of conferences.

• *Office of Justice Programs (OJP)*

http://www.ojp.usdoj.gov/

The OJP site provides up-to-date funding notices and descriptions of programs by grantmaking unit, such as the research-funding National Institute of Justice and the Office of Juvenile Justice and Delinquency Prevention. Program sites also provide application kits and forms, manuals and guidance.

◆ Labor Department (DoL)

http://www.dol.gov

The Labor Department main menu listing "about DoL" leads to a grant and contracts information page that provides an overview of grant and contracting programs and information resources and a working knowledge of various agencies' interests. The grants site also puts valuable tools at grantseekers' fingertips, such as Office of Management and Budget grant-related policy circulars and connections to major information sources, such as the federal government's official grant compendium, the *Catalog of Federal Domestic Assistance*. But most competitive grantmaking comes from the Employment and Training Administration.

• *Employment and Training Administration (ETA)*

http://www.doleta.gov

The ETA home page provides the latest on ETA programs and initiatives. Applicants can click on current solicitations and find information about recent awards and descriptions of successful programs, including welfare-to-work competitive grant projects.

• *Welfare-To-Work (WTW)*

http://wtw.doleta.gov

Applicants can go directly to the WTW home page for the latest information about availability of hundreds of millions of dollars in grants to help individuals make the transition from welfare to employment. The WTW site includes information on technical assistance conferences to help grantseekers write applications for the next competitive round; consult fact sheets, regional contacts, planning guidance and applicable grants rules.

◆ National Aeronautics and Space Administration (NASA)

http://www.nasa.gov/

The National Aeronautics and Space Administration's busy Web site can launch grantseekers on their exploration of education and research funding opportunities at headquarters and distant field centers several ways.

• *NASA Centers*

http://www.nasa.gov/hqpao/nasa_centers.html

The "Welcome to NASA" button leads to the NASA field centers home page, which permits users to seek out opportunities and information by topic or discipline, for example, information technology or deep space systems.

- ***NASA Procurement***

http://www.hq.nasa.gov/office/procurement/index.html

Scrolling down the Office of Procurement home page, also off the main menu, lands users at the same research and announcements of opportunity and connects to the Federal Acquisition Jumpstation, a major intersection of other federal procurement sites. The procurement page includes synopses of opportunities, downloadable solicitation and contract documents, contract and grant award information and procurement regulations.

- ***Office of Earth Science***

http://www.earth.nasa.gov/nra/index.html

- ***Office of Life and Microgravity Sciences and Applications***

http://peer1.idi.usra.edu/

- ***Office of Space Science***

http://www.hq.nasa.gov/office/oss/research.htm

- ***Research Opportunities***

http://www.nasa.gov/research.html

Blasting off from the main menu, visitors will find current funding announcements and program descriptions under four major science offices, including the Office of Space Science (OSS) and the Office of Life and Microgravity Sciences and Applications. On science sites, grantseekers may sign up for a constant stream of e-mail notices of funding opportunities. Alternately, the main menu selection, "research opportunities," leads to current solicitations across funding components.

◆ National Endowment for the Arts (NEA)

http://arts.endow.gov/

The National Endowment for the Arts guidelines and applications page links readers to grant programs by category, upcoming application deadlines and lists of recent awards. Program information includes eligibility, review criteria and instructions for applying. Visitors with grants also may link to administrative information. NEA provides advice on completing application forms as well as the forms themselves, which also are available by e-mail request [webmgr@arts.endow.gov]. Prospective applicants also may electronically request notification of awards and special announcements. Visitors may view NEA's arts.community hyperlinked magazine with features and news about the arts and connections to other arts resources.

◆ National Endowment for the Humanities (NEH)

http://www.neh.fed.us/

The National Endowment for the Humanities' site links users to its guidelines and applications page that lists grant programs by category, upcoming application deadlines and lists of recent awards. Program information includes eligibility, review criteria and instructions for applying. Visitors may access NEH publications, including its annual report, which lists recent awards and a general list of reviewers and they may tap the latest grant award information. NEA provides a handy deadline calendar for prospective applicants and grant administration information for current grantees. The page also directs visitors to state humanities councils.

◆ National Institutes of Health (NIH)

http://www.nih.gov

Because the National Institutes of Health's vast Web site is in constant transition, this $17 billion funding venue requires frequent check-ups. The site is a means not only to gather grant information but keep up with and comment on reforms in the review process and ongoing efforts to streamline the application process. NIH, along with the National Science Foundation, have taken a lead in developing the means to conduct electronic commerce and the biomedical behemoth is using the rapidly growing site to inform researchers and gather feedback on topical grant issues.

Keeping up with NIH isn't easy. The home page links visitors to 25 different institutes and offices outside the director's office, which itself houses 36 separate sites. In addition to NIH's centralized grant alert system, the individual NIH funding component provides detailed information about grant opportunities, including special initiatives and ongoing programs. A few institutes, such as the National Institute of Allergy and Infectious Diseases, provide advance information of grant plans. And most sites brief viewers on research findings, scientific conferences, relevant policy reports, minutes of key advisory meetings and key staff contacts.

Recent NIH Web features include a financial management home page, which provides data on funding-by-disease; and a new legislative home page that can help researchers keep abreast of Congressional proposals that could affect funding.

• *NIH Guide for Grants and Contracts*

http://grants.nih.gov/grants/guide/index.html

The Guide for Grants and Contracts page is the heart of NIH's centralized grants and contracts information system. The electronic guide, delivered via e-mail by subscription administers a week's worth of grant announcements and related notices on program changes and policy issues. The guide provides hyper-text program announcements that permit grantseekers to link to important documents and background materials mentioned in the announcements.

• *Office of Extramural Research (OER)*

http://grants.nih.gov/grants/oer.htm

The Office of Extramural Research is the central location for information about funding opportunities, application kits and other forms, grants policies and requirements, information on grant awards and access to abstracts of previous awards — back to 1992 — via the CRISP biomedical research database. It also is the place to keep up with news about peer review of grant applications. As a special feature, researchers may submit general questions about NIH extramural research and training programs, grants policy and awards data by e-mail.

◆ National Science Foundation (NSF)

http://www.nsf.gov/

The $4.5 billion National Science Foundation is a major funder of research and education grants. A pioneer in developing the Internet, NSF not only provides vast amounts of information useful to grantseekers — from science data to research abstracts — it is a lead agency in using the Internet to streamline the grantmaking process.

Visitors to NSF's home page can immediately access directorates of their choice, from biology to education. Directorate sites provide detailed descriptions of grant programs and, often, special communications to applicants and grantees.

The NSF "Grants and Awards" page, a main menu option, provides listings of or links to everything the NSF grantseeker needs to know. As examples, the page links to an overview of NSF programs; funding opportunities; program deadlines and target dates; award information and abstracts of funded projects; regulations and important notices; grants policy and requirements; and information about outreach programs on proposal preparation and award administration through regional grant conferences.

• *Custom News*

http://www.nsf.gov/home/cns/start.htm

NSF's introduction of a popular customized e-mail information service may tempt users to stay away from the agency's home page. Grantseekers who sign up for the Custom News Service can request automatic e-mail notification of program announcements, forms, news releases, project directories, important notices and reports, dear colleague letters and the "Bulletin," the monthly calendar of upcoming grant competitions.

• *FastLane*

http://www.fastlane.nsf.gov

NSF's FastLane seeks to provide electronic access to proposal forms preparation, proposal review, final project reports and applications. Under FastLane, grantees may check electronically on the status of their proposals, file final project reports and take care of other grant business. FastLane also can be used to pick through recent grant awards by topic, state or institution. NSF's site enables visitors to browse and search a catalog of NSF publications. It provides links to fully search publications and grants. In addition to providing access to its own vast database, NSF links to external research centers, laboratories, selected projects and federal agencies.

• *Office of Budget, Finance and Award Management (BFA)*

http://www.nsf.gov/bfa

• *Budget Internet Information System (BIIS)*

http://ntalpha.bfa.nsf.gov

NSF's Office of Budget, Finance and Award Management offers a wealth of information about appropriations, financial management of grants, cost policy and audit. A bonus is the Budget Internet Information System that permits users to drill down into detailed award information via listings by organization, state and institution and funding rates by state and organization.

◆ Nuclear Regulatory Commission (NRC)

http://www.nrc.gov/

NRC awards approximately $100 million in contracts with commercial firms, nonprofit organizations and universities every year and the agency home page provides details on doing business with the NRC. Users also may request by e-mail to be added to NRC's solicitation mailing list.

◆ Research and Study Opportunities at the Smithsonian Institution

http://www.si.edu/research%2bstudy/

The Smithsonian Opportunities for Research and Study home page offers a wide range of information on fellowships and internships. In particular, it has five main links: Smithsonian Fellowship Program; Fellowships at the Smithsonian Astrophysical Observatory; Native American Community Scholar Awards; Minority Internship Program; and Native American Intern Program. Grantseekers may contact the institution via e-mail to request application forms.

◆ Small Business Administration (SBA)

http://www.sbaonline.sba.gov/sbir/

The home page of the Small Business Administration's Office of Technology merges information about 10 participating agencies in the governmentwide Small Business Innovation Research (SBIR) program — aimed at small businesses — and the companion Small Business Technology Transfer Research (STTR) program — which requires small business-nonprofit partnerships. This central site links to individual agencies' solicitations; provides a master schedule of SBIR/STTR proposal deadlines; and lists upcoming SBIR conferences and/or seminars. Grantseekers also can look at successful proposals and an annual awards list and access the SBIR proposal preparation handbook.

◆ Substance Abuse and Mental Health Services Administration (SAMHSA)

http://www.samhsa.gov/

The Substance Abuse and Mental Health Services Administration home page features a week-in-review option that updates constituents about grant and award announcements, meetings, new publications, data releases and doings of the agency director. The site provides program and service information by sub-agency center, including a description of SAMHSA's competitive knowledge and development and application program, which seeks to develop new knowledge about ways to improve the prevention and treatment of substance abuse and mental illness. It also links to substance abuse information resources and clearinghouses. The SAMHSA grants page provides lists of previous grant recipients and current opportunities; a counterpart contracts page runs current requests for proposals.

◆ Transportation Department (DoT)

http://www.dot.gov

DoT's home page steers users to a grants information and programs site that includes data regarding university research grants. Or grantseekers can take alternate routes to information about funding opportunities — via the Research and Special Programs home page or DoT's operating administrations, including the National Highway Traffic Safety Administration (NHTSA) and the Federal Aviation Administration. At the NHTSA site, for example, users may browse and download active solicitations.

◆ U.S. Agency for International Development (USAID)

http://www.info.usaid.gov

The "Business and Procurement" option on the U.S. Agency for International Development's home page can dispatch universities, nonprofits voluntary organizations and businesses to opportunities for education, research and development project funding. Its announcements and solicitations page permits visitors to link to current grant and contract solicitations and call up recent award notices. The procurement site provides information for small businesses, proposal preparation resources and critical procurement regulation handbooks that outline eligibility and other requirements. Users may check future procurement plans and subscribe to receive new solicitation notices by e-mail.

Federal Publications/Documents/Sources

◆ *Catalog of Federal Domestic Assistance* (CFDA)

http://www.cfda.gov/

Catalog of Federal Domestic Assistance is the official compendium of federal grant programs, must reading for novice and veteran grantseekers alike. Grantseekers can use this site to search the catalog by word, program or agency for more than 1,300 federal assistance programs. Entries include the purpose of the program, a program description, relevant statutory references, general funding information and contacts. Grantseekers may tap into the CFDA at many sites, including the Health and Human Service Department's home page via GrantsNet, where users can search CFDA programs alphabetically.

◆ *Commerce Business Daily* (CBD)

http://CBDNet.gpo.gov

Commerce Business Daily is the official advertiser of federal contract opportunities and CBDNet is the official CBD site. Many agencies, including the Energy Department, the Defense Department, the Agency for International Development, the National Aeronautics and Space Administration and the Environmental Protection Agency also use CBD to solicit cooperative agreement and other grant applications. A major advantage to using the CBD home site is the ability to conduct a variety of searches that can help contractors scope out business possibilities and conduct market research. A simple browse by classification code gives readers a rundown of procurements during the previous 15 days. Other searches can produce award data by category and geographical area. Many public and private sites link to CBD, but the GPO site's not-so-secret edge is a friendly, competent support staff that can walk users through the mechanics of searching.

◆ Federal Acquisition Jumpstation

http://nais.nasa.gov/fedproc/home.html

The Federal Acquisition Jumpstation is billed as a doorway to federal procurements on the Internet. It provides one-stop shopping via links to a hodgepodge of agency grant and contract sites. The resource expects its more than 75 hotlinks to federal contracting activities and other sources of funding information to grow. New links are frequently added as additional federal procurement sites appear on the Internet. The Jumpstation is handiest as a supplement to targeted agency site visits rather than as a substitute.

◆ *Federal Register*

http://www.nara.gov/fedreg/

http://www.access.gpo.gov/su_docs/

The *Federal Register*, managed by the National Archives and Records Administration (NARA), is the federal government's official daily record of agency and regulatory affairs. The document is compulsory reading for grantseekers since many agencies, such as the Education Department and Agriculture Department, use the *Federal Register* to announce upcoming grant competitions. However, not all agencies publish grant notices in the *Federal Register*, although they are required to publicize any activity with regulatory impact, including grants-related rulemaking. Agencies not using the *Federal Register* for grant announcements include the largest domestic grantmaker, the National Institutes of Health and the National Science Foundation, but both post required announcements of upcoming application review and other meetings. The NARA site provides a quick look at next-day register entries and a crash course in how to use the resource. NARA also provides access to the updated Code of Federal Regulations (CFR) as updated. The site links to the Government Printing Office site, where readers can search current and past issues of the register, the CFR and other publications.

◆ General Accounting Office (GAO)

http://www.gao.gov

Congress' watchdog, the General Accounting Office, keeps tabs on government grant programs, processes and issues and reports to lawmakers on what works and what needs fixing. Now, grantseekers can bone up on many grant-relevant issues — from the effectiveness of programs for at-risk and delinquent youths to the adequacy of peer review procedures — by delving into reports and testimony. Visit the GAO home page for information on a range of services: the Daybook, a daily e-mail report of new titles and offerings; availability of back issues of the Daybook by e-mail; e-mail ordering of printed copies of GAO reports; a searchable database of reports and testimony; and access to GAO reports in text and PDF files from the Government Printing Office at GPO Access.

◆ Government Printing Office/GPO ACCESS

http://www.access.gpo.gov/su_docs

A valuable archive of online databases of use to grantseekers, whether they are looking for funding announcements in the latest *Federal Register*, scanning House or Senate bills at any stage of the legislative process or public laws affecting funding opportunities. Grantseekers may search, view and download the latest editions among these primary source documents or scour the electronic shelves for issues going back two years. Documents are available in ASCII text file and in the Adobe Acrobat file format.

◆ Library of Congress/THOMAS

http://thomas.loc.gov/

The THOMAS wing of the Library of Congress home page has given the public unprecedented access to legislative information and served as a gateway to Senate and House home pages and sites of individual committees, such as appropriations committees. Pickings are varied at committee sites, but some panels, such as the House Appropriations Committee provide up-to-date reports of legislative action. THOMAS users can find full text of legislation and the Congressional Record, bill summaries and status and committee reports, searchable by keyword, report or bill number or committee number. Users can look up membership of congressional committees and subcommittees and check hearings schedules.

◆ Office of Management and Budget (OMB)

http://www.whitehouse.gov/omb/index.html

OMB circulars govern all aspects of the federal grants process — administration and cost recovery for overhead and audits. Grantseekers may access circulars; review a list, updated daily, of regulations under review; and consult the President's proposed budget for the coming year.

◆ 555-1212.com

http://www.555-1212.com/

This handy site offers users searchable databases for locating area codes and country codes, e-mail addresses, telephone numbers and Web sites.

◆ America's Charities

http://www.charities.org/

America's Charities, a coalition of national human service nonprofits, provides on its Web site information on workplace solicitation along with basic data on member organizations, including descriptions of organizations, contact information and brief financial data. Users can search America's Charities directories either by category or by the entire list of directories. Also included is volunteer information for those interested in volunteering at America's Charities.

◆ American Journalism Review News Link

http://www.newslink.org/menu.html

American Journalism Review News Link Web site contains weekly articles regarding the state of online journalism. Of particular interest is the index of more than 9,900 newspapers, magazines, TV and radio services worldwide. Grantseekers can link quickly to the news organization's Web site to search for regional news on funding prospects.

◆ American Medical Association Physician Select

http://www.ama-assn.org/aps/amahg.htm

The American Medical Association Physician Select Web site contains "information on virtually every licensed physician in the United States and its possessions, including more than 650,000 doctors of medicine (MD) and doctors of osteopathy or osteopathic medicine (DO)." Profiles include physician medical schools, residency training programs, medical specialty and practice location. Alumni directors looking for lost alumni will love this service.

◆ Ancestry Home Town

http://www.ancestry.com/

This is an excellent site for conducting genealogical research on the Web. Users can search 111 databases including the Social Security Death Index. Family tree searches also are provided. Users can search over 500 million names. Additionally, users can browse through the organization's newsletter, Ancestry Times, online. There is a listing of new databases available and other ancestry resources.

◆ ARCH-Alumni Records Clearinghouse

http://www.arch.org/

The ARCH Project is sponsored by Snow and Associates, an international research organization that locates lost alumni at more than 500 education, fraternal and professional organizations across North America. At this Web site, qualified institutions can send inquiries about lost alumni to other institutions and databases maintained by Snow and Associates. Users are limited to conducting five searches per day.

◆ Biography

http://www.biography.com/

The Arts & Entertainment network Biography Web site contains a BioSearch database of 25,000 personalities and 2,500 videos. Users can search by name or browse through the list alphabetically. Biographical profiles are brief and contain only limited information. "This Week's Top 10 Bios" is also featured on this Web site. Highlights from Biography's magazine is available for viewing, as is an online store where items such as videos may be purchased.

◆ CheckFree Investment Services

http://www.secapl.com/

Surfers can use CheckFree Investment Services' Web site to quickly retrieve information on stock prices. This information is essential in tracking a company's performance or investigating an individual's net worth. Users merely type in a ticker symbol to find current trading levels, 52-week highs and lows and five-year growth. A link to an the "Internet Stock Report" is also available.

◆ Companies Online

http://www.companiesonline.com/

Grantseekers can access the Companies Online Web site, sponsored by Dun and Bradstreet and search the company database by name, city, state, ticker symbol and URL. Users also can browse the list by industry. Company profiles include contact information, annual sales, number of employees, ticker symbol, company trade name(s) and parent company information. A link to the Web site's featured companies of the week offers valuable information such as annual sales and ownership structure.

◆ Corporate America's Most Powerful People

http://forbes.com/tool/toolbox/ceo/

This Internet site, sponsored by *Forbes* magazine, provides a searchable database of the top 800 chief executive officers in the United States. CEOs are ranked alphabetically by company name, state and city, industry and salary. Users also can search the database by company name, state and industry. Information is available for the years 1997, 1998 and 1999. Links to the Super 100, the Top 10 and the "Most over and underpaid" are also available. Users can also view select stories from *Forbes* magazine such as "A King's Pay."

◆ Craig and Vartorella: International Marking and Advertising

http://www.scbell.com/Marketing_&_Fundraising/

This international consulting firm's Web site contains information on the types of services it offers to nonprofits — board development assistance, grantsmanship training, capital and annual campaign assistance, strategic and long-range planning, etc. A history of the firm and its founders, as well as contact information is provided. The Web site also features its article-of-the-month in addition to other free articles that may be obtained via e-mail request. Information on upcoming seminars and free lectures is also provided. The Internet site also contains information on accessing its fee-based database of grant sources in the areas of field and laboratory exploration, healthcare, performing arts and free equipment for nonprofits. The Web site also allows visitors to subscribe to the firm's free e-mail distribution list of grant opportunity alerts and to a discussion group that allows nonprofits to share their experiences in areas of common interest.

◆ Database America

http://www.databaseamerica.com/html/index.htm

Database America is a marketing information company with detailed information on 11 million businesses and 165 million consumers. The Database America Web site contains a small business forum and a people finder database that allows users to search for addresses and phone numbers by name, city and state. A reverse search by phone number also is available. The site additionally contains a fee-based database that provides brief profiles of companies.

◆ EDGAR Database of Corporate Information

http://www.sec.gov/edgarhp.htm

The EDGAR (Electronic Data Gathering, Analysis and Retrieval) Database of Corporate Information was created by the U.S. Securities and Exchange Commission to collect and validate the submission of public documents by companies. As of May 1996, all public domestic companies are required to file their disclosure documents electronically. This means that corporate grantseekers can access copies of companies' 10-Ks, 10-Qs and 8-Ks with a simple key word search.

◆ Facts Online

http://www.facts-online.com/

The Facts Online Internet site contains a database of leading public and private technology companies. Company profiles include name, address, telephone number, business type and description. A subscription is required for full access. When available, profiles also contain links to the business's Web site, CEO's name, toll free and fax numbers and number of employees. Public companies also display annual revenues, net income, date of fiscal year and links to the Securities and Exchange Commission database. The Web site also offers free weekly summaries via e-mail.

◆ FECInfo

http://www.tray.com/FECInfo/index.html-ssi

This Web site accurately describes itself as a, "place to discover who gave what to which Federal candidates and when." The FECInfo Web site provides a wealth of information on corporate and individual political contributions. Visitors can search the extensive database by contributor name, state, zip code and employer/occupation; or by U.S. House, Senate or Presidential candidate name. The site also lists Political Action Committee contributions and ranks the top 200 individual/corporate contributors by state. After providing a free Web site for over four years, in March 200, FECInfo began to move some of their more specialized and enhanced databases and searches to a subscription basis.

◆ Federal Acquisition Jumpstation

http://nais.nasa.gov/fedproc/home.html

A handy but contract-oriented jumping off point to business opportunities governmentwide. This no-frills hub links to grants and contracts opportunities pages in various agencies, but there are gaping omissions, even in terms of government buying. Home page offerings include the Education Department's "Grants and Contracts" page; National Institutes of Health's "Grants and Contracts" and "Grants and Research" pages; the U.S. Geological Survey's "Contract and Grant Information" page; and the National Science Foundation's grants and program areas page.

◆ Federal Information Exchange (FEDIX)

http://www.sciencewise.com/fedix

One of the strongest tools grantseekers can use to shop for research and technology funding, FEDIX is a free one-stop retrieval service of timely grant and contract opportunities at seven federal sources. Supported under a cooperative agreement from the Energy Department, it lets grantseekers go straight to agencies' funding news without stumbling through sometimes circuitous individual sites. From the FEDIX main menu, users can look easily for grant and contract opportunities by agency, subject or audience. Agency selection permits users to scan notices of active competitions from *Commerce Business Daily* and the *Federal Register*, look at descriptions of ongoing funding opportunities and obtain application tips, budget forms and grant administration guidance. FEDIX is limited to certain agencies only — a drawback — and its value varies somewhat by agency. Grantseekers can miss a program here and there at participating agencies if they depend on FEDIX alone for information. But the service is a fine starting place in the grant search for those agencies. It is a must for keeping track of opportunities at the Air Force Office of Scientific Research and the Office of Naval Research (ONR), for example, providing an online look at ONR's program guide sometimes months before the printed version is available. Other areas that may be researched are: the Department of Defense; the Department of Agriculture; and the Agency for International Development.

◆ Fortune 500

http://www.pathfinder.com/fortune/fortune500/index.html

U.S. grantseekers will want to visit the online version of the Fortune 500, the "gold standard of corporate rankings." Users can search Fortune's database of companies or browse through its rankings. Companies are ranked by sales, profits and assets. Stock quotes, previous Fortune 500 and Fortune Global 500 rankings are also included in each company's profile.

◆ Fortune Global 500

http://www.pathfinder.com/fortune/global500/index.html

International grantseekers will want to visit the Fortune Global 500 Web site for information on the world's largest multinational companies. Companies are ranked by their performance, industry and country. Within the searchable database, grantseekers additionally can rank companies by revenues, profits, assets, equity or number of employees.

◆ Hoover's MasterList Database

http://www.hoovers.com/

The Hoover's MasterList Database is an Internet subscription service that contains information on the largest and fastest growing companies in the United States. Entries in the Hoover's database contain a description of a company and its history, a list of corporate officers including salary information, financial data with relevant links to other resources and a list of competitors. Users can become online members so as to be able to access additional database information.

◆ Inc. 500

http://www.inc.com/500/about.html

The Inc. 500 Web site contains *Inc.* magazine's annual list of America's fastest growing private companies. Users can search the list by company name, keyword, state or business sector. Company profiles include name, headquarters location, URL (if available), industry and business sector type and revenue, profit and employee increases or decreases. Users can search the entire list of companies or can view the companies that made the 1999 list. Included on the Web site are company spotlights, a Hall of Fame section and various Inc. 500 stories and articles from 1988 to 1999.

◆ Internet Millionaires Page

http://www.pulver.com:80/million/

The Internet Millionaires Page Web site lists the major shareholders of publicly traded Internet-related companies, such as Lycos, Netscape, UUnet, etc,; provides the number of shares each investor holds; and calculates the value of the holdings. Stock quotes are updated every 15 minutes. The Web site also has a list of some upcoming Internet related companies and their major shareholders.

◆ LibertyNet: Home Page of the Philadelphia Region

http://www.libertynet.org/

The LibertyNet: Home Page of the Philadelphia Region Internet site contains information on local community groups, services, healthcare, businesses, educational institutions and government agencies. While there are few foundations listed on the site, such as the Independent Foundation, grantseekers will find numerous connections to businesses, services and other nonprofit organizations.

◆ Martindale-Hubbell Lawyer Locator

http://lawyers.martindale.com/marhub

The Martindale-Hubbell Lawyer Locator allows users to search this legal directory online. Searches can be conducted by name, law firm, area of practice, location or language. Grantseekers also can locate U.S. government lawyers and corporate law departments.

◆ Metacrawler

http://www.metacrawler.com/

Metacrawler provides a service that simultaneously searches nine search engines. The directory contains 20 different categories which includes business, education, finance, society and a reference section.

◆ Microsoft Library

http://library.microsoft.com/

The Microsoft Library Web site is a great online reference for corporate grantseekers. The Web site connects to more than 30,000 commercial entries. The Microsoft Library also offers links to library-related Web sites, such as the Library of Congress or the Internet Public Library. Additional resources include Internet search tools, specific Internet and computer resources and basic Microsoft information, including Bill Gates and executive staff info, press releases, financial info and technical support.

◆ Minnesota Attorney General's Consumer Protection Office

http://www.ag.state.mn.us/home/charities/default.shtml

Grantseekers now can search through the financial data of more than 5,500 nonprofits and charities registered with the Charities Division of the Minnesota Attorney General's Office. The site contains only limited information, including contact information, brief purpose and description of the organization, year established, assets, contributions and salary of the top five officers and employees. The data is collected from a number of source documents, including tax returns. Grantseekers can search the database by name or city/state. Other links include: a guide to charities laws; checking on charities; charity resources; and environmental update.

◆ Mother Jones 400

http://www.motherjones.com/mother_jones/ND98/400intro.html

The Mother Jones 400 Web page contains an interactive database of top campaign contributors. Grantseekers can search the database for information on the political donations and affiliations of America's top executives. The Mother Jones database is searchable by rank, industry/affiliation, state, city, donor and amount of donation.

◆ National Teaching & Learning Forum

http://129.219.88.111/ipeds

The National Teaching & Learning Forum site contains an interactive database of faculty salaries from more than 4,000 colleges and universities. Users can enter up to 24 different school names before conducting a search. The database discloses salaries for full professors, associate professors, assistant professors and instructors. Visitors also can study faculty salary differences based on gender and learn more about ethnic minority group representation. The site also offers a grant opportunities page that offers users the ability to search among 35 different programs.

◆ Newtithing Group

http://www.newtithing.org

The Newtithing Group describes itself as, "a philanthropic research organization committed to increasing charitable giving, personal fulfillment and the productivity of donations to the world's charitable sectors." The Web site offers educational tools such as the Newtithing Advisor, an online budgeting and charitable giving calculator, ongoing news and speaking engagements. Any and all profits that might result from the Newtithing Group are donated annually to charity.

◆ Philanthropic Digest Index

http://www.tc.umn.edu/nlhome/g248/bergq003/wa/PD_Index.html

The Philanthropic Digest Index Web site contains a list of major grants given by individual donors. A majority of the grants listed are in the $1 million to $25 million range. The index provides the donors name, grant amount, recipient name and year and/or month the gift was made. The information provided is compiled by Waltman Associates. A link takes you to their home page where they offer other products, such as the Directory of Corporate and Nonprofit Boards and the National Directory of College and University Trustees.

◆ PointCast Network

http://www.entrypoint.com/

The PointCast Network Web site offers an innovative way to receive important information, tailored to your needs. PointCast, Inc., has created the PointCast Network (PCN), a free service that broadcasts personalized news and information directly to a viewer's computer screen. PCN's SmartScreen technology automatically turns a static screen saver into a listing of current headlines, sports scores, stock quotes, etc. Getting up-to-date news while your computer would normally be idle seems like an important and useful way to stay informed of news on companies and industries and perhaps even national funding opportunities.

◆ PR Newswire

http://www.prnewswire.com/

PR Newswire, "the leading source of immediate news from corporations worldwide for media, business, the financial community and the individual investor," offers corporate grantseekers online access to news, press releases and investment profiles. This site is a one-stop shop for corporate information. The Web site also offers "today's latest stories," with links to up-to-the-minute news stories.

◆ Prospect Research Online

http://www.rpbooks.com/

Prospect Research Online (PRO) is a subscription online service that combines information from four main areas into one comprehensive system: corporate research, major gift announcements, executive biographies and donor/board Lists. PRO offers information on corporate donations and sponsorship along with news, interviews and press releases regarding corporate philanthropy. PRO has developed detailed descriptions of approximately 1,000 corporations in the United States and Canada. PRO's entries include financial information, a list officers and directors, giving guidelines, contact information, restrictions and giving history. The site also offers a people finder service.

◆ Research-It!

http://www.itools.com:80/research-it/

The Research-It! Web site contains a variety of handy research tools. The site includes a dictionary, thesaurus, language translator, biographical dictionaries, maps, area code and zip code directories, currency converter, stock quotes and ticker symbols, UPS and Federal Express tracking and an index of mailing lists.

◆ The Star-Ledger New Jersey Top 100

http://www.nj.com/business/top100/

New Jersey's top 100 companies are ranked by annual sales in this Web site's database. Visitors to this site can search through the rankings of the top sellers and top employers for companies in the state of New Jersey. Company profiles contain the following: year founded; sales figures; number of employees (in New Jersey and worldwide); hiring trend; names of the chairman, chief executive officer and president; company description; and descriptions of any recent developments. The site also includes feature stories and company and executive profiles that describe and analyze business trends.

◆ Starting Point

http://www.stpt.com/

The Starting Point Web site offers many links to many different types of searches. Users will find links to a people finder, travel center, city guide and weather center. The Web site offers personal services such as a calendar and address book. Users of this site can find information on government, women and family, finance, international news, health and fitness, shopping, sports and recreation, entertainment and career and education, just to name a few. Links to several sites, such as CDNow and Reel.com are also provided.

◆ StockMaster

http://www.stockmaster.com/

The StockMaster Web site provides grantseekers with 20 minute delayed stock and mutual fund quotes and historical charts since 1993. Grantseekers can search for stock by name or ticker symbol and may find out the following information: news; profiles; financials; earning history; competitors; and SEC filings.

◆ Switchboard

http://www.switchboard.com/

The Switchboard site contains a handy database to conveniently look up phone numbers, addresses and e-mail addresses for individuals and businesses. Users can search for businesses by name or by business category. The database contains millions of residential and business listings. The Web site allows users to shop online, search for old classmates, enter various message boards and view maps and directions.

◆ Tile.net

http://tile.net/

Users have a choice of searching: 1) Mailing lists on the Internet, arranged by name, subject, description, country or sponsoring organization; 2) Usenet newsgroups, listed by description or newsgroup hierarchy; 3) FTP sites, arranged by contents, country, Internet domain name or site name; 4) Computer poduct vendors, searchable by company name, product, zip code, state (if applicable), country or date last updated; or 5) Internet and Web design companies.

◆ United States Post Office

http://www.usps.gov/

The U.S. Post Office Web site contains no information on grant programs; however, it does offer some services that are useful to the grantseeker, including information on postal rates, a post office locator, a stamps online service and a database of zip codes.

◆ Wealth of Internet Resources

http://users.rowan.edu/~au/

This Web site, created by Valerie Au at Rowan University's Office of Development, contains a list of links to a variety of grantseeking resource sites. Links are grouped into a number of different categories, including corporations, education, foundations, government and politics, online discussions, online vendors, people, phone numbers and zip codes, professional groups, search engines, research home pages and traveling.

◆ WebActive

http://www.webactive.com/

WebActive is a weekly publication designed to offer progressive activists an up-to-date resource on the World Wide Web to find other organizations and individuals with similar values and interests. The WebActive home page offers information on online activism for social, political and environmental causes. The site is comprehensive and graphically sophisticated, with significant information offered on a variety of different issues, each of which has its own set of links and some of which allow the user to download movies or pamphlets. Sponsored by Internet audio/video pioneer Real Networks, Inc., it focuses on progressive politics. Much of its contents and offered in Real Audio format. WebActive contains the following features: Radio Nation; Pacifica Network News; Democracy NOW!; Hightower Radio; WebActive Directory; Soapbox; and CounterSpin.

◆ Webgator

http://www.inil.com/users/dguss/wgator.htm

This Internet site, primarily aimed at private investigators, contains some useful tools for prospect researchers. Links are provided to associations, organizations and state licensing agencies; bankruptcy, property and miscellaneous records; companies, corporations and uniform commercial code listings; federal and national government records; government directories; student and alumni databases; missing persons; medical related directories and databases; newspapers; and telephone and e-mail directories. There is also a what's new feature that contains links to several Web sites and is updated monthly.

◆ Who Owns the Shore?

http://www.phillynews.com/packages/njshore/homeindex.html

This Internet site, maintained by the *Philadelphia Inquirer*, offers users a database containing 90,000 property records listing the values of homes on the New Jersey Shore. Users can search by city or county, property address, property value, owner's name and owner's city and state. This Web site also offers other relevant information such as: shore town histories and profiles; Catholic organizations in the area; and photos of some of the most expensive homes on the shore.

Resources

◆ Academe Today

http://www.today@chronicle.com/

A superb news and information service available free to subscribers of the weekly *Chronicle of Higher Education*, it provides advance word on articles coming up in the next issue, academic resources on the Internet, actions in Washington, DC, and information on new grant competitions. A cautionary note, however: grant information is not comprehensive (selections are geared to an university audience and certain categories of grants are overlooked) and competitions advertised as new on a certain day may have appeared weeks or days earlier in primary sources.

◆ America's Promise

http://www.americaspromise.org/

America's Promise – The Alliance for Youth is led by General Colin Powell and is dedicated to mobilizing individuals, groups and organizations from every part of American life, to build and strengthen the character and competence of our youth. The America's Promise site offers a wealth of information about the organization and its mission, but most importantly, it presents the organization's "Report to the Nation," which details the steps America's Promise has taken in its effort to be a nationwide catalyst, urging public, private and nonprofit organizations to focus their combined talents and resources to improve the lives of our nation's youth. As a result, more than 450 corporations, nonprofit organizations, philanthropic foundations, service providers, communities and national, state and local governments, have joined the nationwide Alliance for youth.

◆ American Philanthropy Review

http://philanthropy-review.com

http://www.charitychannel.com

American Philanthropy Review is best known for its nonprofit CharityChannel discussion forums. These forums have more than 20,000 participants discussing topics such as grants, foundations, tax law, college and university advancement, healthcare philanthropy, sponsorship, arts fundraising and more. The site also allows forum participants to share documents with each other on its GuestShare page. The site details subscription information for each forum.

◆ Applied Research and Development International

http://www.ardi.org

Applied Research and Development International, Inc. (ARDI) advocates the importance of effective leadership and management and conducting applied research which creates, enhances and facilitates utilization of knowledge. ARDI's Web site provides searchable links to product descriptions, a research directory and an Access Management Assistance Providers database.

◆ Aspen Publishers Grants and Nonprofit Resources

http://www.aspenpublishers.com/

On this publisher's site, under the Grants and Nonprofit heading, users can see the catalog of Aspen's nonprofit publications, such as *Foundation and Corporate Grants Alert, Federal Grants and Contacts Weekly* and *Giving By Industry: A Reference Guide to the New Corporate Philanthropy.*

◆ Associated Grantmakers of Massachusetts

http://www.agmconnect.org/

Associated Grantmakers of Massachusetts, Inc. (AGM) is a statewide association of corporate and foundation grantmakers. AGM's mission is to support and advance effective and responsible philanthropy throughout the state. The site offers links to library resources, an annual report, lists of the board of directors and staff, information on the association's events, descriptions of services for nonprofits and grantmakers and links to other philanthropic organizations and sites of interest. Foundations and corresponding links are listed by category such as: private/family; public; community; and corporate. Users may also purchase books from the AGM resource library which offers information on grantmaking, grantseeking and organization management.

◆ Association for Professional Researchers for Advancement

http://www.aprahome.org/

The Association for Professional Researchers for Advancement is "the" association for grantseekers and prospect researchers. Its Web site contains information on the association's mission and goals, its board of directors, its membership services and meetings and conferences. Grantseekers also will find links to a number of online resources, including the Foundation Center, Philanthropy Related Links and Northwestern University's Research Page.

◆ Associations, Foundations and Institutes

http://info.rutgers.edu/orsp/assnsit1.html

The Associations, Foundations and Institutes Web site serves as a hotlist for 13 associations, foundations and institutes that fund university research. Although the list is not comprehensive, it offers a good starting point for the major sites. In addition, it links to the University of Waterloo, Ontario, Canada Scholarly Societies Project Web page which is a fairly comprehensive site that has converted many of the existing gopher links to Web pages. The guide contains both alphabetical and subject listings. This Web site provides links to the Foundation Center, the Council on Foundations and the Grantsmanship Center.

◆ Benton Foundation's Best Practice Toolkit

http://www.benton.org/cpphome.html

This site provides tools and resources to help nonprofits make effective use of communications technologies effectively. Links include: technology funding for nonprofits; nonprofit-related electronic newsletters; and fundraising on the Internet.

◆ Better Business Bureau Philanthropy Advisory Service

http://www.bbb.org/about/pas.html

While the Better Business Bureau Philanthropic Advisory Service's mission is to "educate donors," its Web page contains a number of publications for nonprofits, including the Standards for Charitable Solicitations. The site also offers a number of reports on nonprofits; however, the information is not to be used for fundraising purposes.

◆ Board Café

http://www.compasspoint.org/publications/board_cafe/boardcafe.html

This Web site offers a free subscription to Board Café, an online newsletter. An online form must be submitted. This newsletter is a collaborative project of the National Center of Nonprofit Boards and CompassPoint Nonprofit Services.

◆ Business for Social Responsibility

http://www.bsr.org

This membership organization is a US-based global resource for companies seeking to sustain their commercial success in ways that demonstrate respect for ethical values, people, communities and the environment. More than 1,400 companies are members of or affiliated with BSR. Member companies, representing nearly every sector of the global economy, include American Express, AT&T, British Telecom, Starbucks Corporation, Dayton Hudson, DuPont, Ford, General Motors, Honeywell, Home Depot, Johnson & Johnson, L.L. Bean, Mattel, Motorola, Merrill Lynch, Toms of Maine, Time Warner, Stonyfield Farm Yogurt, Wal-Mart and Walt Disney.

◆ Business Week

http://www.businessweek.com/index.html

The Business Week Internet site provides sample stories from the award winning *Business Week* magazine. Corporate grantseekers, who do not receive the magazine's print version, will want to periodically browse the page to keep apprised of news and trends in the business world. Users can search past issues and are supplied with links to other business resources.

◆ Campaign Service Consultants

http://people.ne.mediaone.net/cscunningham/

This site, sponsored by nonprofit consulting firm, Campaign Service Consultants, offers grantseekers a wealth of links. From the home page, access the Foundation Web Links pages, which has more than 700 foundation and foundation-related links; the Corporate Web Link page, which lists more than 500 corporate giving related links; and the Fundraising Web Links page, which offers links to sites representing a variety of areas: advocacy, boards, marketing, financial management, general fundraising, research aids, grantseeking, volunteers and software. The site also has grant searching tips.

◆ CFRNET

cfrnet@listserv.unc.edu

The CFRNET mailing list provides a forum for those involved in building partnerships between educational institutions and corporations and foundations; however, many types of nonprofits are subscribed to CFRNET. Discussion topics include: corporate and foundation giving trends, solicitation strategies, stewardship programs, proposal writing, prospect tracking, gift-in-kind programs and issues related to employment and recruiting. To subscribe, send the following e-mail to listserv@unc.edu (with the subject line blank): subscribe cfrnet [your name].

◆ Charity Village

http://www.charityvillage.com/cvhome.html

Charity Village is Canada's supersite for the nonprofit sector, including 3,000 pages of news, jobs, information and resources for executives, staffers, donors and volunteers. Visitors will find an online newsletter; links to nonprofit organizations, associations and foundations; a job bank; listings of periodicals and other online resources; events; news; volunteer information; and more. Grantseekers may also subscribe to Village Vibes, Charity Village's weekly e-mail newsflash service. To subscribe, send the following e-mail to vibes@istar.ca: subscribe villagevibes [your name].

◆ *Chronicle of Philanthropy*

http://www.philanthropy.com

The *Chronicle of Philanthropy* is "the" newspaper of the nonprofit world. Published every other week, it is the No. 1 news source for charity leaders, fund raisers, grantmakers and other people involved in the philanthropic arena. The Web site offers the complete contents of the new issue, an archive of articles from the past two years and more than four years worth of grant listings. The site includes links to products and services, conferences, workshops and seminars.

◆ Cleveland State University Office of Research and Economic Development

http://www.csuohio.edu/uored/

This Cleveland State University Web site provides grantseekers with information dealing with grants, contracts and cooperative agreements. Users are guided through the process of drafting a proposal. Topics include idea development, grantseeking basics, sponsor identification and proposal preparation. The site also contains a list of faculty and staff grant awards, news and events, policies and procedures, funding sources and grant forms.

◆ Coalescence Inc.

http://www.dowelldogood.com

Coalescence is a resource for organizations, conferences and award programs that promote and recognize community improvement.

◆ COMMUNISERVE — Information Services

http://members.surfsouth.com/~jperdew/info.htm

This Web site offers a great deal of information to grantseekers, including about 250 links to various sites of interest. Included services are an overview on the basics of grantseeking and a grant application preparation service. Many links are available in the following areas: telecommunications and telemedicine, arts and humanities, energy and environment, social issues, politics, African-American topics, economic development, job hunting and media sites.

◆ Community Wealth Online

http://www.communitywealth.org

A site that might interest innovative and entrepreneurial nonprofits, Community Wealth Online offers case studies, models, tips and news about well-known and little-known entrepreneurial efforts to generate resources to promote social change.

◆ CompuMentor

http://www.compumentor.org

Since 1987, CompuMentor has been providing low-cost, volunteer-based computer assistance to schools and nonprofits. The Web site offers a software redistribution program, consulting services and resource center.

◆ Consultants ONTAP

http://www.ontap.org

Consultants ONTAP is a searchable database of consultants and technical assistance providers who work with Northern California nonprofit community. Users can search for a consultant by area of expertise or view an alphabetical listing. Good advice on how to choose a consultant is also provided.

◆ Council for the Advancement and Support of Education

http://www.case.org/

The Council for the Advancement and Support of Education (CASE), a nonprofit serving institutional advancement professionals in colleges, universities and independent elementary and secondary schools, maintains a site that offers information on such resources as a National Clearinghouse for Corporate Matching Gift Information; a National Clearinghouse for Ethics in Educational Fundraising; a tracking service for legislative and public affairs actions affecting education; fundraising training courses; books, videos and other publications; links to numerous related sites, including links to U.S. and Canadian college and university home pages; and consulting services. The Web site is available in Spanish and French; provides a link to CASE Europe; offers recent CASE news; and provides a list of the board of trustees along with a staff directory.

◆ Council of Michigan Foundations

http://www.cmif.org/

The Council of Michigan Foundations (CMF) Web site contains information on the regional association of grantmakers. The council, which represents the philanthropic programs of approximately 468 foundations and corporations, strives to enhance, improve and increase philanthropy in Michigan. Grantseekers will find information about the council's services and programs, press releases and upcoming events. A publications catalog is also available online. Current CMF programs include the K-12 Education in Philanthropy project and the Great Lakes Environmental Collaborative.

◆ Council on Foundations

http://www.cof.org/

The home page of the Council on Foundations provides information on the association's mission, press releases and legislative updates, conferences and workshops, a job bank, membership information and a list of publications. Of particular interest to grantseekers is a listing of its corporate and foundation members, along with links to their home pages.

◆ CyberVPM

http://www.cybervpm.com

CyberVPM is an online networking resource for volunteer program managers. The Web site offers a free E-newsletter on volunteer program management. The site also offers advice to volunteers.

◆ Delaware Valley Grantmakers

http://www.libertynet.org/dvg

Delaware Valley Grantmakers is a nonprofit membership association comprised of 140 organizations representing corporations, private foundations, community foundations, donor-advised funds, charitable trusts and grantmaking public charities located in southeastern Pennsylvania, southern New Jersey and Delaware. The primary mission is to promote effective philanthropy by providing grantmakers with continuing education, communication and information exchange, provide a focus for collaborative grantmaking, public policy development, community problem solving and enhancing the environment for the growth of philanthropy and communicating the message of its role and value in our society. The Delaware Valley Grantmakers Web site contains links to the association's members and other Internet resources, common grant and report forms and information on its publications.

◆ Donors Forum of Chicago

http://www.donorsforum.org/

The Donors Forum of Chicago Web site links grantseekers to its philanthropic database. Users may search the grants database by foundation name, beneficiary type, grant purpose, support type or recipient name. More than 90 private and corporate foundations are included in the database.

◆ Financial Aid, Foundations, Funding and Grants

http://www.rsccd.org/home/sacacc/webscout/gf/gffram.htm

Rancho Santiago Community College sponsors this Web site. It offers a variety of links to grantseekers. Users will find links to corporate information, grants listings, financial aid information and related software, venture capital sites, foundation-related sites and scholarship data.

◆ Foundation Center

http://fdncenter.org/

The Foundation Center home page provides grantseekers with a wealth of information on the location of its five libraries and more than 200 cooperating collections; training and seminars held around the country on proposal writing; funding trends and analysis, including highlights of foundation giving, as well as lists of the top 100 foundations, top 50 corporate foundations and top 25 community foundations ranked by assets and giving. The center's Philanthropy News Digest contains weekly updates from foundations on recent awards, personnel changes and other notices. The site's fundraising process page provides the nuts and bolts of researching funding sources. Grantseekers also will find a list of the center's most recent publications and links to grantmakers on the Web.

◆ Foundations.org

http://www.foundations.org/index.html

The Foundations.org site, sponsored by the Northern California Community Foundation, provides a directory of foundations and grantmakers. The Web site provides a corporate and private foundations and grantmakers directory, as well as a community foundations directory. Grantseekers can link to each foundation's home page, as well as to other grants-related directories, such as charities, fundraising events and the government.

◆ Funding for Technology

http://www.mcrel.org/resources/technology/funding.asp

This informative site, from the Mid-continent Research for Education and Learning organization, offers grantseekers a listing of reports, articles, bibliographies, strategies, proposal writing tips and funding sources.

◆ Fundraising Online

http://www.fundraisingonline.com

This Web site provides links to interviews, workshops, news about fundraising and sights to see. Recent news topics include: fundraising over the Internet; e-mailing donors; and online fundraising sources.

◆ Fundraising Resources and Listservs

http://www.lib.ua.edu/smr/pr3.htm

The fundraising resources listed on this site include electronic journals, grantseeking-related sites, fundraising listservs and library-related listservs. The site is sponsored by Southern Media Resources.

◆ Fundsnet Services

http://www.fundsnetservices.com

Fundsnet Services offers an ever-expanding (more than 700 at press time) list of foundation, corporate and community funder links on its directory-like site. Also noted are new grant initiatives and programs, news and other resources.

◆ Grant Seeker's Guide to the Internet: Revised and Revisited

http://www.nonprofit.net/info/guide.html

New grantseekers will love this site's non-technical explanation of the Internet, its tools and a list of online funding resources. The Web site also contains information on connecting to the Internet, including hardware and software requirements and Internet providers. Links to several foundation's Web sites, such as the Benton Foundation are provided, as are links to philanthropy information Web sites such as Internet Resources for Nonprofits and the Foundation Center.

◆ GrantScape

http://www.grantscape.com

The GrantScape Web site — sponsored by Aspen Publishers, Inc., the publisher of *Corporate Philanthropy Report*, *Federal Grants and Contracts Weekly*, *computer.grants.alert* and the GrantScape Electronic Fundraising Database — is an unique resource for information for private- and public-sector grantseekers. The site offers information on a daily funding opportunity (Funder of the Day); a searchable archive of five newsletters; links to related Internet sites; tips for grantseekers; and a basic guide called Grantseeking 101 for those new to the grantseeking vocation. Grantseekers also can search through the company's catalog of publications for information on its newsletters, books, directories and electronic products.

◆ The Grantsmanship Center

http://www.tgci.com/

The Grantsmanship Center (TGC) is a leading source of fundraising training and information for the nonprofit sector. TGC's Internet site provides an overview of its grantsmanship and fundraising training programs, its online subscription service, lists and links to nonprofit resources, issues of TGC magazine online and a list of publications. The site also offers daily grant announcements from federal government agencies in the *Federal Register* and an index of links to grantmaking foundation Web sites.

◆ GrantsWeb

http://sra.rams.com/cws/sra/resource.htm

An alternative starting point for grantseekers, GrantsWeb is a hodgepodge of useful information that links to a variety of federal and private sources of funds. The site provides a quick overview of government grant programs, linking to FEDIX and to agency solicitations, procurements and program announcements via the Texas Research Administrators Group (TRAM) and a glimpse of private sources through a link to the Foundation Center. It also links to the bilingual Natural Sciences and Engineering Research Council of Canada. GrantsWeb connects to a handful of university sites, some providing extensive information and links as well as their own unique features. The site also provides access to key databases and leads to grants-related professional societies, grants management training resources and discussion groups.

◆ Grant-related Links

http://www.sccoe.k12.ca.us/edr3.html

The Grant-related Links Internet site, sponsored by the Santa Clara County Office of Education, provides a list of links to sites in five major areas: education grants, federal grants, math and science grants, technology grants and other grant resources. Financial aid and scholarship information is provided. There also is a link to a funding update, which provides a searchable listing of current education funding opportunities.

◆ Guidestar

http://www.guidestar.org/

The Guidestar site offers grantseekers information on the programs and finances of more than 620,000 American charities and nonprofit organizations; up-to-date news stories on philanthropy; and a forum for donors and volunteers. The Guidestar nonprofit database is searchable by name, keyword, field of activity, location or revenue. The Web site offers a helpful online glossary of pertinent terms, press releases and a frequently asked questions section.

◆ HandsNet

http://www.handsnet.orgt

The goal of HandsNet is to give organizations the power and resources to integrate effective online communications strategies so as to strengthen their programs and policies for children, families and people in need. The Web site offers a service called WebClipper for a yearly fee. The service tracks the topics that you specify and brings you updates via e-mail. However, a free trial membership is available.

◆ ideaList

http://www.idealist.org/

This Web site, sponsored by Action Without Borders, contains a searchable directory of 20,000 nonprofit Web sites in 140 countries. The directory is searchable by keyword and location. The site also offers a list of tools for nonprofits including finding a consultant, nonprofit guides and products, nonprofit services and conferences. Information also is provided for volunteer and job opportunities and internships. Users can subscribe to the site's newsletter via e-mail.

◆ iGive

http://www.igive.com

The idea behind iGive is to build an online community that allows members to aid worthwhile causes or charities through purchases made via this Web site. All one has to do to become a member is sign up online. Every time a member enters onto this Web site or makes a purchase, iGive and its sponsors make a donation to the member's chosen charity or organization.

◆ IKNOW

http://www.iknow.org/

IKNOW offers "Interactive knowledge for nonprofits worldwide." The Web site has a directory of key issues for nonprofits which includes: volunteerism, fundraising, education and governance.

◆ Impact Online

http://www.impactonline.org

Impact Online is a nonprofit organization that aims to help people become involved within their communities. Impact Online offers a free online matching service called Volunteer Match, a Virtual Volunteering research project, as well as advice and information on volunteering on its site.

◆ Independent Sector

http://www.indepsec.org/

The Independent Sector, "a national leadership forum, working to encourage philanthropy, volunteering, nonprofit initiative and citizen action," provides information on its Web site on the latest government actions that affect the industry as well as a list of member organizations, publications, board members and frequently asked questions. Users of this Web site also can search the member database by location or by category.

◆ Institute for Global Communications

http://www.igc.org

The Institute for Global Communications (IGC) is a nonprofit organization that sponsors the Progressive Directory, which offers connections to organizations working toward peace, environmental protection, social and economic justice, human rights, health and nonviolent conflict resolution. Links are available to several sites such as Peacenet, Econet, Antiracismnet and Womensnet. The IGC also offers Internet services, electronic publishing services and more to members of the Association for Progressive Communications, a global computer communications and information network dedicated to serving non-governmental organizations and citizen activists working for social justice, environmental sustainability and related issues. The Web site offers a calendar of events, action alerts and more than 1300 links to browse.

◆ Internal Revenue Service (IRS)

http://www.irs.ustreas.gov/prod/bus_info/eo/eo-appl.html

The IRS provides a list of questions used in determining whether an organization is eligible to apply for recognition of exemption from Federal income taxation under § 501(a) of the Internal Revenue Code and, if so, how to proceed.

◆ Internet Nonprofit Center

http://www.nonprofit-info.org/

The Internet Nonprofit Center Web site is one of the premier locations for information on nonprofits on the World Wide Web. The site is divided into four main sections: the library, serving as a repository for publications, information and data about nonprofit organizations and the nonprofit sector; the gallery of organizations, providing links to nonprofit home pages; the parlor, containing information on the Internet Nonprofit Center and other related topics and including access to a chat room; and the heliport, providing links to additional resources of special interest to donors and volunteers. Additionally, the site contains the Nonprofit Locator that allows users to find any nonprofit organization in the U.S. by searching a database of over a million tax-exempt entities. The database is searchable by keyword and state.

◆ Internet Prospector

http://www.internet-prospector.org/

The Internet Prospector Web page contains links to private, corporate and public funding resources on the Internet. The Web site also contains information on online news resources, lists of both online and print biographical resources and archives of its free monthly electronic newsletter, Internet Prospector. Grantseekers also will find information on how to subscribe to the mailing list PRSPCT-L.

◆ David Lamb's Prospect Research Page

http://staff.washington.edu/dlamb/

David Lamb, director of prospect research at the University of Washington, has developed a Web site that provides a variety of research links for grantseekers. The site contains links to information on companies and executives, foundations, news sources, directories, real estate, search engines and general reference sources. Links also are provided for other research-related sites pages, including the Association of Professional Researchers for Advancement. Users can fill out an online form to submit Web sites for possible consideration of being added to the page. Contact information is also provided such as e-mail address, mailing address, phone and fax numbers.

◆ LitLamp

http://www.litlamp.com

LitLamp is a place where sponsors and their agencies can find marketing opportunities that create meaningful relationships with desirable audiences. The Web site offers a searchable profile database.

◆ Meta-Index of Nonprofit Sites

http://www.pj.org/links_metaindex.cfm

The Meta-Index of Nonprofit Sites is a feature of the Philanthropy News Network Web site. It gives grantseekers access to a variety of resources, including a general list of nonprofit organizations and activists. The index divides nonprofits into five main categories: human rights, civil liberties and politics, health and human services, environmental issues and animal rights and miscellaneous.

◆ National Center for Charitable Statistics

http://nccs.urban.org

The National Center for Charitable Statistics (NCCS) is "the national repository of data on the nonprofit sector in the United States." The NCCS seeks to develop and distribute high quality data on nonprofit organizations and their activities for use in research on the relationships between the nonprofit sector, government, the commercial sector and the broader civil society. The site offers resources such as IRS forms, data such as a glossary and state profiles, in addition to databases, projects and publications.

◆ National Charities Information Bureau

http://www.give.org/

The National Charities Information Bureau's (NCIB) mission is to promote informed giving and to enable more contributors to make sound giving decisions. NCIB's Web page provides grantseekers with a quick reference guide to 400 national charities and a help desk to field questions and comments. Grantseekers also will find NCIB's guidelines for evaluating a charity, tips on how to make a charitable contribution and instructions on how to order a full report for a specific charity. Users may receive an introductory issue of the *Wise Giving Guide* free. NCIB members receive the four quarterly issues of the guide free of charge. The *Wise Giving Guide* indicates whether an organization meets NCIB Standards and, if not, which ones it does not meet. The guide also contains articles on current issues in the charitable sector. The Web site also offers a charity report of the week.

◆ National Society of Fund Raising Executives

http://www.nsfre.org

The National Society of Fund Raising Executives (NSFRE) is "the professional association for individuals responsible for generating philanthropic support for a wide variety of nonprofit, charitable organizations." Founded in 1960, NSFRE is made up of more than 20,000 members in 154 chapters throughout North America. The site provides links to the Latest News, a directory of consultants and a fundraising resource center.

◆ NETSource

http://www.usc.edu/source/

NETSource is maintained by the University of Southern California Development Research Department. The site provides a myriad of links to resources for prospect researchers and other development professionals. Its index contains such categories as corporate intelligence, directories, newspapers and magazines, fundraising and foundation information, genealogy, legal research, planned giving, prospect research and others.

◆ Nonportal

http://www.nonportal.org

Nonportal is a project of the Gilbert Center. The Gilbert Center is made up of Michael Gilbert and a group of his colleagues from around the world. They are a modern, virtual organization that operates entirely online. The site offers a section on Nonprofit Online news, as well as several nonprofit related links such as: Free Management Library; Action Without Borders; Virtual Volunteering; and About Nonprofits. There is also a link to the Gilbert Center.

◆ Nonprofit Charitable Organizations

http://nonprofit.about.com/jobs/nonprofit/mpremail.htm

This nonprofit information Web site includes articles, searches, related topics and links. Users may post questions on a bulletin board or may e-mail Stan Hutton, a nonprofit management professional, who oversees this site.

◆ Nonprofit Cyber-Accountability

http://www.bway.net/~hbograd/cyb-acc.html#HBograd

Nonprofit Cyber-Accountability Web site is a collection of articles, essays and papers on the Web's use by nonprofits. The site's creator, Harriet Bograd, poses in her introduction to the topic two important questions: 1) How to use the Web to make information more available to the public and government regulators? and 2) How should solicitations on the Internet be regulated, if at all? Instead of a long disseration on the top, she cleverly links grantseekers to brief topic paragraphs then links grantseekers to more detailed articles or online resources. Links include: Investigating Nonprofits; Philanthropic Resource, Inc.; Internet Nonprofit Center; and German Charities Institute. Grantseekers also can subscribe to the mailing list via the Web site.

◆ Nonprofit GENIE

http://www.genie.org

The Nonprofit GENIE is sponsored by the California Endowment, the California Wellness Foundation, the James Irvine Foundation, the David and Lucille Packard Foundation and others. Links are provided to all of the above mentioned foundations, as well as to FAQs, Nonprofit Genie publications, grantmakers' opinions and the Resource Oasis. The Resource Oasis contains links to 13 management support organizations that sponsor the Nonprofit GENIE and offer a wide range of expert help on fundraising, strategic planning, meeting facilitation, financial management and other topics vital to the success of a nonprofit organization.

◆ Nonprofit Online News

http://www.gilbert.org/news

The site offers current nonprofit news online. Grantseekers can subscribe via e-mail to a free weekly e-mail edition of Nonprofit Online News. Users of this site are invited to e-mail the Gilbert Center with any relevant news or comments. The site is filled with many useful links to nonprofit related information. There is a link to the Gilbert Center which can connect users to the other services they offer, such as Nonportal.

◆ Nonprofit Resources Catalogue

http://www.clark.net/pub/pwalker/

The online Nonprofit Resources Catalogue, created in 1994, has grown to include links to more than 2,890 research and informational sites. Of particular interest to nonprofits are links to fundraising and general nonprofit resources. Links also are provided for sites relating to general reference, health and human services, the Internet, news sources, the government and United Ways. The Web site was last updated on 05/11/97, however, most of the links are still active and useful.

◆ Nonprofit Tech

http://www.nonprofit-tech.org

Nonprofit Tech was created to work with the nonprofit sector to increase organizational effectiveness. The site seeks to inform, educate and support nonprofits in their efforts to implement and use technology. There is a list of nonprofit partners and member and project clients. Services that Nonprofit Tech offers are: the tech library for nonprofits; the tech forum; and the tech e-group.

◆ NonProfit Times

http://www.nptimes.com/

The *NonProfit Times* Web site provides monthly electronic articles on nonprofit management. Grantseekers should visit the site periodically to keep updates on news and trends in the nonprofit industry. Additionally, grantseekers can search through back issues of the periodical. Also included is Salary Survey 2000, detailing current salaries in the nonprofit sector according to a *NonProfit Times* report.

◆ Nonprofit ToolKIT

http://www.nptoolkit.org

The New York Foundation for the Arts and Arts Wire, with funding from the Charles Stewart Mott Foundation, created Nonprofit ToolKIT, a monthly online magazine designed to serve the technology needs of the nonprofit community. Each issue of Nonprofit ToolKIT is focused on a different topic in technology planning and the magazine is structured to capitalize on the learning opportunities presented by that topic.

◆ The Office of Research and Sponsored Programs at Northwestern University

http://www.nwu.edu/orsp/

The Office of Research and Sponsored Programs at Northwestern University Web site contains information on Northwestern's fundraising goals and office setup. The most useful information to grantseekers, however, is a list of prospective research and fundraising links, such as: Non-Government Funding Sources; The American Society of Mechanical Engineers; National Science Foundation; and the Department of Education.

◆ Philanthropy News Network

http://www.pj.org/

Philanthropy News Network, formerly Philanthropy Journal of North Carolina, offers grantseekers news and information in a variety of areas including corporate giving, foundations, education, technology, fundraising, laws, taxes, people, volunteers and nonprofit jobs. The site also is the home of Philanthropy Links and the Meta-Index of Nonprofit Sites.

◆ Philanthropy Related Links

http://www.pj.org/links.cfm

This Web site, linked to the home page of the Philanthropy News Network, contains several good links and resources for grantseekers. The site provides direct links to many foundations, nonprofits and corporate research sources, including Carnegie Corporation of New York, SEC's EDGAR and FRED databases and the National Science Foundation. The site also links to philanthropy-related publications, the Meta-Index of Nonprofit Organizations and a list of mailing lists.

◆ Proposal Writing Internet Resources

http://www.library.wisc.edu/libraries/Memorial/grants/proposal.htm

This Web site comes from the Grants Information Center located at the University of Wisconsin. This Web site focuses on the proposal writing process. There is a link to several resources available in print at the university. The rest of the links include information on proposals and related topics that are found on the Internet, such as: Elements of a Grants Proposal; Getting Funded: It Takes More Than Just a Good Idea; Guide to Proposal Planning and Writing; and Some Reasons Why Proposals Fail.

◆ Prospect Research Tips from Waltham Associates

http://www.tc.umn.edu/nlhome/g248/bergq003/wa/rsrchtips.html

This Internet site, sponsored by the nonprofit consultant firm of Waltham and Associates, provides a list of links to aid grantseekers. Users will find links to periodicals and journals such as *Town & Country* magazine, databases such as SEC's EDGAR and Hoover's, other prospect research sources like the Internet Prospector and general reference sites. Links to the Philanthropy Index, the Dow Jones and to KnowX Public Records Searches are also provided. There is even a link for online UPS tracking.

◆ PRSPCT-L

listserv@Bucknell.edu

This mailing list is a forum for discussion of issues related to prospect research. Areas of discussion include fundraising resources, techniques, ethics and job announcements. To subscribe, send the following e-mail message (with the subject line blank) to LISTSERV@BUCKNELL.EDU: subscribe prspct-l [your name].

◆ SAMI Funding Sources

http://www.learner.org/sami/

SAMI is a rural math and science initiative funded by the Annenberg/CPB Math and Science Project and by the US West Foundation. The ultimate goal of the project is to improve math and science education in rural settings. The SAMI Funding Sources Web site is an information-packed source for grantseekers. It offers users several categories of information: funding information resources; teacher help; and science and classroom resources. Within the rural and general categories, funding opportunities are broken down into federal, foundation, corporate and other. Users can browse the site's database by filling out an online form for the appropriate area of interest.

◆ TALK-AMPHILREV

majordomo@tab.com

This unmoderated list was implemented by the editors of American Philanthropy Review. It serves as a "big tent" list where development professionals congregate and benefit from the experience and expertise of those in differing disciplines of fund development. The list is open to both in-house and outside professionals involved in any aspect of philanthropy. Unlike most lists, it welcomes short, relevant commercial postings. To subscribe, send the following e-mail message (with the subject line blank) to majordomo@tab.com: subscribe talk-amphilrev [your name].

◆ UK Fundraising

http://www.fundraising.co.uk/

The UK Fundraising Internet site promotes itself as a resource for charity and nonprofit fundraisers in the United Kingdom. Grantseekers can participate in a companion e-mail discussion list called FundUK. The Web site also offers additional resources, including links to grants and funding opportunities, books, magazines, courses, events and other non-profit related items and sites. A link is also provided for Grant Writer Online, a suite of software and services for nonprofits.

◆ University of Virginia Research Sponsors

http://www.cs.virginia.edu/~seas/resdev/sponsors.html

The University of Virginia Research Sponsors Web site assists grantseekers in identifying research funding and scholarship opportunities. Grantseekers who visit this site will find a list of Internet sites containing information of interest to researchers in all fields of science and technology. There also are links to government agencies, foundations, associations and other searchable databases and gopher resources. These links include: the Department of Energy; the Environmental Protection Agency; the Fullbright Scholars Program; and Polaris Grants Central. The Web site also provides a link to a list of universities around the world.

◆ Young Nonprofit Professionals Network

http://www.ynpn.org

The Young Nonprofit Professionals Network (YNPN) promotes "an efficient, viable and inclusive nonprofit sector that supports the growth, learning and development of young professionals." This mission is geared towards the young people involved in the San Francisco Bay Area nonprofit community. The Web site offers news, a calendar of events, resource links, committees, an e-mail list and a discussion group.

Index to Sites by Alphabetical Order

3M in the Community 1
555-1212.com 163
7-Eleven Stores 1

A

AARP Andrus Foundation 61
Abelard Foundation 61
Abell Foundation 61
Able Trust 61
Academe Today 175
Achelis Foundation 62
Adobe Philanthropic Council 1
Aetna Foundation 2
Agency for Healthcare Research and Quality (AHRQ) 143
Agriculture Department (USDA) 143
Ahmanson Foundation 62
Aid to Artisans 62
Air Force Office of Scientific Research (AFOSR) 146
Akron Community Foundation 62
Alaska Conservation Foundation 63
Alaska Science and Technology Foundation 63
Alberta Foundation for the Arts 63
Albertson Foundation, J. A. and Kathryn 63
Albion Community Foundation 64
Alcoholic Beverage Medical Research Foundation 64
Alger Regional Community Foundation 64
Allegheny Foundation 64
Allen Charitable Foundation, Paul G. 65
Allen Foundation 65
Allen Foundation for the Arts 65
Alliance Healthcare Foundation 65
Alliant Energy Foundation 2
Alpert Foundation, Herb 66
Altman Foundation, Jenifer 66
Amateur Athletic Foundation of Los Angeles 66
America's Charities 163
America's Promise 175
American Association of Museums 66
American Association of Physics Teachers 67
American Association of School Libraries 67
American Association of University Women 67

American Brain Tumor Association 67
American Express Company 2
American Federation for Aging Research 68
American Foundation for AIDS Research 68
American Foundation for the Blind 68
American Health Assistance Foundation 68
American Historical Association 69
American Journalism Review News Link 163
American Legion Child Welfare Foundation 69
American Medical Association 69
American Medical Association Physician Select 163
American Music Center 69
American Philanthropy Review 175
Ameritech Corporation 3
Amway 3
Amy Foundation 70
Ancestry Home Town 164
Annenberg Foundation 70
Appalachian Community Fund 70
Apple Computer 3
Applied Research and Development International 176
Arca Foundation 70
ARCH-Alumni Records Clearinghouse 164
ARCO Foundation 4
Arizona Cardinals Charities 4
Arizona Commission on the Arts 71
Arizona Community Foundation 71
Army Research Office (ARO) 146
Art Council of Northwest Florida 71
Arthritis Foundation 71
Ashland Foundation 4
ASM International Foundation 72
Aspen Publishers Grants and Nonprofit Resources 176
Associated Grantmakers of Massachusetts 176
Association for Professional Researchers for Advancement 176
Associations, Foundations and Institutes 177
AT&T Foundation 5
Atkinson Charitable Foundation 72
Atlanta Women's Foundation 72
Aurora Foundation 72
Autodesk Foundation 5
Avon Products Foundation 5

B

Babcock Foundation, Mary Reynolds 73
Bader Foundation, Helen 73
Bagnoud Foundation, Francois-Xavier 73
Baltimore Gas and Electric Company Corporate Contributions 6

Bank of America Foundation . . . 6
BankBoston and the Community . . . 6
Bankers Trust Foundation . . . 7
Baptist Community Ministries . . . 73
Baraga County Community Foundation . . . 74
Battle Creek Community Foundation . . . 74
Bauman Foundation . . . 74
Baxter International Corporate Citizenship . . . 7
Bell Atlantic Foundation . . . 7
BellSouth Foundation . . . 8
Ben & Jerry's Foundation . . . 8
Benton Foundation . . . 74
Benton Foundation's Best Practice Toolkit . . . 177
Berger Foundation, H. N. and Frances C. . . . 75
Bernardine Franciscan Sisters Foundation . . . 75
Better Business Bureau Philanthropy Advisory Service . . . 177
Beveridge Foundation, Frank Stanley . . . 75
Biehl Foundation, Amy . . . 76
Big Ben Foundation, Inc. . . . 75
Bingham Foundation, William . . . 76
Biography . . . 164
Blakemore Foundation . . . 76
Blandin Foundation . . . 76
Blank Foundation, Arthur M. Family . . . 77
Blowitz-Ridgeway Foundation . . . 77
Blue Cross and Blue Shield of Michigan Community Sponsored Events . . . 8
Board Café . . . 177
BOC Group . . . 9
Bodman Foundation . . . 77
Boeing . . . 9
Bonner Foundation, Corella and Bertram F. . . . 77
Booth Ferris Foundation . . . 78
Borden Foundation, Mary Owen . . . 78
Boston Foundation . . . 78
Bowne Foundation, Robert . . . 78
BPAmoco Corporation . . . 9
Bradley Foundation, Lynde and Harry . . . 79
Brain Foundation, Joe . . . 79
Brainerd Foundation . . . 79
Bread and Roses Community Fund . . . 79
Bremer Foundation, Otto . . . 80
Bristol-Myers Squibb Foundation . . . 9
British Telecom in the Community . . . 10
Brookdale Foundation Group . . . 80
Brooklyn Union . . . 10
Brother's Brother Foundation . . . 80
Brown Brothers Harriman & Company Community Involvement . . . 10
Brown Foundation, James Graham . . . 80

Budget Internet Information System (BIIS) 157
Bullitt Foundation 81
Burger King 11
Burroughs Wellcome Fund 81
Bush Charitable Foundation, Edyth 81
Bush Foundation for Family Literacy, Barbara 81
Business for Social Responsibility 178
Business Week 178

C

Cable & Wireless Corporate Community Involvement 11
Cabot Corporation Social Responsibility 11
Cadillac Area Community Foundation 82
California Community Foundation 82
California Endowment 82
California HealthCare Foundation 82
California Wellness Foundation 83
Campaign Service Consultants 178
Cancer Treatment Research Foundation 83
Canon U.S.A. Society and Environment 12
Canyon Research 83
Captain Planet Foundation 83
CarEth Foundation 84
CARLISLE Foundation 84
Carnegie Corporation of New York 84
Carnegie Endowment for International Peace 84
Carolina Power & Light in the Community 12
Carthage Foundation 85
Carver Charitable Trust, Roy J. 85
Casey Foundation, Annie E. 85
Castle Foundation, Samuel N. and Mary 85
Catalog of Federal Domestic Assistance (CFDA) 159
Catholic Campaign for Human Development 86
Center for Theology and the Natural Sciences 86
Centers for Disease Control and Prevention (CDC) 144
Central Indiana Community Foundation 86
Century Foundation 86
Ceridian Corporation Community Involvement 12
CFRNET 178
Champlin Foundations 87
Charity Village 179
CheckFree Investment Services 164
Chesapeake Bay Trust 87
Chevron Corporation 13
Chi Chi Rodriguez Youth Foundation 87
Chiang Ching-kuo Foundation for International Scholarly Exchange 87
Chinook Fund 88
Chronicle of Philanthropy 179

Cisco Systems Community Involvement 13
Citigroup Foundation 13
CJ Foundation for SIDS 88
Clark Foundation, Edna McConnell 88
Clark Foundation, Robert Sterling 88
Cleveland Foundation 89
Cleveland State University Office of Research and Economic Development. 179
Clipper Ship Foundation 89
Clorox Community Affairs 14
Coalescence Inc.. 179
Coca-Cola Scholars Foundation 14
Coleman Foundation 89
Comdisco, Inc.. 14
Commerce Business Daily (CBD) 160
Commerce Department (DoC) 144
Commonwealth Fund 89
COMMUNISERVE — Information Services 180
Community Foundation of Sarasota County 90
Community Wealth Online 180
Companies Online 165
Compaq Computer Corporate Contributions 14
CompuMentor 180
Computer Associates 15
Conoco 15
Conseco Community Action Report 15
Consultants ONTAP 180
Cooper Foundation 90
Cooperative State Research Education and Extension Service (CSREES) 143
Corporate America's Most Powerful People 165
Corporation for National Service (CNS) 146
Cottonwood Foundation 90
Council for the Advancement and Support of Education 181
Council of Michigan Foundations 181
Council on Foundations 181
Craig and Vartorella: International Marking and Advertising 165
Crail-Johnson Foundation 90
Cummings Foundation, Nathan 91
Custom News 157
CyberVPM 181

D

D. C. Commission on the Arts and Humanities 91
Dai Nippon Printing Company-Dynamic Corporate Citizenship 16
Daiwa Anglo-Japanese Foundation 91
Dana Foundation, Charles A. 92
Database America 166
Davis Foundations, Arthur Vining 92
Defense Department (DoD) 146

Defense Department Research and Engineering (DDR&E) 146
Delaware Valley Grantmakers 182
Delmas Foundation, Gladys Krieble 92
Delta Air Lines 16
Dial Corporation 16
DJ&T Foundation 93
Do Right Foundation 93
Dodge Foundation, Geraldine R 93
Dole Food Company 17
Donnelly & Sons Company, R.R. 17
Donors Forum of Chicago 182
Downing Foundation, J.C. 94
Draper Laboratories Community Outreach, Charles Stark 17
Dreyer's Grand Ice Cream Corporate Philanthropy 18
Dreyfus Foundation, Camille and Henry 94
Drucker Foundation for Nonprofit Management, Peter F. 94
Dunn Foundation 95
DuPont-Social Responsibility 18

E

Eastern Enterprises Foundation 18
Eastman Chemical Company and the Community 19
Eaton Corporation 19
Echoing Green Foundation 95
Economic Development Administration (EDA) 145
Eddie Bauer, Inc. 19
EDGAR Database of Corporate Information 166
Education Department (ED) 147
Edugate 147
Electronic Data Systems (EDS) Community Affairs 19
Electronic Frontier Foundation 95
EMI Group 20
Employment and Training Administration (ETA) 153
Energy Department (DoE) 148
Energy Foundation 95
Enron 20
Environmental Protection Agency (EPA) 149
Epilepsy Foundation 96
Estée Lauder Companies 20
Eurasia Foundation 96
Evans Foundation, Lettie Pate 96
ExxonMobil Corporation 20

F

Facts Online 166
Fannie Mae Foundation 21
Fargo-Moorhead Area Foundation 96
FastLane 157

FECInfo 166
Federal Acquisition Jumpstation 160, 167
Federal Information Exchange (FEDIX) 167
Federal Register 160
Feinstein Foundation 97
Fels Fund, Samuel S. 97
Fetzer Institute 97
Fina 21
Financial Aid, Foundations, Funding and Grants 182
Fleet Bank 21
Flinn Foundation 97
FMC Foundation 21
Food and Nutrition Service (FNS) 144
Ford Foundation 98
Ford Motor Company 22
Fortune 500 167
Fortune Global 500 168
Foundation Center 182
Foundation for Anesthesia Education and Research 98
Foundation for Exceptional Children 98
Foundation for Microbiology 99
Foundation for Seacoast Health 99
Foundation for the Carolinas 99
Foundations.org 183
France Telecom 22
Fred Meyer Stores 22
Freddie Mac 22
Freedom Forum 100
Friends of the Environment Foundation 100
Fuji Bank Group-Corporate Citizen 22
Fujitsu-Social Commitment 23
Fund for the City of New York 100
Funding for Technology 183
Fundraising Online 183
Fundraising Resources and Listservs 183
Fundsnet Services 183

G

Gap, Inc. Community Relations 23
Gates Foundation, Bill and Melinda 101
Genentech, Inc., Corporate Responsibility 23
General Accounting Office (GAO) 161
General Electric Co. 23
General Mills 24
General Motors Corporation-Philanthropy 24
Gerbode Foundation, Wallace Alexander 101
Getty Trust, J. Paul 101
Gill Foundation 102

Gillette Company 24
Glaxo Wellcome in the Community 24
Glenn Foundation for Medical Research. 102
Global Fund for Women. 102
Gold Foundation, Arnold P. 102
Goldman Fund, Richard and Rhoda 103
Government Printing Office/GPO ACCESS 161
Grant Seeker's Guide to the Internet: Revised and Revisited 184
Grant-related Links 185
Grants and Contracts Information (OCFO). 148
GrantScape. 184
Grantsmanship Center, The 184
GrantsWeb 185
Green Bay Packers Foundation. 103
GTE Foundation. 25
Guardian National Insurance Company. 25
Guggenheim Foundation, Harry Frank 103
Guggenheim Memorial Foundation, John Simon 103
Guidestar 185
Gund Foundation, George 104
Gunk Foundation 104

H

H. E. Butt Grocery. 25
Haas Fund, Walter and Elise 104
Hallmark Cards 25
HandsNet 185
Harmony Foundation. 104
Hartford Foundation for Public Giving. 105
Hartford Foundation, John A.. 105
Haynes and Dora Haynes Foundation, John Randolph 105
Health and Human Services Department (HHS) 150
Health Resources and Services Administration (HRSA) 151
Healthcare Foundation of New Jersey. 106
Hearst Foundations, William Randolph 106
HEI Charitable Foundation. 26
Heinz Endowments 106
Henson Foundation, Jim 107
Hershey Foods Corporation. 26
Hewlett Foundation, William and Flora 107
Hewlett Packard Corporate Philanthropy 26
Hitachi Foundation. 26
Hogg Foundation for Mental Health. 107
Home Depot. 27
Hoover's MasterList Database 168
Housing and Urban Development (HUD). 151
Houston Endowment 108
Howard Hughes Medical Institute 108

Humboldt Area Foundation 108
Huntington Bancshares Incorporated 27

I

I Have a Dream Foundation. 108
ideaList 186
IGA 27
iGive 186
IKNOW 186
Impact Online. 186
Inc. 500 168
Independent Sector. 186
Institute for Global Communications 187
Institute of Museum and Library Services (IMLS) 151
Intel and the Community 27
Internal Revenue Service (IRS) 187
International Business Machines (IBM) Philanthropy. 28
International Paper 28
International Trade Administration (ITA) 145
Internet Millionaires Page. 168
Internet Nonprofit Center 187
Internet Prospector 187
Intimate Brands 28
Ipalco. 29
Irvine Health Foundation 109
Itochu-Contributing to Society 29
Ittleson Foundation 109

J

Jacksonville Jaguars Foundation 29
Japan Foundation 109
JCPenney Community Involvement 30
JM Family Enterprises. 30
John AIDS Foundation, Elton 109
Johnson & Johnson 30
Johnson Foundation, Magic 110
Johnson Foundation, Robert Wood 110
Johnson Foundation, Walter S. 110
Jones Foundation, W. Alton 111
Justice Department (DoJ) 152
Justice Information Electronic Newsletter (JUSTINFO) 152
Juvenile Diabetes Foundation International. 111
Juvenile Justice Electronic List (JUVJUST) 152

K

Kaiser Family Foundation, Henry J. 111
Kansas City Power & Light Company Community Outlets. 31
Kansas Health Foundation 111

Kauffman Foundation, Ewing Marion 112
Kazanjian Economics Foundation, Calvin K. 112
Kellogg Foundation, W. K. 112
Kennedy Center Fund for New American Plays 112
Kennedy, Jr. Foundation, Joseph P. 113
Kentucky Foundation for Women 113
Kettering Foundation 113
Kimberly-Clark 31
Kingfisher in the Community 31
KN Energy 32
Knight Foundation, John S. and James L. 114
Kodak Corporation 32
Kornfeld Foundation, Emily Davie and Joseph S. 114

L

Labor Department (DoL) 153
Lamb's Prospect Research Page, David 188
LEF Foundation 114
LEGOLAND California 32
Levi Strauss & Company 32
LibertyNet: Home Page of the Philadelphia Region 169
Library of Congress/THOMAS 161
Limited Inc. Foundation, The 33
Lindbergh Foundation, Charles A. and Anne Morrow 115
LitLamp 188
Long Island Community Foundation 115
Lotus Development Corporation Philanthropy Program 33
Lowe Foundation, Edward 115
Lowe's Companies 33
Lubrizol Foundation 34
Lucas Educational Foundation, George 116
Ludwick Family Foundation 116

M

MacArthur Foundation, John D. and Catherine T. 116
Maddie's Fund 117
Mailman Family Foundation, A. L. 117
ManitoFoundation 117
Marin Community Foundation 117
Markle Foundation, John and Mary R. 118
Marks & Spencer 34
Martindale-Hubbell Lawyer Locator 169
Mary Kay 34
Massachusetts Environmental Trust 118
Mattel, Inc. 34
Mayday Fund 118
McCarthy Family Foundation 118
McCormick Tribune Foundation, Robert R. 119

McDonald's-Our Community 35
McDonnell Foundation, James S. 119
McGregor Fund 119
MCI WorldCom 35
Meadows Foundation 120
Medina Foundation 120
Medtronic Foundation 35
Mellon Foundation, Andrew W. 120
Men's Wearhouse 35
Merck & Co. 36
Mertz-Gilmore Foundation, Joyce 120
Metacrawler 169
Meta-Index of Nonprofit Sites 188
Metropolitan Life Insurance Company 36
Meyer Memorial Trust 121
Microsoft Community Affairs 36
Microsoft Library 169
Mid Atlantic Arts Foundation 121
Milbank Memorial Fund 121
Milken Family Foundation 121
Millipore Foundation 37
Minnesota Attorney General's Consumer Protection Office 170
Mintz Levin Community Service 37
Mitsubishi Electric America Foundation 37
Monsanto Fund 37
Montana Community Foundation 122
Morgan and Company Community Relations, J. P. 38
Mother Jones 400 170
Motorola 38
Mott Foundation, Charles Stewart 122
Ms. Foundation for Women 122
Museum Loan Network 123

N

NASA Centers 153
NASA Procurement 154
National Aeronautics and Space Administration (NASA) 153
National Center for Charitable Statistics 188
National Center for Environmental Research (NCER) 150
National Charities Information Bureau 189
National Council for Social Studies Online 123
National Criminal Justice Reference Service (NCJRS) 152
National Endowment for the Arts (NEA) 155
National Endowment for the Humanities (NEH) 155
National Foundation for the Improvement of Education 123
National Geographic Society Education Foundation 124
National Institute of Standards and Technology (NIST) 145
National Institutes of Health (NIH) 155

National Oceanic and Atmospheric Administration (NOAA) 145
National Rivers Coalition 124
National Science Foundation (NSF) 156
National Science Teachers Association Awards Programs. 124
National Security Education Program (NSEP) 147
National Semiconductor Community Care 38
National Society of Fund Raising Executives 189
National Teaching & Learning Forum 170
National Telecommunications and Information Administration (NTIA) 145
National Trust for Historic Preservation 124
NatWest Group Community Relations-Group Community Review. 39
NEC Foundation of America 39
Nellie Mae Foundation. 39
NETSource. 189
New Israel Fund. 125
Newtithing Group 170
NIH Guide for Grants and Contracts 156
Nonportal. 189
Nonprofit Charitable Organizations. 190
Nonprofit Cyber-Accountability 190
Nonprofit Gateway. 144
Nonprofit GENIE 190
Nonprofit Online News 190
Nonprofit Resources Catalogue 191
Nonprofit Tech. 191
NonProfit Times 191
Nonprofit ToolKIT 191
Nordstrom 40
Norman Foundation 125
Nortel Networks. 40
Northeast Utilities Community Services. 40
Northern States Power Company Community Involvement 41
Northwest Airlines. 41
Norton Endowment Foundation, Laird 125
Novartis Foundation for Sustainable Development. 41
Novell 41
Nuclear Regulatory Commission (NRC). 157

O

Occidental Petroleum Corporation. 42
Office of Budget, Finance and Award Management (BFA). 157
Office of Earth Science 154
Office of Environmental Management 148
Office of Extramural Research (OER) 156
Office of Justice Programs (OJP) 152
Office of Life and Microgravity Sciences and Applications 154
Office of Management and Budget (OMB). 161
Office of Naval Research (ONR) 147

Office of Procurement and Assistance Management . . . 148
Office of Research and Development (ORD) . . . 150
Office of Research and Sponsored Programs at Northwestern University, The . . . 192
Office of Resource and Management . . . 149
Office of Science (OS) . . . 149
Office of Science Grants and Contracts . . . 149
Office of Space Science . . . 154
Olfactory Research Fund . . . 126
Olin Corporation . . . 42
Open Society Institute . . . 126
Orchard Foundation . . . 126
Orthopaedic Research and Education Foundation . . . 126
Oshman's SuperSports USA . . . 42
Ottinger Foundation . . . 127
Owens Corning World Community Support . . . 42

P

Pacific Gas & Electric Contributions Program . . . 43
Packard Foundation, David and Lucile . . . 127
Patagonia Environmental Grants Program . . . 43
PECO Energy Community Development . . . 43
Perkins Family Restaurants . . . 43
Pet Life Foundation . . . 127
Pew Charitable Trusts . . . 127
Pfizer . . . 44
Philadelphia Foundation . . . 128
Philanthropic Digest Index . . . 171
Philanthropy News Network . . . 192
Philanthropy Related Links . . . 192
Phillips Petroleum Company-Our Citizenship . . . 44
Pillsbury Company . . . 44
PointCast Network . . . 171
Points of Light Foundation . . . 128
Pollock-Krasner Foundation . . . 128
PR Newswire . . . 171
Princess Grace Foundation - USA . . . 128
Proctor & Gamble Community Center . . . 44
Proposal Writing Internet Resources . . . 192
Prospect Research Online . . . 171
Prospect Research Tips from Waltham Associates . . . 193
PRSPCT-L . . . 193
Prudential Foundation . . . 45
Puerto Rico Community Foundation . . . 129
Puffin Foundation . . . 129

Q

Quad/Graphics . . . 45
Quaker Oats Foundation . . . 45
Quantum Corporation . . . 46
Quantum Foundation . . . 129

R

Ralston Purina Company . . . 46
Rand Merchant Bank Social Responsibility . . . 46
Reebok . . . 47
Research and Study Opportunities at the Smithsonian Institution . . . 158
Research Opportunities . . . 154
Research-It! . . . 172
Retirement Research Foundation . . . 129
Reynolds Foundation, Z. Smith . . . 130
Rhone-Poulenc Foundation . . . 47
Ripken, Jr. Foundation, Kelly and Cal . . . 130
Rippel Foundation, Fannie E. . . . 130
Rite Aid . . . 47
Robinson Foundation, Jackie . . . 130
Rockefeller Brothers Fund . . . 131
Rockefeller Family Fund . . . 131
Rockefeller Foundation . . . 131
Rohm and Haas and the Community . . . 47
Rolex Awards for Enterprise . . . 48
Rosenberg Foundation . . . 132
Rothschild Foundation, Judith . . . 132
Rural Utilities Service (RUS) . . . 144

S

Sage Foundation, Russell . . . 132
SAMI Funding Sources . . . 193
Samsung Group Social Activities . . . 48
San Antonio Area Foundation . . . 132
San Diego Community Foundation . . . 133
Scaife Family Foundation . . . 133
Scaife Foundation, Sarah . . . 133
Sears, Roebuck and Company . . . 48
Sega Foundation . . . 49
Sierra Club Foundation . . . 133
Sloan Foundation, Alfred P. . . . 134
Small Business Administration (SBA) . . . 158
SmithKline Beecham Community Partnership . . . 49
Sobrato Family Foundation . . . 134
Sonoco Foundation . . . 49
Sonoma County Community Foundation . . . 134
Sonora Area Foundation . . . 134
Soros Foundations Network . . . 135
Southern Poverty Law Center . . . 135
Southwire Company-Our Work in the Community . . . 50
Spencer Foundation . . . 135
Sprint Corporation . . . 50
St. Luke's Charitable Health Trust . . . 135
Starbucks Corporation . . . 50

Star-Ledger New Jersey Top 100, The 172
Starting Point 172
Stern Family Fund 136
StockMaster 172
Stolichnaya 50
Stonyfield Farm 51
Stride Rite Foundation 51
Substance Abuse and Mental Health Services Administration (SAMHSA) 158
Sun Microsystems 51
Surdna Foundation 136
Switchboard 173

T

TALK-AMPHILREV 193
Tandy Corporation 51
TAPPI Foundation 136
Target Stores 52
Templeton Foundation, John 136
Tesoro Hawaii Foundation 52
Texaco Foundation 52
Texas Instruments Corporate Citizenship 52
Think Quest 53
Thomson Financial Services Community Spirit 53
Tile.net 173
Tom's of Maine 53
Toshiba America Foundation 53
Toynbee Prize Foundation 137
Toyota USA Foundation 54
Transportation Department (DoT) 159
Triangle Community Foundation 137
Trillium Foundation 54
Trinity Grants Program 137
Trust Fund for Children with Special Health Care Needs 138
Turner Foundation 138

U

U.S. Agency for International Development (USAID) 159
U.S. Army Medical Research and Materiel Command (USAMRMC) 147
U.S.-Japan Foundation 138
UK Fundraising 194
Union Carbide 54
Unisys Social Responsibility 54
United Hospital Fund of New York 138
United Parcel Service 55
United States Post Office 173
United Technologies Community Involvement 55
University of Virginia Research Sponsors 194
Upjohn Institute, W.E. 139

US West 55
USG Corporation 55

V

Valero Energy Corporation 56
Valley Foundation 139
Vastar Resources, Inc. 56
Victoria Foundation 139
Virginia Environmental Endowment 139
Vision Service Plan 56
Vulcan Inc. 56

W

Walgreens 57
Wallace-Reader's Digest Funds 140
Wal-Mart Foundation 57
Warhol Foundation for the Visual Arts, Andy 140
Wealth of Internet Resources 173
WebActive 174
Webgator 174
Weeden Foundation 140
Weill Foundation for Music, Kurt 140
Weingart Foundation 141
Welfare-To-Work (WTW) 153
Wendy's International, Inc. 57
Wenner-Gren Foundation for Anthropological Research 141
Wheat Ridge Ministries 141
Whirlpool Foundation 58
Whitaker Foundation 141
Who Owns the Shore? 174
Wilburforce Foundation 142
Windermere Foundation 58
Woods Charitable Fund 142
Wray Trust 142
WRQ 58

Y

Yahoo! Inc. 59
Yorkshire Electricity 59
Young Nonprofit Professionals Network 194

Z

ZDNet 59

Index to Corporate and Foundation Sites by Major Category of Giving

Arts

3M in the Community . . . 1
Achelis Foundation . . . 62
Adobe Philanthropic Council . . . 1
Aetna Foundation . . . 2
Ahmanson Foundation . . . 62
Aid to Artisans . . . 62
Alberta Foundation for the Arts . . . 63
Albion Community Foundation . . . 64
Allen Foundation for the Arts . . . 65
Alliant Energy Foundation . . . 2
Alpert Foundation, Herb . . . 66
American Association of Museums . . . 66
American Association of School Libraries . . . 67
American Express Company . . . 2
American Historical Association . . . 69
American Music Center . . . 69
Amway . . . 3
ARCO Foundation . . . 4
Arizona Commission on the Arts . . . 71
Art Council of Northwest Florida . . . 71
Ashland Foundation . . . 4
AT&T Foundation . . . 5
Aurora Foundation . . . 72
Avon Products Foundation . . . 5
Baltimore Gas and Electric Company Corporate Contributions . . . 6
Bank of America Foundation . . . 6
BankBoston and the Community . . . 6
Bankers Trust Foundation . . . 7
Baraga County Community Foundation . . . 74
Bauman Foundation . . . 74
Bell Atlantic Foundation . . . 7
Benton Foundation . . . 74
Beveridge Foundation, Frank Stanley . . . 75
Bingham Foundation, William . . . 76
Blakemore Foundation . . . 76
Blandin Foundation . . . 76
Blank Family Foundation, Arthur M. . . . 77
Boeing . . . 9
BPAmoco Corporation . . . 9
Brooklyn Union . . . 10

Bush Charitable Foundation, Edyth . . . 81
Cable & Wireless Corporate Community Involvement . . . 11
Cabot Corporation Social Responsibility . . . 11
Cadillac Area Community Foundation . . . 82
California Community Foundation . . . 82
Carolina Power & Light in the Community . . . 12
Ceridian Corporation Community Involvement . . . 12
Clark Foundation, Robert Sterling . . . 88
Cleveland Foundation . . . 89
Clorox Community Affairs . . . 14
Community Foundation of Sarasota County . . . 90
Compaq Computer Corporate Contributions . . . 14
Conoco . . . 15
Conseco Community Action Report . . . 15
Cooper Foundation . . . 90
Cottonwood Foundation . . . 90
Cummings Foundation, Nathan . . . 91
D. C. Commission on the Arts and Humanities . . . 91
Dai Nippon Printing Company-Dynamic Corporate Citizenship . . . 16
Davis Foundations, Arthur Vining . . . 92
Delmas Foundation, Gladys Krieble . . . 92
Delta Air Lines . . . 16
Dial Corporation . . . 16
Dodge Foundation, Geraldine R. . . . 93
Dole Food Company . . . 17
Eastman Chemical Company and the Community . . . 19
EMI Group . . . 20
Estée Lauder Companies . . . 20
Evans Foundation, Lettie Pate . . . 96
ExxonMobil Corporation . . . 20
Fargo-Moorhead Area Foundation . . . 96
Fels Fund, Samuel S. . . . 97
Fleet Bank . . . 21
Flinn Foundation . . . 97
Ford Foundation . . . 98
Ford Motor Company . . . 22
Freedom Forum . . . 100
Gap, Inc. Community Relations . . . 23
General Electric Co. . . . 23
General Mills . . . 24
General Motors Corporation-Philanthropy . . . 24
Gerbode Foundation, Wallace Alexander . . . 101
Getty Trust, J. Paul . . . 101
Glaxo Wellcome in the Community . . . 24
Goldman Fund, Richard and Rhoda . . . 103
Guggenheim Memorial Foundation, John Simon . . . 103
Gund Foundation, George . . . 104
Gunk Foundation . . . 104

H. E. Butt Grocery . . . 25
Haas Fund, Walter and Elise . . . 104
Harmony Foundation . . . 104
Hartford Foundation for Public Giving . . . 105
Hearst Foundations, William Randolph . . . 106
HEI Charitable Foundation . . . 26
Heinz Endowments . . . 106
Henson Foundation, Jim . . . 107
Hershey Foods Corporation . . . 26
Hewlett Foundation, William and Flora . . . 107
Hewlett Packard Corporate Philanthropy . . . 26
Hitachi Foundation . . . 26
Houston Endowment . . . 108
Huntington Bancshares Incorporated . . . 27
International Business Machines (IBM) Philanthropy . . . 28
International Paper . . . 28
Itochu-Contributing to Society . . . 29
Japan Foundation . . . 109
JCPenney Community Involvement . . . 30
JM Family Enterprises . . . 30
Kennedy Center Fund for New American Plays . . . 112
Kentucky Foundation for Women . . . 113
Kimberly-Clark . . . 31
KN Energy . . . 32
Knight Foundation, John S. and James L. . . . 114
Kodak Corporation . . . 32
LEF Foundation . . . 114
Limited Inc. Foundation, The . . . 33
Marin Community Foundation . . . 117
Marks & Spencer . . . 34
McGregor Fund . . . 119
Meadows Foundation . . . 120
Medtronic Foundation . . . 35
Mellon Foundation, Andrew W. . . . 120
Men's Wearhouse . . . 35
Merck & Co. . . . 36
Mertz-Gilmore Foundation, Joyce . . . 120
Metropolitan Life Insurance Company . . . 36
Meyer Memorial Trust . . . 121
Microsoft Community Affairs . . . 36
Mid Atlantic Arts Foundation . . . 121
Monsanto Fund . . . 37
Montana Community Foundation . . . 122
Morgan and Company Community Relations, J. P. . . . 38
Motorola . . . 38
Mott Foundation, Charles Stewart . . . 122
Museum Loan Network . . . 123
National Trust for Historic Preservation . . . 124

Nordstrom . . . 40
Novell . . . 41
Open Society Institute . . . 126
Owens Corning World Community Support . . . 42
Packard Foundation, David and Lucile . . . 127
Pew Charitable Trusts. . . . 127
Pollock-Krasner Foundation . . . 128
Princess Grace Foundation - USA . . . 128
Proctor & Gamble Community Center . . . 44
Prudential Foundation . . . 45
Puerto Rico Community Foundation. . . . 129
Puffin Foundation . . . 129
Quantum Corporation . . . 46
Ralston Purina Company. . . . 46
Rhone-Poulenc Foundation. . . . 47
Rockefeller Brothers Fund . . . 131
Rockefeller Foundation . . . 131
Rohm and Haas and the Community . . . 47
Rothschild Foundation, Judith . . . 132
Samsung Group Social Activities . . . 48
San Antonio Area Foundation . . . 132
San Diego Community Foundation. . . . 133
Sonoco Foundation. . . . 49
Sonoma County Community Foundation . . . 134
Sonora Area Foundation. . . . 134
Soros Foundations Network . . . 135
Sprint Corporation . . . 50
Surdna Foundation . . . 136
Target Stores . . . 52
Texaco Foundation. . . . 52
Texas Instruments Corporate Citizenship . . . 52
Tom's of Maine . . . 53
Triangle Community Foundation . . . 137
Union Carbide . . . 54
Unisys Social Responsibility . . . 54
United Technologies Community Involvement. . . . 55
US West. . . . 55
USG Corporation. . . . 55
Valero Energy Corporation . . . 56
Vastar Resources, Inc. . . . 56
Wallace-Reader's Digest Funds . . . 140
Warhol Foundation for the Visual Arts, Andy . . . 140
Weill Foundation for Music, Kurt. . . . 140
Weingart Foundation . . . 141
Woods Charitable Fund . . . 142
Wray Trust . . . 142

Civic

Abell Foundation . . . 61
Akron Community Foundation . . . 62
Albion Community Foundation. . . . 64
Alger Regional Community Foundation . . . 64
Allegheny Foundation . . . 64
Alliant Energy Foundation . . . 2
American Association of University Women . . . 67
American Express Company . . . 2
American Historical Association . . . 69
Ameritech Corporation. . . . 3
Appalachian Community Fund . . . 70
Arca Foundation. . . . 70
ARCO Foundation . . . 4
Arizona Community Foundation . . . 71
Ashland Foundation . . . 4
Atkinson Charitable Foundation . . . 72
Atlanta Women's Foundation . . . 72
Avon Products Foundation . . . 5
Bader Foundation, Helen . . . 73
Baltimore Gas and Electric Company Corporate Contributions. . . . 6
Bank of America Foundation . . . 6
Bankers Trust Foundation . . . 7
Baptist Community Ministries. . . . 73
Baraga County Community Foundation . . . 74
Battle Creek Community Foundation . . . 74
Bauman Foundation. . . . 74
Benton Foundation . . . 74
Berger Foundation, H. N. and Frances C. . . . 75
Beveridge Foundation, Frank Stanley . . . 75
Blandin Foundation . . . 76
Blank Family Foundation, Arthur M. . . . 77
Boston Foundation. . . . 78
Bradley Foundation, Lynde and Harry . . . 79
Bread and Roses Community Fund. . . . 79
Bremer Foundation, Otto . . . 80
Bristol-Myers Squibb Foundation. . . . 9
Brooklyn Union. . . . 10
Brown Foundation, James Graham . . . 80
Cable & Wireless Corporate Community Involvement . . . 11
Cadillac Area Community Foundation . . . 82
California Community Foundation . . . 82
California Wellness Foundation . . . 83
CarEth Foundation . . . 84
Carnegie Corporation of New York . . . 84
Carnegie Endowment for International Peace . . . 84
Carthage Foundation . . . 85
Casey Foundation, Annie E. . . . 85

Catholic Campaign for Human Development 86
Central Indiana Community Foundation 86
Century Foundation 86
Chinook Fund 88
Citigroup Foundation 13
Clark Foundation, Edna McConnell 88
Clark Foundation, Robert Sterling 88
Cleveland Foundation 89
Clorox Community Affairs 14
Coleman Foundation 89
Community Foundation of Sarasota County 90
Computer Associates 15
Conoco 15
Conseco Community Action Report 15
Cummings Foundation, Nathan 91
Delta Air Lines 16
Do Right Foundation 93
Dodge Foundation, Geraldine R. 93
Dole Food Company 17
Donnelly & Sons Company, R.R. 17
Downing Foundation, J.C. 94
Draper Laboratories Community Outreach, Charles Stark 17
Drucker Foundation for Nonprofit Management, Peter F. 94
DuPont-Social Responsibility 18
Eastman Chemical Company and the Community 19
Eaton Corporation 19
Eddie Bauer, Inc. 19
Electronic Frontier Foundation 95
Eurasia Foundation 96
ExxonMobil Corporation 20
Fannie Mae Foundation 21
Fargo-Moorhead Area Foundation 96
Feinstein Foundation 97
Fels Fund, Samuel S. 97
Ford Foundation 98
Foundation for the Carolinas 99
France Telecom 22
Freedom Forum 100
Friends of the Environment Foundation 100
Fuji Bank Group-Corporate Citizen 22
Fund for the City of New York 100
General Motors Corporation-Philanthropy 24
Gerbode Foundation, Wallace Alexander 101
Gill Foundation 102
Global Fund for Women 102
Green Bay Packers Foundation 103
GTE Foundation 25
Guardian National Insurance Company 25

Gund Foundation, George 104
H. E. Butt Grocery. 25
Haas Fund, Walter and Elise 104
Hallmark Cards 25
Haynes and Dora Haynes Foundation, John Randolph 105
Heinz Endowments 106
Hershey Foods Corporation. 26
Hewlett Foundation, William and Flora 107
Hewlett Packard Corporate Philanthropy 26
Houston Endowment 108
Humboldt Area Foundation 108
Huntington Bancshares Incorporated 27
IGA 27
Intel and the Community 27
International Business Machines (IBM) Philanthropy. 28
JCPenney Community Involvement 30
JM Family Enterprises. 30
Johnson Foundation, Walter S. 110
Jones Foundation, W. Alton 111
Kansas City Power & Light Company Community Outlets. 31
Kauffman Foundation, Ewing Marion. 112
Kellogg Foundation, W. K.. 112
Kettering Foundation 113
Kimberly-Clark 31
KN Energy 32
Knight Foundation, John S. and James L. 114
Kodak Corporation. 32
Levi Strauss & Company 32
Limited Inc. Foundation, The 33
Long Island Community Foundation. 115
Lotus Development Corporation Philanthropy Program 33
Lowe Foundation, Edward. 115
MacArthur Foundation, John D. and Catherine T.. 116
Mailman Family Foundation, A. L.. 117
Manito Foundation 117
Marin Community Foundation 117
Markle Foundation, John and Mary R. 118
McCormick Tribune Foundation, Robert R. 119
McGregor Fund 119
Meadows Foundation 120
Medina Foundation 120
Medtronic Foundation 35
Mellon Foundation, Andrew W. 120
Merck & Co. 36
Mertz-Gilmore Foundation, Joyce 120
Metropolitan Life Insurance Company 36
Meyer Memorial Trust 121
Microsoft Community Affairs 36

Millipore Foundation 37
Mintz Levin Community Service 37
Montana Community Foundation 122
Morgan and Company Community Relations, J. P. 38
Motorola 38
Mott Foundation, Charles Stewart 122
Ms. Foundation for Women 122
NatWest Group Community Relations-Group Community Review 39
New Israel Fund 125
Norman Foundation 125
Northeast Utilities Community Services 40
Orchard Foundation 126
Ottinger Foundation 127
Owens Corning World Community Support 42
Pacific Gas & Electric Contributions Program 43
Packard Foundation, David and Lucile 127
Pew Charitable Trusts 127
Philadelphia Foundation 128
Points of Light Foundation 128
Proctor & Gamble Community Center 44
Puerto Rico Community Foundation 129
Quantum Foundation 129
Rand Merchant Bank Social Responsibility 46
Reebok 47
Retirement Research Foundation 129
Reynolds Foundation, Z. Smith 130
Rockefeller Brothers Fund 131
Rockefeller Family Fund 131
Rockefeller Foundation 131
Rohm and Haas and the Community 47
Rolex Awards for Enterprise 48
Rosenberg Foundation 132
Sage Foundation, Russell 132
San Antonio Area Foundation 132
San Diego Community Foundation 133
Scaife Foundation, Sarah 133
Sierra Club Foundation 133
Sloan Foundation, Alfred P. 134
Sobrato Family Foundation 134
Sonora Area Foundation 134
Soros Foundations Network 135
Southern Poverty Law Center 135
Southwire Company-Our Work in the Community 50
Sprint Corporation 50
Stern Family Fund 136
Sun Microsystems 51
Surdna Foundation 136
Texaco Foundation 52

Thomson Financial Services Community Spirit . . . 53
Toynbee Prize Foundation . . . 137
Triangle Community Foundation . . . 137
Trillium Foundation . . . 54
Trinity Grants Program . . . 137
Turner Foundation . . . 138
U.S.-Japan Foundation . . . 138
Unisys Social Responsibility . . . 54
Upjohn Institute, W.E. . . . 139
US West . . . 55
Vastar Resources, Inc. . . . 56
Victoria Foundation . . . 139
Weeden Foundation . . . 140
Weingart Foundation . . . 141
Whirlpool Foundation . . . 58
Wilburforce Foundation . . . 142
Woods Charitable Fund . . . 142
Yahoo! Inc. . . . 59

Education

3M in the Community . . . 1
7-Eleven Stores . . . 1
Abell Foundation . . . 61
Achelis Foundation . . . 62
Adobe Philanthropic Council . . . 1
Aetna Foundation . . . 2
Ahmanson Foundation . . . 62
Akron Community Foundation . . . 62
Albertson Foundation, J. A. and Kathryn . . . 63
Albion Community Foundation . . . 64
Alger Regional Community Foundation . . . 64
Allegheny Foundation . . . 64
Allen Foundation . . . 65
Alliant Energy Foundation . . . 2
Alpert Foundation, Herb . . . 66
American Association of Physics Teachers . . . 67
American Association of School Libraries . . . 67
American Association of University Women . . . 67
American Legion Child Welfare Foundation . . . 69
Ameritech Corporation . . . 3
Amway . . . 3
Amy Foundation . . . 70
Annenberg Foundation . . . 70
Apple Computer . . . 3
ARCO Foundation . . . 4
Ashland Foundation . . . 4
ASM International Foundation . . . 72

AT&T Foundation 5
Atkinson Charitable Foundation 72
Aurora Foundation. 72
Autodesk Foundation 5
Avon Products Foundation 5
Bader Foundation, Helen 73
Bank of America Foundation 6
Bankers Trust Foundation 7
Baraga County Community Foundation 74
Bauman Foundation. 74
Baxter International Corporate Citizenship. 7
Bell Atlantic Foundation 7
BellSouth Foundation. 8
Benton Foundation. 74
Berger Foundation, H. N. and Frances C. 75
Beveridge Foundation, Frank Stanley. 75
Bingham Foundation, William. 76
Blandin Foundation 76
Bodman Foundation 77
Boeing 9
Bonner Foundation, Corella and Bertram F. 77
Booth Ferris Foundation 78
Borden Foundation, Mary Owen 78
Bowne Foundation, Robert 78
BPAmoco Corporation 9
Bradley Foundation, Lynde and Harry 79
Brain Foundation, Joe 79
Bremer Foundation, Otto 80
Bristol-Myers Squibb Foundation. 9
British Telecom in the Community 10
Brooklyn Union. 10
Brother's Brother Foundation. 80
Brown Foundation, James Graham 80
Burger King 11
Burroughs Wellcome Fund. 81
Bush Charitable Foundation, Edyth 81
Bush Foundation for Family Literacy, Barbara 81
Cable & Wireless Corporate Community Involvement 11
Cabot Corporation Social Responsibility 11
Cadillac Area Community Foundation 82
California Community Foundation 82
Canyon Research. 83
Carnegie Corporation of New York 84
Carolina Power & Light in the Community 12
Carver Charitable Trust, Roy J. 85
Castle Foundation, Samuel N. and Mary. 85
Center for Theology and the Natural Sciences 86
Ceridian Corporation Community Involvement 12

Champlin Foundations. 87
Chesapeake Bay Trust 87
Chevron Corporation. 13
Chiang Ching-kuo Foundation for International Scholarly Exchange 87
Cisco Systems Community Involvement 13
Citigroup Foundation 13
Clark Foundation, Edna McConnell 88
Cleveland Foundation 89
Clorox Community Affairs. 14
Coca-Cola Scholars Foundation 14
Coleman Foundation 89
Community Foundation of Sarasota County 90
Compaq Computer Corporate Contributions. 14
Conoco. 15
Conseco Community Action Report. 15
Cooper Foundation. 90
Crail-Johnson Foundation. 90
Daiwa Anglo-Japanese Foundation. 91
Dana Foundation, Charles A. 92
Davis Foundations, Arthur Vining 92
Delmas Foundation, Gladys Krieble. 92
Delta Air Lines. 16
Dial Corporation 16
Do Right Foundation 93
Dodge Foundation, Geraldine R. 93
Donnelly & Sons Company, R.R. 17
Downing Foundation, J.C. 94
Draper Laboratories Community Outreach, Charles Stark. 17
Dreyer's Grand Ice Cream Corporate Philanthropy. 18
Dreyfus Foundation, Camille and Henry. 94
DuPont-Social Responsibility. 18
Eastern Enterprises Foundation 18
Eastman Chemical Company and the Community 19
Eaton Corporation 19
Echoing Green Foundation 95
Eddie Bauer, Inc. 19
Electronic Data Systems (EDS) Community Affairs. 19
Electronic Frontier Foundation. 95
Enron. 20
Epilepsy Foundation. 96
Estée Lauder Companies 20
Evans Foundation, Lettie Pate 96
ExxonMobil Corporation 20
Fargo-Moorhead Area Foundation 96
Fels Fund, Samuel S. 97
Fetzer Institute. 97
Fina 21
Fleet Bank 21

Flinn Foundation 97
FMC Foundation 21
Ford Foundation 98
Ford Motor Company 22
Foundation for Anesthesia Education and Research 98
Foundation for Exceptional Children 98
Foundation for Seacoast Health 99
France Telecom 22
Fred Meyer Stores 22
Freedom Forum 100
Fuji Bank Group-Corporate Citizen 22
Fujitsu-Social Commitment 23
Gap, Inc. Community Relations 23
Gates Foundation, Bill and Melinda 101
Genentech, Inc., Corporate Responsibility 23
General Electric Co. 23
General Mills 24
General Motors Corporation-Philanthropy 24
Gillette Company 24
Glaxo Wellcome in the Community 24
Goldman Fund, Richard and Rhoda 103
Green Bay Packers Foundation 103
GTE Foundation 25
Guardian National Insurance Company 25
Guggenheim Foundation, Harry Frank 103
Gund Foundation, George 104
H. E. Butt Grocery 25
Haas Fund, Walter and Elise 104
Hartford Foundation for Public Giving 105
Haynes and Dora Haynes Foundation, John Randolph 105
Hearst Foundations, William Randolph 106
HEI Charitable Foundation 26
Heinz Endowments 106
Hershey Foods Corporation 26
Hewlett Foundation, William and Flora 107
Hewlett Packard Corporate Philanthropy 26
Hitachi Foundation 26
Houston Endowment 108
Howard Hughes Medical Institute 108
Huntington Bancshares Incorporated 27
I Have a Dream Foundation 108
IGA 27
Intel and the Community 27
International Business Machines (IBM) Philanthropy 28
International Paper 28
Intimate Brands 28
Ipalco 29
Itochu-Contributing to Society 29

Japan Foundation . . . 109
JCPenney Community Involvement . . . 30
JM Family Enterprises . . . 30
John AIDS Foundation, Elton . . . 109
Johnson Foundation, Magic . . . 110
Johnson Foundation, Walter S. . . . 110
Kansas City Power & Light Company Community Outlets . . . 31
Kauffman Foundation, Ewing Marion . . . 112
Kazanijian Economics Foundation, Calvin K. . . . 112
Kellogg Foundation, W. K. . . . 112
Kimberly-Clark . . . 31
Kingfisher in the Community . . . 31
KN Energy . . . 32
Knight Foundation, John S. and James L. . . . 114
Kodak Corporation . . . 32
Kornfeld Foundation, Emily Davie and Joseph S. . . . 114
LEGOLAND California . . . 32
Levi Strauss & Company . . . 32
Limited Inc. Foundation, The . . . 33
Lindbergh Foundation, Charles A. and Anne Morrow . . . 115
Lotus Development Corporation Philanthropy Program . . . 33
Lowe's Companies . . . 33
Lubrizol Foundation . . . 34
Lucas Educational Foundation, George . . . 116
Ludwick Family Foundation . . . 116
MacArthur Foundation, John D. and Catherine T. . . . 116
Mailman Family Foundation, A. L. . . . 117
Manito Foundation . . . 117
Marin Community Foundation . . . 117
Markle Foundation, John and Mary R. . . . 118
Marks & Spencer . . . 34
McCarthy Family Foundation . . . 118
McCormick Tribune Foundation, Robert R. . . . 119
McDonald's-Our Community . . . 35
McGregor Fund . . . 119
MCI WorldCom . . . 35
Meadows Foundation . . . 120
Medtronic Foundation . . . 35
Mellon Foundation, Andrew W. . . . 120
Men's Wearhouse . . . 35
Merck & Co. . . . 36
Metropolitan Life Insurance Company . . . 36
Meyer Memorial Trust . . . 121
Microsoft Community Affairs . . . 36
Milken Family Foundation . . . 121
Millipore Foundation . . . 37
Mintz Levin Community Service . . . 37
Mitsubishi Electric America Foundation . . . 37

Monsanto Fund 37
Montana Community Foundation 122
Morgan and Company Community Relations, J. P. 38
Motorola 38
Mott Foundation, Charles Stewart 122
National Council for Social Studies Online 123
National Foundation for the Improvement of Education 123
National Geographic Society Education Foundation 124
National Science Teachers Association Awards Programs 124
National Semiconductor Community Care 38
NatWest Group Community Relations-Group Community Review 39
NEC Foundation of America 39
Nellie Mae Foundation 39
Nordstrom 40
Nortel Networks 40
Northeast Utilities Community Services 40
Northern States Power Company Community Involvement 41
Novell 41
Olin Corporation 42
Orthopaedic Research and Education Foundation 126
Owens Corning World Community Support 42
Pacific Gas & Electric Contributions Program 43
Packard Foundation, David and Lucile 127
PECO Energy Community Development 43
Pew Charitable Trusts 127
Pfizer 44
Philadelphia Foundation 128
Phillips Petroleum Company-Our Citizenship 44
Pillsbury Company 44
Princess Grace Foundation - USA 128
Proctor & Gamble Community Center 44
Prudential Foundation 45
Puerto Rico Community Foundation 129
Quaker Oats Foundation 45
Quantum Corporation 46
Quantum Foundation 129
Ralston Purina Company 46
Rand Merchant Bank Social Responsibility 46
Reynolds Foundation, Z. Smith 130
Rhone-Poulenc Foundation 47
Ripken, Jr. Foundation, Kelly and Cal 130
Robinson Foundation, Jackie 130
Rockefeller Brothers Fund 131
Rockefeller Foundation 131
Rohm and Haas and the Community 47
Sage Foundation, Russell 132
Samsung Group Social Activities 48
San Antonio Area Foundation 132

San Diego Community Foundation . . . 133
Sega Foundation . . . 49
Sloan Foundation, Alfred P. . . . 134
Sobrato Family Foundation . . . 134
Sonoco Foundation . . . 49
Sonoma County Community Foundation . . . 134
Sonora Area Foundation . . . 134
Soros Foundations Network . . . 135
Southwire Company-Our Work in the Community . . . 50
Spencer Foundation . . . 135
Sprint Corporation . . . 50
Starbucks Corporation . . . 50
Stride Rite Foundation . . . 51
Sun Microsystems . . . 51
Tandy Corporation . . . 51
TAPPI Foundation . . . 136
Target Stores . . . 52
Templeton Foundation, John . . . 136
Tesoro Hawaii Foundation . . . 52
Texaco Foundation . . . 52
Texas Instruments Corporate Citizenship . . . 52
Think Quest . . . 53
Thomson Financial Services Community Spirit . . . 53
Tom's of Maine . . . 53
Toshiba America Foundation . . . 53
Toyota USA Foundation . . . 54
Triangle Community Foundation . . . 137
Trillium Foundation . . . 54
U.S.-Japan Foundation . . . 138
Union Carbide . . . 54
Unisys Social Responsibility . . . 54
United Parcel Service . . . 55
United Technologies Community Involvement . . . 55
Upjohn Institute, W.E. . . . 139
US West . . . 55
USG Corporation . . . 55
Valero Energy Corporation . . . 56
Vastar Resources, Inc. . . . 56
Victoria Foundation . . . 139
Vulcan Inc. . . . 56
Walgreens . . . 57
Wallace-Reader's Digest Funds . . . 140
Wal-Mart Foundation . . . 57
Weingart Foundation . . . 141
Wendy's International, Inc. . . . 57
Whirlpool Foundation . . . 58
Woods Charitable Fund . . . 142
ZDNet . . . 59

Environment

3M in the Community 1
Adobe Philanthropic Council 1
Ahmanson Foundation. 62
Alaska Conservation Foundation. 63
Alpert Foundation, Herb 66
Altman Foundation, Jenifer. 66
Amway 3
ARCO Foundation 4
Arizona Community Foundation. 71
Ashland Foundation 4
Baltimore Gas and Electric Company Corporate Contributions. 6
Bankers Trust Foundation 7
Baraga County Community Foundation 74
Bauman Foundation. 74
Baxter International Corporate Citizenship. 7
Beveridge Foundation, Frank Stanley. 75
Blandin Foundation 76
Blank Family Foundation, Arthur M. 77
BOC Group 9
Bodman Foundation 77
Brainerd Foundation. 79
Bullitt Foundation 81
Cable & Wireless Corporate Community Involvement 11
Cabot Corporation Social Responsibility 11
Cadillac Area Community Foundation 82
California Community Foundation 82
Canon U.S.A. Society and Environment. 12
Captain Planet Foundation. 83
Carolina Power & Light in the Community 12
Castle Foundation, Samuel N. and Mary. 85
Chesapeake Bay Trust 87
Chevron Corporation. 13
Community Foundation of Sarasota County 90
Compaq Computer Corporate Contributions. 14
Conoco. 15
Cottonwood Foundation 90
Cummings Foundation, Nathan 91
Dai Nippon Printing Company-Dynamic Corporate Citizenship 16
Dole Food Company 17
Downing Foundation, J.C. 94
Dunn Foundation. 95
DuPont-Social Responsibility. 18
Eddie Bauer, Inc. 19
Enron. 20
Estée Lauder Companies 20
ExxonMobil Corporation 20
Ford Foundation. 98

Ford Motor Company . . . 22
France Telecom . . . 22
Friends of the Environment Foundation . . . 100
Gap, Inc. Community Relations . . . 23
General Motors Corporation-Philanthropy . . . 24
Gerbode Foundation, Wallace Alexander . . . 101
Gillette Company . . . 24
Glaxo Wellcome in the Community . . . 24
Guardian National Insurance Company . . . 25
Gund Foundation, George . . . 104
Haas Fund, Walter and Elise . . . 104
HEI Charitable Foundation . . . 26
Heinz Endowments . . . 106
Hershey Foods Corporation . . . 26
Hewlett Foundation, William and Flora . . . 107
Hewlett Packard Corporate Philanthropy . . . 26
Home Depot . . . 27
International Business Machines (IBM) Philanthropy . . . 28
International Paper . . . 28
Ipalco . . . 29
Itochu-Contributing to Society . . . 29
Ittleson Foundation . . . 109
Jones Foundation, W. Alton . . . 111
Kimberly-Clark . . . 31
LEF Foundation . . . 114
Lindbergh Foundation, Charles A. and Anne Morrow . . . 115
Lowe's Companies . . . 33
Manito Foundation . . . 117
Marin Community Foundation . . . 117
Marks & Spencer . . . 34
Massachusetts Environmental Trust . . . 118
McCarthy Family Foundation . . . 118
McDonald's-Our Community . . . 35
Mellon Foundation, Andrew W. . . . 120
Merck & Co. . . . 36
Mertz-Gilmore Foundation, Joyce . . . 120
Meyer Memorial Trust . . . 121
Microsoft Community Affairs . . . 36
Montana Community Foundation . . . 122
Morgan and Company Community Relations, J. P. . . . 38
Mott Foundation, Charles Stewart . . . 122
National Rivers Coalition . . . 124
New Israel Fund . . . 125
Norman Foundation . . . 125
Northeast Utilities Community Services . . . 40
Norton Endowment Foundation, Laird . . . 125
Occidental Petroleum Corporation . . . 42
Olin Corporation . . . 42

Orchard Foundation. 126
Owens Corning World Community Support 42
Pacific Gas & Electric Contributions Program 43
Packard Foundation, David and Lucile 127
Patagonia Environmental Grants Program 43
PECO Energy Community Development 43
Pew Charitable Trusts. 127
Phillips Petroleum Company-Our Citizenship. 44
Proctor & Gamble Community Center 44
Quantum Corporation 46
Rockefeller Family Fund 131
Rockefeller Foundation 131
Samsung Group Social Activities 48
San Diego Community Foundation. 133
Sierra Club Foundation. 133
Sonoco Foundation. 49
Southwire Company-Our Work in the Community 50
Starbucks Corporation 50
Stolichnaya 50
Stonyfield Farm. 51
Surdna Foundation 136
Tesoro Hawaii Foundation 52
Tom's of Maine 53
Triangle Community Foundation 137
Turner Foundation 138
Union Carbide 54
United Technologies Community Involvement 55
Valero Energy Corporation 56
Vastar Resources, Inc. 56
Victoria Foundation 139
Virginia Environmental Endowment 139
Wal-Mart Foundation 57
Weeden Foundation 140
Whitaker Foundation 141
Wilburforce Foundation 142
Wray Trust 142
WRQ 58
Yorkshire Electricity 59

Health

3M in the Community 1
AARP Andrus Foundation 61
Abell Foundation 61
Able Trust 61
Achelis Foundation 62
Adobe Philanthropic Council 1
Aetna Foundation. 2

Ahmanson Foundation . . . 62
Albion Community Foundation . . . 64
Alcoholic Beverage Medical Research Foundation . . . 64
Alger Regional Community Foundation . . . 64
Allen Charitable Foundation, Paul G. . . . 65
Allen Foundation . . . 65
Alliance Healthcare Foundation . . . 65
Altman Foundation, Jenifer . . . 66
American Brain Tumor Association . . . 67
American Federation for Aging Research . . . 68
American Foundation for AIDS Research . . . 68
American Foundation for the Blind . . . 68
American Health Assistance Foundation . . . 68
American Legion Child Welfare Foundation . . . 69
American Medical Association . . . 69
ARCO Foundation . . . 4
Arthritis Foundation . . . 71
AT&T Foundation . . . 5
Aurora Foundation . . . 72
Avon Products Foundation . . . 5
Bader Foundation, Helen . . . 73
Bagnoud Foundation, Francois-Xavier . . . 73
Baltimore Gas and Electric Company Corporate Contributions . . . 6
Bank of America Foundation . . . 6
Bankers Trust Foundation . . . 7
Baraga County Community Foundation . . . 74
Baxter International Corporate Citizenship . . . 7
Bell Atlantic Foundation . . . 7
Bernardine Franciscan Sisters Foundation . . . 75
Beveridge Foundation, Frank Stanley . . . 75
Bingham Foundation, William . . . 76
Blowitz-Ridgeway Foundation . . . 77
Blue Cross and Blue Shield of Michigan Community Sponsored Events . . . 8
Borden Foundation, Mary Owen . . . 78
Brain Foundation, Joe . . . 79
Bremer Foundation, Otto . . . 80
Bristol-Myers Squibb Foundation . . . 9
Brookdale Foundation Group . . . 80
Brother's Brother Foundation . . . 80
Brown Foundation, James Graham . . . 80
Bush Charitable Foundation, Edyth . . . 81
Cable & Wireless Corporate Community Involvement . . . 11
Cadillac Area Community Foundation . . . 82
California Community Foundation . . . 82
California Endowment . . . 82
California HealthCare Foundation . . . 82
California Wellness Foundation . . . 83
Cancer Treatment Research Foundation . . . 83

Castle Foundation, Samuel N. and Mary 85
Ceridian Corporation Community Involvement 12
Champlin Foundations 87
Cisco Systems Community Involvement 13
CJ Foundation for SIDS 88
Clark Foundation, Edna McConnell 88
Clorox Community Affairs 14
Coleman Foundation 89
Commonwealth Fund 89
Community Foundation of Sarasota County 90
Compaq Computer Corporate Contributions 14
Conoco 15
Conseco Community Action Report 15
Crail-Johnson Foundation 90
Cummings Foundation, Nathan 91
Dana Foundation, Charles A. 92
Davis Foundations, Arthur Vining 92
Dole Food Company 17
Eastman Chemical Company and the Community 19
Eaton Corporation 19
Epilepsy Foundation 96
Estée Lauder Companies 20
ExxonMobil Corporation 20
Fargo-Moorhead Area Foundation 96
Fetzer Institute 97
Fleet Bank 21
Flinn Foundation 97
Ford Foundation 98
Ford Motor Company 22
Foundation for Seacoast Health 99
France Telecom 22
Fund for the City of New York 100
Gap, Inc. Community Relations 23
Gates Foundation, Bill and Melinda 101
Genentech, Inc., Corporate Responsibility 23
General Mills 24
General Motors Corporation-Philanthropy 24
Gillette Company 24
Glaxo Wellcome in the Community 24
Glenn Foundation for Medical Research 102
Gold Foundation, Arnold P. 102
Goldman Fund, Richard and Rhoda 103
Green Bay Packers Foundation 103
Guardian National Insurance Company 25
Hartford Foundation for Public Giving 105
Hartford Foundation, John A. 105
Healthcare Foundation of New Jersey 106
Hearst Foundations, William Randolph 106

HEI Charitable Foundation . . . 26
Hershey Foods Corporation . . . 26
Hewlett Packard Corporate Philanthropy . . . 26
Hogg Foundation for Mental Health . . . 107
Home Depot . . . 27
Houston Endowment . . . 108
Huntington Bancshares Incorporated . . . 27
Irvine Health Foundation . . . 109
Ittleson Foundation . . . 109
JCPenney Community Involvement . . . 30
John AIDS Foundation, Elton . . . 109
Johnson & Johnson . . . 30
Johnson Foundation, Magic . . . 110
Johnson Foundation, Robert Wood . . . 110
Juvenile Diabetes Foundation International . . . 111
Kaiser Family Foundation, Henry J. . . . 111
Kansas Health Foundation . . . 111
Kellogg Foundation, W. K. . . . 112
Kennedy, Jr. Foundation, Joseph P. . . . 113
Kimberly-Clark . . . 31
Kodak Corporation . . . 32
Kornfeld Foundation, Emily Davie and Joseph S. . . . 114
Levi Strauss & Company . . . 32
Limited Inc. Foundation, The . . . 33
Lindbergh Foundation, Charles A. and Anne Morrow . . . 115
MacArthur Foundation, John D. and Catherine T. . . . 116
Marks & Spencer . . . 34
Mary Kay . . . 34
Mayday Fund . . . 118
McCarthy Family Foundation . . . 118
McCormick Tribune Foundation, Robert R. . . . 119
McDonald's-Our Community . . . 35
McDonnell Foundation, James S. . . . 119
McGregor Fund . . . 119
Meadows Foundation . . . 120
Medtronic Foundation . . . 35
Men's Wearhouse . . . 35
Merck & Co. . . . 36
Metropolitan Life Insurance Company . . . 36
Meyer Memorial Trust . . . 121
Microsoft Community Affairs . . . 36
Milbank Memorial Fund . . . 121
Milken Family Foundation . . . 121
Mitsubishi Electric America Foundation . . . 37
Morgan and Company Community Relations, J. P. . . . 38
Ms. Foundation for Women . . . 122
Northeast Utilities Community Services . . . 40
Novartis Foundation for Sustainable Development . . . 41

Orthopaedic Research and Education Foundation 126
Owens Corning World Community Support 42
Packard Foundation, David and Lucile 127
Pew Charitable Trusts 127
Pfizer 44
Phillips Petroleum Company-Our Citizenship 44
Proctor & Gamble Community Center 44
Prudential Foundation 45
Puerto Rico Community Foundation 129
Quad/Graphics 45
Quaker Oats Foundation 45
Quantum Foundation 129
Retirement Research Foundation 129
Ripken, Jr. Foundation, Kelly and Cal 130
Rippel Foundation, Fannie E. 130
Rite Aid 47
Rockefeller Brothers Fund 131
Rockefeller Foundation 131
Rohm and Haas and the Community 47
San Antonio Area Foundation 132
San Diego Community Foundation 133
Sears, Roebuck and Company 48
Sega Foundation 49
SmithKline Beecham Community Partnership 49
Sobrato Family Foundation 134
Sonoco Foundation 49
Sonoma County Community Foundation 134
Sonora Area Foundation 134
St. Luke's Charitable Health Trust 135
Stolichnaya 50
Stride Rite Foundation 51
Target Stores 52
Templeton Foundation, John 136
Texas Instruments Corporate Citizenship 52
Triangle Community Foundation 137
Trust Fund for Children with Special Health Care Needs 138
United Hospital Fund of New York 138
Valero Energy Corporation 56
Valley Foundation 139
Vastar Resources, Inc. 56
Vision Service Plan 56
Walgreens 57
Wal-Mart Foundation 57
Weingart Foundation 141
Whirlpool Foundation 58
Yahoo! Inc. 59

Humanities

Ahmanson Foundation 62
American Association of School Libraries 67
American Music Center 69
Baltimore Gas and Electric Company Corporate Contributions 6
Blakemore Foundation 76
Community Foundation of Sarasota County 90
Delmas Foundation, Gladys Krieble 92
Getty Trust, J. Paul 101
National Trust for Historic Preservation 124
Sonoma County Community Foundation 134
Vastar Resources, Inc. 56

International

3M in the Community 1
Allen Foundation 65
Amway 3
ARCO Foundation 4
AT&T Foundation 5
Bankers Trust Foundation 7
Baptist Community Ministries 73
Baxter International Corporate Citizenship 7
Biehl Foundation, Amy 76
BPAmoco Corporation 9
British Telecom in the Community 10
Brother's Brother Foundation 80
Cable & Wireless Corporate Community Involvement 11
Carnegie Corporation of New York 84
Carnegie Endowment for International Peace 84
Chevron Corporation 13
Chiang Ching-kuo Foundation for International Scholarly Exchange 87
Cisco Systems Community Involvement 13
Citigroup Foundation 13
Compaq Computer Corporate Contributions 14
Conoco 15
Conseco Community Action Report 15
Daiwa Anglo-Japanese Foundation 91
Delmas Foundation, Gladys Krieble 92
DuPont-Social Responsibility 18
Eurasia Foundation 96
Ford Foundation 98
Gates Foundation, Bill and Melinda 101
General Electric Co. 23
Glaxo Wellcome in the Community 24
Global Fund for Women 102
Guggenheim Memorial Foundation, John Simon 103
HEI Charitable Foundation 26

Hewlett Foundation, William and Flora 107
Hewlett Packard Corporate Philanthropy 26
Itochu-Contributing to Society 29
Japan Foundation 109
Kellogg Foundation, W. K. 112
Kennedy, Jr. Foundation, Joseph P. 113
Levi Strauss & Company 32
MacArthur Foundation, John D. and Catherine T. 116
McDonnell Foundation, James S. 119
Merck & Co. 36
Mertz-Gilmore Foundation, Joyce 120
Morgan and Company Community Relations, J. P. 38
Mott Foundation, Charles Stewart 122
New Israel Fund 125
Nortel Networks 40
Novartis Foundation for Sustainable Development 41
Owens Corning World Community Support 42
Pollock-Krasner Foundation 128
Reebok 47
Rockefeller Brothers Fund 131
Rockefeller Foundation 131
SmithKline Beecham Community Partnership 49
Soros Foundations Network 135
Think Quest 53
Trinity Grants Program 137
U.S.-Japan Foundation 138
United Technologies Community Involvement 55

Religion

Amy Foundation 70
Baptist Community Ministries 73
Beveridge Foundation, Frank Stanley 75
Bonner Foundation, Corella and Bertram F. 77
Bremer Foundation, Otto 80
Castle Foundation, Samuel N. and Mary 85
Catholic Campaign for Human Development 86
Center for Theology and the Natural Sciences 86
Cummings Foundation, Nathan 91
Davis Foundations, Arthur Vining 92
Dole Food Company 17
Fetzer Institute 97
Goldman Fund, Richard and Rhoda 103
Haas Fund, Walter and Elise 104
Manito Foundation 117
Men's Wearhouse 35
New Israel Fund 125
Pew Charitable Trusts 127
Templeton Foundation, John 136

Trinity Grants Program 137
Wheat Ridge Ministries 141

Science

Achelis Foundation 62
Alaska Science and Technology Foundation 63
Allen Charitable Foundation, Paul G. 65
American Association of Physics Teachers 67
American Brain Tumor Association 67
American Federation for Aging Research 68
American Foundation for AIDS Research 68
American Foundation for the Blind 68
American Health Assistance Foundation 68
Arthritis Foundation 71
Bagnoud Foundation, Francois-Xavier 73
Bingham Foundation, William 76
Burroughs Wellcome Fund 81
Cabot Corporation Social Responsibility 11
Cancer Treatment Research Foundation 83
Carver Charitable Trust, Roy J. 85
Center for Theology and the Natural Sciences 86
Dana Foundation, Charles A. 92
Downing Foundation, J.C. 94
Dreyfus Foundation, Camille and Henry 94
Energy Foundation 95
Epilepsy Foundation 96
Foundation for Anesthesia Education and Research 98
Foundation for Microbiology 99
Fund for the City of New York 100
Genentech, Inc., Corporate Responsibility 23
Glenn Foundation for Medical Research 102
GTE Foundation 25
Hewlett Packard Corporate Philanthropy 26
Howard Hughes Medical Institute 108
Itochu-Contributing to Society 29
Ittleson Foundation 109
Juvenile Diabetes Foundation International 111
Kimberly-Clark 31
Limited Inc. Foundation, The 33
Mary Kay 34
McCarthy Family Foundation 118
McDonnell Foundation, James S. 119
Medtronic Foundation 35
Milken Family Foundation 121
Millipore Foundation 37
National Science Teachers Association Awards Programs 124
NEC Foundation of America 39

Olfactory Research Fund 126
Packard Foundation, David and Lucile 127
Pet Life Foundation 127
Rhone-Poulenc Foundation 47
Rockefeller Foundation 131
Sloan Foundation, Alfred P. 134
Soros Foundations Network 135
TAPPI Foundation 136
Texas Instruments Corporate Citizenship 52
Think Quest 53
Toshiba America Foundation 53
Toyota USA Foundation 54
Wenner-Gren Foundation for Anthropological Research 141
Whitaker Foundation 141

Social Services

3M in the Community 1
AARP Andrus Foundation 61
Abelard Foundation 61
Abell Foundation 61
Able Trust 61
Achelis Foundation 62
Adobe Philanthropic Council 1
Ahmanson Foundation 62
Akron Community Foundation 62
Albion Community Foundation 64
Alger Regional Community Foundation 64
Allegheny Foundation 64
Allen Charitable Foundation, Paul G. 65
Alliant Energy Foundation 2
Amateur Athletic Foundation of Los Angeles 66
American Association of University Women 67
American Express Company 2
American Foundation for the Blind 68
American Legion Child Welfare Foundation 69
Ameritech Corporation 3
Amway 3
ARCO Foundation 4
Arizona Cardinals Charities 4
Arizona Community Foundation 71
Ashland Foundation 4
AT&T Foundation 5
Atlanta Women's Foundation 72
Aurora Foundation 72
Avon Products Foundation 5
Bader Foundation, Helen 73
Bagnoud Foundation, Francois-Xavier 73

Baltimore Gas and Electric Company Corporate Contributions. 6
Bank of America Foundation 6
BankBoston and the Community 6
Bankers Trust Foundation 7
Baptist Community Ministries. 73
Baraga County Community Foundation 74
Battle Creek Community Foundation 74
Baxter International Corporate Citizenship. 7
Bell Atlantic Foundation 7
Ben & Jerry's Foundation. 8
Berger Foundation, H. N. and Frances C. 75
Bernardine Franciscan Sisters Foundation. 75
Beveridge Foundation, Frank Stanley. 75
Big Ben Foundation, Inc.. 75
Bingham Foundation, William. 76
Blank Family Foundation, Arthur M. 77
Blowitz-Ridgeway Foundation 77
Blue Cross and Blue Shield of Michigan Community Sponsored Events 8
Bodman Foundation 77
Boeing 9
Borden Foundation, Mary Owen. 78
Boston Foundation. 78
Brain Foundation, Joe 79
Bremer Foundation, Otto 80
British Telecom in the Community. 10
Brookdale Foundation Group 80
Brooklyn Union. 10
Brother's Brother Foundation. 80
Brown Brothers Harriman & Company Community Involvement. 10
Brown Foundation, James Graham 80
Burger King 11
Bush Charitable Foundation, Edyth 81
Cable & Wireless Corporate Community Involvement 11
Cabot Corporation Social Responsibility 11
Cadillac Area Community Foundation 82
California Community Foundation. 82
California Wellness Foundation 83
CARLISLE Foundation. 84
Carolina Power & Light in the Community 12
Casey Foundation, Annie E.. 85
Catholic Campaign for Human Development 86
Central Indiana Community Foundation 86
Ceridian Corporation Community Involvement 12
Cisco Systems Community Involvement 13
Cleveland Foundation 89
Clipper Ship Foundation 89
Clorox Community Affairs. 14
Comdisco, Inc.. 14

Commonwealth Fund . . . 89
Community Foundation of Sarasota County . . . 90
Compaq Computer Corporate Contributions . . . 14
Computer Associates . . . 15
Conoco . . . 15
Conseco Community Action Report . . . 15
Cooper Foundation . . . 90
Cottonwood Foundation . . . 90
Crail-Johnson Foundation . . . 90
Dai Nippon Printing Company-Dynamic Corporate Citizenship . . . 16
Delta Air Lines . . . 16
Dial Corporation . . . 16
DJ&T Foundation . . . 93
Do Right Foundation . . . 93
Dodge Foundation, Geraldine R. . . . 93
Dole Food Company . . . 17
Downing Foundation, J.C. . . . 94
Draper Laboratories Community Outreach, Charles Stark . . . 17
Dreyer's Grand Ice Cream Corporate Philanthropy . . . 18
DuPont-Social Responsibility . . . 18
Eastman Chemical Company and the Community . . . 19
Electronic Data Systems (EDS) Community Affairs . . . 19
Enron . . . 20
Estée Lauder Companies . . . 20
ExxonMobil Corporation . . . 20
Fannie Mae Foundation . . . 21
Fargo-Moorhead Area Foundation . . . 96
Feinstein Foundation . . . 97
FMC Foundation . . . 21
Ford Foundation . . . 98
Ford Motor Company . . . 22
Foundation for the Carolinas . . . 99
France Telecom . . . 22
Fred Meyer Stores . . . 22
Fuji Bank Group-Corporate Citizen . . . 22
Gap, Inc. Community Relations . . . 23
General Electric Co. . . . 23
General Motors Corporation-Philanthropy . . . 24
Gill Foundation . . . 102
Gillette Company . . . 24
Global Fund for Women . . . 102
Goldman Fund, Richard and Rhoda . . . 103
Green Bay Packers Foundation . . . 103
Guggenheim Memorial Foundation, John Simon . . . 103
Gund Foundation, George . . . 104
H. E. Butt Grocery . . . 25
Haas Fund, Walter and Elise . . . 104
Hallmark Cards . . . 25

Hartford Foundation for Public Giving . . . 105
Healthcare Foundation of New Jersey . . . 106
Hearst Foundations, William Randolph . . . 106
HEI Charitable Foundation . . . 26
Heinz Endowments . . . 106
Hershey Foods Corporation . . . 26
Hewlett Foundation, William and Flora . . . 107
Hitachi Foundation . . . 26
Hogg Foundation for Mental Health . . . 107
Home Depot . . . 27
Houston Endowment . . . 108
Huntington Bancshares Incorporated . . . 27
International Business Machines (IBM) Philanthropy . . . 28
Intimate Brands . . . 28
Itochu-Contributing to Society . . . 29
Jacksonville Jaguars Foundation . . . 29
JCPenney Community Involvement . . . 30
JM Family Enterprises . . . 30
Johnson & Johnson . . . 30
Johnson Foundation, Magic . . . 110
Johnson Foundation, Walter S. . . . 110
Kansas City Power & Light Company Community Outlets . . . 31
Kauffman Foundation, Ewing Marion . . . 112
Kennedy, Jr. Foundation, Joseph P. . . . 113
Kimberly-Clark . . . 31
Kodak Corporation . . . 32
Kornfeld Foundation, Emily Davie and Joseph S. . . . 114
Levi Strauss & Company . . . 32
Limited Inc. Foundation, The . . . 33
Long Island Community Foundation . . . 115
Lowe's Companies . . . 33
Ludwick Family Foundation . . . 116
Maddie's Fund . . . 117
Mailman Family Foundation, A. L. . . . 117
Marin Community Foundation . . . 117
Marks & Spencer . . . 34
McCarthy Family Foundation . . . 118
McCormick Tribune Foundation, Robert R. . . . 119
McDonald's-Our Community . . . 35
McGregor Fund . . . 119
Meadows Foundation . . . 120
Medina Foundation . . . 120
Medtronic Foundation . . . 35
Men's Wearhouse . . . 35
Merck & Co. . . . 36
Meyer Memorial Trust . . . 121
Microsoft Community Affairs . . . 36
Milken Family Foundation . . . 121

Millipore Foundation . . . 37
Mintz Levin Community Service . . . 37
Monsanto Fund . . . 37
Montana Community Foundation . . . 122
Morgan and Company Community Relations, J. P. . . . 38
Mott Foundation, Charles Stewart . . . 122
Ms. Foundation for Women . . . 122
National Semiconductor Community Care . . . 38
NatWest Group Community Relations-Group Community Review . . . 39
NEC Foundation of America . . . 39
New Israel Fund . . . 125
Nordstrom . . . 40
Nortel Networks . . . 40
Northeast Utilities Community Services . . . 40
Northern States Power Company Community Involvement . . . 41
Northwest Airlines . . . 41
Novartis Foundation for Sustainable Development . . . 41
Open Society Institute . . . 126
Owens Corning World Community Support . . . 42
Pacific Gas & Electric Contributions Program . . . 43
PECO Energy Community Development . . . 43
Pew Charitable Trusts . . . 127
Philadelphia Foundation . . . 128
Phillips Petroleum Company-Our Citizenship . . . 44
Points of Light Foundation . . . 128
Proctor & Gamble Community Center . . . 44
Prudential Foundation . . . 45
Puerto Rico Community Foundation . . . 129
Quad/Graphics . . . 45
Quaker Oats Foundation . . . 45
Quantum Corporation . . . 46
Ralston Purina Company . . . 46
Reebok . . . 47
Retirement Research Foundation . . . 129
Ripken, Jr. Foundation, Kelly and Cal . . . 130
Rippel Foundation, Fannie E. . . . 130
Rohm and Haas and the Community . . . 47
Rosenberg Foundation . . . 132
Samsung Group Social Activities . . . 48
San Antonio Area Foundation . . . 132
San Diego Community Foundation . . . 133
Scaife Family Foundation . . . 133
Sears, Roebuck and Company . . . 48
Sega Foundation . . . 49
SmithKline Beecham Community Partnership . . . 49
Sobrato Family Foundation . . . 134
Sonoco Foundation . . . 49
Sonoma County Community Foundation . . . 134

Sonora Area Foundation . . . 134
Sprint Corporation . . . 50
Starbucks Corporation . . . 50
Stolichnaya . . . 50
Target Stores . . . 52
Tesoro Hawaii Foundation . . . 52
Tom's of Maine . . . 53
Toynbee Prize Foundation . . . 137
Triangle Community Foundation . . . 137
Trillium Foundation . . . 54
Trinity Grants Program . . . 137
Unisys Social Responsibility . . . 54
United Parcel Service . . . 55
United Technologies Community Involvement . . . 55
US West . . . 55
USG Corporation . . . 55
Valero Energy Corporation . . . 56
Vastar Resources, Inc. . . . 56
Vision Service Plan . . . 56
Walgreens . . . 57
Wal-Mart Foundation . . . 57
Weingart Foundation . . . 141
Whirlpool Foundation . . . 58
Windermere Foundation . . . 58
Woods Charitable Fund . . . 142
Yahoo! Inc. . . . 59

Youth

Achelis Foundation . . . 62
Akron Community Foundation . . . 62
Amateur Athletic Foundation of Los Angeles . . . 66
American Legion Child Welfare Foundation . . . 69
Annenberg Foundation . . . 70
Arizona Cardinals Charities . . . 4
Arizona Community Foundation . . . 71
Aurora Foundation . . . 72
Babcock Foundation, Mary Reynolds . . . 73
Bader Foundation, Helen . . . 73
Bagnoud Foundation, Francois-Xavier . . . 73
Baraga County Community Foundation . . . 74
Blank Family Foundation, Arthur M. . . . 77
Blowitz-Ridgeway Foundation . . . 77
Bodman Foundation . . . 77
Borden Foundation, Mary Owen . . . 78
Bowne Foundation, Robert . . . 78
Brooklyn Union . . . 10
Cable & Wireless Corporate Community Involvement . . . 11

Captain Planet Foundation . . . 83
CARLISLE Foundation . . . 84
Carver Charitable Trust, Roy J. . . . 85
Casey Foundation, Annie E. . . . 85
Castle Foundation, Samuel N. and Mary . . . 85
Chesapeake Bay Trust . . . 87
Chi Chi Rodriguez Youth Foundation . . . 87
Citigroup Foundation . . . 13
CJ Foundation for SIDS . . . 88
Clark Foundation, Edna McConnell . . . 88
Clorox Community Affairs . . . 14
Comdisco, Inc. . . . 14
Computer Associates . . . 15
Crail-Johnson Foundation . . . 90
Dial Corporation . . . 16
Donnelly & Sons Company, R.R. . . . 17
Downing Foundation, J.C. . . . 94
Dunn Foundation . . . 95
Fargo-Moorhead Area Foundation . . . 96
Ford Foundation . . . 98
Foundation for Exceptional Children . . . 98
Freddie Mac . . . 22
Fund for the City of New York . . . 100
Gates Foundation , Bill and Melinda . . . 101
Gillette Company . . . 24
Goldman Fund, Richard and Rhoda . . . 103
Green Bay Packers Foundation . . . 103
Guardian National Insurance Company . . . 25
Hartford Foundation for Public Giving . . . 105
Heinz Endowments . . . 106
Hogg Foundation for Mental Health . . . 107
I Have a Dream Foundation . . . 108
Intimate Brands . . . 28
Jacksonville Jaguars Foundation . . . 29
JM Family Enterprises . . . 30
Johnson Foundation, Magic . . . 110
Johnson Foundation, Walter S. . . . 110
Kansas Health Foundation . . . 111
Kauffman Foundation, Ewing Marion . . . 112
KN Energy . . . 32
Kornfeld Foundation, Emily Davie and Joseph S. . . . 114
Ludwick Family Foundation . . . 116
Mailman Family Foundation, A. L. . . . 117
Mattel, Inc. . . . 34
McCarthy Family Foundation . . . 118
Meadows Foundation . . . 120
Men's Wearhouse . . . 35
Mott Foundation, Charles Stewart . . . 122

Orchard Foundation 126
Oshman's SuperSports USA 42
Packard Foundation, David and Lucile 127
Perkins Family Restaurants 43
Pillsbury Company 44
Rosenberg Foundation 132
Samsung Group Social Activities 48
Sobrato Family Foundation 134
Stride Rite Foundation 51
Trust Fund for Children with Special Health Care Needs 138
Victoria Foundation 139
Virginia Environmental Endowment 139
Vision Service Plan 56
Wallace-Reader's Digest Funds 140
Wendy's International, Inc. 57
WRQ 58

9 780834 218000

Printed in Germany
by Amazon Distribution
GmbH, Erfurt

17087820R00145